THE MAK

THE ENGLISH

THE CORNISH LANDSCAPE

CORNWALL
N
ATLANTIC
OCEAN
Morwenstow
Kilkhampton
STRATTON
BUDE
Daymer Bay
Harlyn Bay
St Constantine
St Eval
Mawgan Porth
St Columb Minor
NEWQUAY
Goss Moor
Cubert
Mitchell
Perranporth
Ladock
ST AGNES
Probus
TRURO
Portreath
Poldice
Malpas
St Michael Penkevil
REDRUTH
St Clement
Tregothnan
Gwennap
Trelissick
Dolcoath
Devoran
CAMBORNE
Perran Wharf
Feock
ST IVES
Gwithian
Gurnards Head
Halsetown
Zennor
Towednack
HAYLE
Ponsanooth
Restronguet
Mylor
Morvah
Trencrom Hill
Lelant
Rosemanowas
St Gerrans
PENWITH
Chysauster
St Erth
Rame
PENRYN
Flushing
Porthcuel
Lanyon Quoit
Ludgvan
CARNMENELLIS
Mabe
ST MAWES
Botallack
MOOR
FALMOUTH
Pendennis
St Just
Madron
MARAZION
Cape Cornwall
PENZANCE
St Hilary
Godolphin
Sancreed
St Michaels Mount
Newlyn
Breage
PENINSULA
HELSTON
Helford River
St Buryan
Mousehole
Porthleven
Sennen
Lamorna
GOONHILLY
DOWNS
LANDS END
CROUSA
DOWNS
Gunwalloe
Mullion
Ruan
Grade
LIZARD

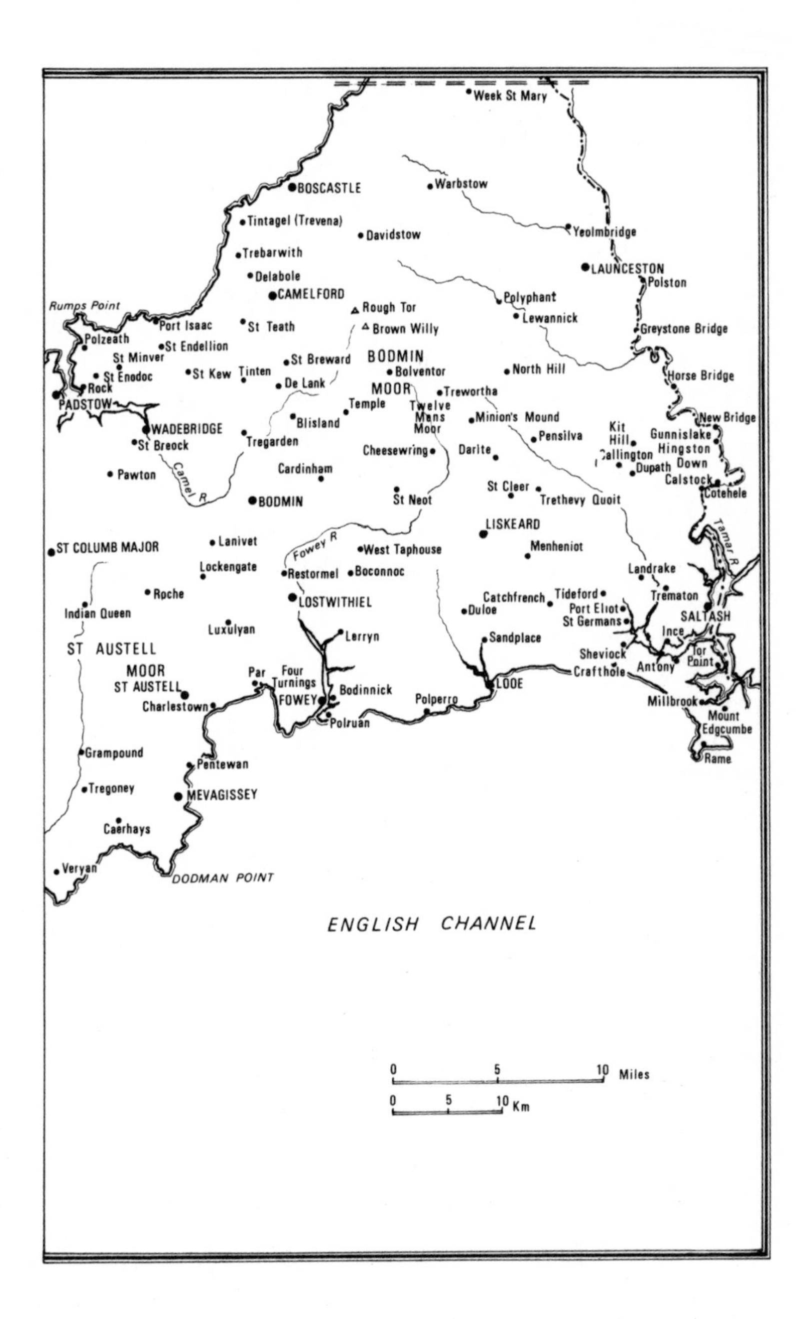
Week St Mary
BOSCASTLE
Warbstow
Tintagel (Trevena)
Davidstow
Yeolmbridge
Trebarwith
Delabole
LAUNCESTON
Polston
CAMELFORD
Polyphant
Rumps Point
Rough Tor
Lewannick
Port Isaac
St Teath
Brown Willy
Greystone Bridge
Polzeath
St Endellion
St Minver
St Breward
BODMIN
St Enodoc
St Kew
Tinten
Bolventor
North Hill
Horse Bridge
Rock
De Lank
MOOR
Trewortha
PADSTOW
Temple
Twelve Mans Moor
Minion's Mound
New Bridge
Blisland
Kit Hill
Gunnislake
WADEBRIDGE
Pensilva
St Breock
Tregarden
Cheesewring
Darite
Callington
Hingston Down
Dupath
Pawton
Cardinham
Camel R
Calstock
St Cleer
Cotehele
BODMIN
St Neot
Trethevy Quoit
LISKEARD
Tamar R
Lanivet
ST COLUMB MAJOR
Fowey R
West Taphouse
Menheniot
Lockengate
Landrake
Restormel
Boconnoc
Roche
Catchfrench
Tideford
Trematon
Indian Queen
LOSTWITHIEL
Duloe
Port Eliot
SALTASH
St Germans
Luxulyan
Lerryn
Sandplace
Ince
ST AUSTELL
Sheviock
Tor Point
MOOR
Antony
Four Turnings
Par
Crafthole
ST AUSTELL
Bodinnick
LOOE
Charlestown
FOWEY
Polperro
Millbrook
Polruan
Mount Edgcumbe
Grampound
Rame
Pentewan
Tregoney
MEVAGISSEY
Caerhays
Veryan
DODMAN POINT
ENGLISH CHANNEL
0
5
10
Miles
0
5
10
Km

THE MAKING OF THE ENGLISH LANDSCAPE
Edited by W. G. Hoskins and Roy Millward

The Making of the English Landscape, W. G. Hoskins
West Riding of Yorkshire, Arthur Raistrick
Dorset, Christopher Taylor
The Northumberland Landscape, Robert Newton
The Shropshire Landscape, Trevor Rowley
The Suffolk Landscape, Norman Scarfe
The Cambridgeshire Landscape, Christopher Taylor
The Oxfordshire Landscape, Frank Emery
The Northamptonshire Landscape, John Steane
The Sussex Landscape, Peter Brandon
The Gloucestershire Landscape, H. P. R. Finberg
The Staffordshire Landscape, David Palliser
The East Riding of Yorkshire Landscape, K. J. Allison
The Hertfordshire Landscape, Lionel Munby
The Bedfordshire and Huntingdonshire Landscape, Peter Bigmore
The Buckinghamshire Landscape, Michael Reed
The Somerset Landscape, Michael Havinden
The Cornish Landscape, W. G. V. Balchin

THE MAKING OF THE WELSH LANDSCAPE

The South Wales Landscape, Moelwyn Williams

THE MAKING OF THE ENGLISH LANDSCAPE

The Cornish Landscape

by

W. G. V. BALCHIN

HODDER AND STOUGHTON

LONDON SYDNEY AUCKLAND TORONTO

British Library Cataloguing in Publication Data
Balchin, W. G. V.
The Cornish Landscape.—Rev. ed.—(Making of the English landscape series; 2)
1. Cornwall—Historical geography
I. Title II. Series
911'.423'7 DA670.C8

ISBN 0-340-20197-5

 Printed in Great Britain for Hodder and Stoughton Limited, Mill Road, Dunton Green, Sevenoaks, Kent by St Edmundsbury Press, Bury St Edmunds, Suffolk. Photoset by Rowland Phototypesetting Ltd, Bury St Emunds, Suffolk. Hodder and Stoughton Editorial Office: 47 Bedford Square, London WC1B 3DP.

For

LILY

A constant companion through
forty-four years of fieldwork

in

CORNWALL

Editor's Introduction

THE APPEARANCE OF a revised edition of *The Cornish Landscape* marks an important stage in *The Making of the English Landscape* series. Almost thirty years ago W. G. V. Balchin's 'illustrated essay' was the first of the county volumes in this ambitious survey of the history of the English landscape planned by W. G. Hoskins. The series arose out of a dissatisfaction with much of the topographical writing of the 1930s, a discontent that is still with us in the 1980s when one scans the ceaseless torrent of guide-book journalism in the travel columns of the Sunday papers. The approach of all the authors who have contributed the eighteen published volumes of the series to date has been determined by the belief that the visible landscape is itself an expression of centuries of history, a history whose clues may be revealed through patient exploration in the field but whose full explanation can only be reached through evidence locked up in national and county records.

W. G. Hoskins laid the foundation of *The Making of the English Landscape* books when he returned to the University College at Leicester after the Second World War to establish the Department of English Local History. As a post-graduate research department it was able to turn all its energy towards local studies; after more than thirty years the harvest has indeed been rich. From the beginning it was Professor Hoskins' intention that these riches should be made accessible to those outside the walls of Academe, and the first channel through which his work became known to the general public was a series of twenty-minute talks on the BBC's Third Programme. Those talks were the inspiration for the present series of books.

Much has changed since the introductory volume and the three county essays – Cornwall, Lancashire and Gloucestershire – appeared in the mid-fifties. The series itself underwent a change of format in 1970 with the publication of Christopher Taylor's *Dorset* and Arthur Raistrick's *West Riding of York-*

shire. The text was doubled in length, but the aim of our authors remained the same, to reveal some of the riches of our county landscapes to the ordinary reader and to encourage him to explore further through the activities and publications of local historical and archaeological groups and societies. Another, less radical change, overtook the series in 1981 with a decision to publish only in paperback.

An underlying theme of all the books has been the influence of a changing economy and society on the English landscape. The many acres of ridge-and-furrow in the Midland counties are the visible relic of a long lost medieval ordering of life. But as the series progressed into the 1970s one was made aware of the problems presented by contemporary changes in achieving a complete survey of the landscape history of England's counties. The greatest challenge came with the upheaval in Britain's local government that erased whole counties from the map. Wales and Scotland suffered most. Brecknockshire, a recognisable unit over almost two thousand years, was swallowed up in a vast sprawling borderland administration that took to itself the old name of Powys. Scotland fared perhaps even worse, where no more exciting name than Highland Region could be found for the whole of the country to the north of the Great Glen. England lost Rutland, a county whose shape had been known since the end of the twelfth century. New names such as Avon and Humberside, lacking historical roots, appeared on the map. For the historian of landscape the only acceptable piece of the 1974 reorganisation, made legal on the first day of April, was the creation of Cumbria. Cumberland, Westmorland and pieces of Lancashire on the northern shore of Morecambe Bay were joined together to give administrative unity to the Lake District and to revive memories of a forgotten Dark Age kingdom of Cumbria. As Professor Hoskins wrote of the series in 1976, 'I had to consider whether we should stick to the old counties as we have known them or adopt the new set-up. As the series was by then so far advanced under the old and well-loved names, we decided to retain them and go on as before.'

The years between the 1950s and the 1980s have seen deeper changes that have influenced our approach to the history of our counties' landscapes. It has been a time of intensive research in several related fields of knowledge where material discoveries and fresh ideas have inevitably influenced the thinking of our several authors. Place-names, their meaning and origins, are fundamental to the work of the local historian. With pleasure one records the debt of the landscape historian to the publications of the English Place-Name Society. One also notes the increasing thoroughness of research in this field. During the years between the 1914 and 1939 wars, when the ground-work of English place-name studies became firmly established, one volume sufficed to analyse the names of a single county. Of late the volumes have multiplied and the letter-press has become smaller and more closely set. Cheshire, still incomplete, runs to five volumes and the fifth volume itself has expanded into three separate parts.

The quantity of material that needs to be considered by anyone who tackles the history of his county has grown immensely. Archaeology has long ceased to be a study only of potsherds and palstaves from centuries long before the Romans. The spade and the far more refined tools and methods of the modern archaeologist have penetrated all the later centuries of history and we have professional journals that report the findings of excavations at medieval sites as well as those that date back only to the eighteenth and nineteenth centuries. Archaeology has something to contribute to every period of landscape history and its findings are frequently set out in immense detail. For instance, the Devon Archaeological Society published in 1982 the results of excavations at Okehampton Castle. The report on the findings in the Bailey alone covers 142 pages. The same journal bears witness to the growth of research into the character of prehistoric landscapes. In a *Review of the Prehistoric and Historic Environment on Dartmoor* the striking results of pollen analysis in unravelling the changes of vegetation in this upland are recorded. By 1981 thirty-four sites had been investigated for their yield of pollen that had been preserved in peat-bogs from the centuries of prehistory. When the first volumes of *The Making of the English Landscape* appeared in the 1950s it seemed reasonable to assume that the continuous history of man's relationship with the countryside began in the depths of a primeval woodland that, it was believed, still covered much of Anglo-Saxon Britain. Over the past two decades evidence has been gathered in abundance to show that prehistory has contributed much to the landscape that lies around us today. Professor Hoskins has argued that many Devon farms are the descendants over a timespan of twenty centuries and more of Iron Age estates and that some of the deep, sunk lanes began as the deliberately hollowed out boundaries of those estates at a time before the Romans knew this land.

In the East Midlands evidence from quite a different source has revealed a fresh prehistoric dimension in the landscapes of Leicestershire and Nottinghamshire. Air surveys made by J. Pickering and D. N. Riley annually through the 1970s have yielded thousands of photographs whose archaeological information, hidden at ground level but visible in crop-marks from the air, has been plotted on maps of a scale of six inches to the mile. The Vale of Belvoir, once believed to have remained heavily forested until after the Saxon settlements because of its heavy clay soils, is now shown 'to have been exploited since Roman times and possibly earlier' and 'the Trent valley shows a density of prehistoric settlement never before suspected'. In his second Introduction, written for this series in 1976, William Hoskins suggested that 'Everything is older than we think.' In so many places local research has come to confirm that belief.

Towns are an important element in the evolution of the English landscape, if not the most important if we judge our society from the places where most people live. Here too the years since the beginning of the series have seen a vast expansion of research. Professor Maurice Beresford's *New Towns of the Middle Ages*, published in 1967, was a landmark in urban studies that presented not only the principles that lay behind the foundation of the medieval new town but also, in its valuable gazetteer outlined the histories of hundreds of English and Welsh boroughs, both the successful and the failed. Urban History has established itself as an academic discipline in its own right, publishing transactions and organising conferences where the results of research are aired. The volume of publications on urban topics has been immense. Of late, and with a random choice we find a *History of Hull*, from the twelfth century to the present day, and a *History of Modern Leeds*, both published in 1980. That mammoth undertaking, *The Victoria History of the Counties of England*, started almost a century ago, looks towards its completion at some unknown future date. In the eighth volume on *Staffordshire* published in 1979, part of the ambitiously planned twenty volumes that will cover the county, we find ninety closely printed double-column pages on the county town. As one reviewer has written, this is 'the first scholarly account of the county town to cover the whole of its history'.

For each county in the series the authors of *The Making of the English Landscape* have attempted to lay before the general reader the findings of research in a wide variety of related fields, as well as the insights of the 'classic' topographical writings published over the past two hundred years. Even so, as WGH wrote in an earlier Editor's Introduction, 'after so many books and articles and theses have been written, there is so much that remains unknown, and no doubt questions that I and others, have still not perceived . . . in the end, I look upon landscape history as an enlargement of consciousness, a new way of looking at familiar scenes which adds to the enjoyment of life. For those who have eyes to see, the face of Britain will never look the same again.'

Leicester, 1983 — Roy Millward

Preface

NEARLY THIRTY YEARS have elapsed since the first version of *Cornwall* appeared in The Making of the English Landscape series. During this period not only has Cornwall continued to change but we have also seen a veritable explosion in literary source material dealing with the Principality. Whereas in the immediate post-war period data were difficult to locate, there is now an embarrassment of riches, as nearly every topic touched upon in this broad survey seems to have been the subject of specialist investigation and publication in the intervening period. This has made the task of rewriting the original book both easier and more difficult: easier because of the increased accessibility of essential data, but more difficult in that one becomes increasingly conscious of the immense amount of interesting information that has had to be omitted to keep within the limits set by the series – despite the fact that the present text is over twice the length of the original.

The main purpose of the book remains a broad survey of the evolution of the present landscape with the hope that it will assist not only the many visitors to, but also the residents of, Cornwall to appreciate their environmental surroundings more fully, and as a result to dig deeper into the now more readily-available literature. Each chapter, therefore, lists in conclusion the more important sources where expanded accounts may be located. To all these authors and to many colleagues who commented upon the original version I owe my thanks. I am also particularly indebted for assistance to many friends in Cornwall, notably Professor Charles Thomas of the Institute of Cornish Studies at Redruth, Mr H. L. Douch and Mr R. D. Penhallurick of the County Museum in Truro, Mr G. E. M. Trinick of the National Trust at Lanhydrock, Mr P. Sargeant of the Nature Conservancy at Trelissick and Mr Charles Woolf of Newquay. Thanks are also due to Mrs Glenys Bridges and Mr G. B. Lewis who assisted with the maps and to Mr Alan Cutliffe who assisted with the photographic illustrations. Last but by no means least my thanks are further due to the Leverhulme Trust for the award of an Emeritus Fellowship to speed the completion of a long-standing project.

All Saints Day, 1982 W. G. V. BALCHIN

Contents

List of Plates

List of maps

ACKNOWLEDGEMENTS

The publishers would like to thank the following for permission to reproduce their photographs:
Aerofilms Ltd: Plates 4, 5, 21, 25, 28, 29, 31, 46, 50, 51, 52
F. L. Attenborough: Plate 35
W. G. V. Balchin: Plates 1, 3, 9, 10, 15, 19, 20, 23, 24, 26, 30, 32, 33, 34, 36, 44, 48, 53, 54, 58, 59, 60, 61, 62, 63
British Travel and Holidays Association: Plates 2, 49
B. A. Butt: Plates 39, 55
Central Office of Information: Plates 22, 43
O. G. S. Crawford: Plate 16
Herbert Hughes: Plate 41
Studio St Ives: Plates 14, 17, 27, 40
Woolf-Greenham Collection: Plates 6, 7, 8, 11, 12, 13, 18, 37, 38, 42, 45, 47, 56, 57

Figures 1 and 19 together with the general map have been prepared by the author. Figures 2 to 17 inclusive are extracts from the Ordnance Survey's six-inch maps of Cornwall (dates as noted) which have been reproduced with the sanction of the Controller of H.M. Stationery Office. Figure 18 has been supplied by Miss Alice Coleman, Director of the Second Land Utilisation Survey of Britain.

The general reader will find the Ordnance Survey's 1:50,000 Landranger maps an invaluable accompaniment to the text. The following five sheets cover Cornwall: 190, 200, 201, 203, 204. For detailed field-work the Ordnance Survey's 1:25,000 Pathfinder maps should be used. Reference to an index map will identify any particular sheet needed.

National Grid references for all places mentioned in the text of the book are given in brackets immediately after the index entry: the National Grid reference system is explained on all Ordnance Survey maps and enables places to be located quickly.

Introduction

ONE OF THE first impressions gained by the sensitive traveller in Cornwall is of a landscape that has a unity and a quality of its very own. Although of England it is in many ways un-English. The fields and farms, hamlets and hedges, mines and monuments, all speak of past centuries, of times when Cornwall, surrounded on three sides by the sea and divided on the fourth by the river Tamar, was isolated from the rest of England. Protected by its geographical position from the more violent results of the successive invasions which have swept through the English plain, Cornwall has preserved many of the very early elements which through the centuries have contributed to the making of the landscape. Here one finds historical geography written in the field rather than in the library: a living reality which makes a journey through Cornwall of lasting value and interest to the informed traveller.

The physical landscape upon which this story is written has its own unique qualities. A broad view of the peninsula reveals a series of wind-swept, rolling, plateau surfaces cut in granites and slates, rising in step-like sequence from the coast to the interior. Frequently ill-drained, exposed, and covered with *Erica* heathland at lower levels and *Molinia* and *Calluna* moorland at higher levels, one cannot avoid the use of adjectives such as 'bleak' and 'dull' to describe much of the scene. But there are two unfailing compensations. The flatter surfaces are interrupted by deep picturesque valleys, often steep sided, sheltered and well wooded, and in their lower parts drowned by the sea to form attractive estuaries. Secondly, where the upland surfaces reach the sea we find the glory of Cornwall, for on the coast tremendous cliffs drop several hundred feet sheer to the Atlantic swell. These magnificent volcanic and granitic cliffs, interspersed with sandy bays eroded in the less resistant slates and shales, form that beautiful and rugged coastal fringe of Cornwall which appeals so much to the holiday-maker.

But can we persuade the visitor to leave his beloved cliffs

and beaches and venture inland for a while? For in a day he may walk not only through fields and lanes, through farms and hamlets, through tiny fishing ports and torn-up mining areas, but also through 4,000 years of time during which man has visibly moulded the landscape. Here he may see the land of the megalith builder, walk through fields reclaimed by Celtic farmers, or linger on a farm recorded in the Domesday Book and already old even then. He may make his way over the moors by Cornish wayside crosses, eat his lunch in an unspoiled Anglo-Saxon village, pause for tea in a minute medieval fishing port, and dine in a twentieth-century tourist town. All these features, and many more, constitute the man-made landscape, which is superimposed in a complex and almost complete cover upon the physical foundation of rock and earth.

The traveller will find much to puzzle him, but it is a landscape well worth deciphering. Understanding will come most easily if he regards the landscape as a document, a palimpsest in which the writings of different ages partially obscure one another. With patience he will be able to decipher each writing, unravel their individual meanings, and trace the continuity between them. This will take him far, but it will not give the whole explanation: for unlike the palimpsest, the cultural landscape has been influenced by the parchment upon which it is inscribed. The facts of physical geography have guided, and at times controlled, the making of the human landscape. Hence, in interpreting the man-made aspects, the intelligent traveller must employ a dual code of reference – the physical stage or *scena* and then the actions of the men who have lived and acted upon it for the past four thousand years.

The traveller will see a landscape abundantly scattered with hamlets. This is the Celtic under-writing. Small settlements of only two or three farmhouses and labourers' cottages, carrying Celtic names, are common at cross-roads. In some will be found the parish church, but often this stands alone, with only the rectory or vicarage near by. Between the hamlets stretch open farmland of mixed pasture and arable, in which the fields are characteristically small, irregular-shaped enclosures bounded by massive granite or slate-walled hedges. Set down in the chequerboard pattern of fields, at remarkably regular intervals, are isolated farmsteads, joined to each other by narrow and often tunnel-like lanes where trees and bushes grow on the top of monumental hedgebanks. These narrow lanes, when seen on the map, have no systematic plan. They wander from farm to farm and have clearly evolved piecemeal over the centuries in response to local needs. Even the modern motor roads occasionally assume the same pattern, for they in turn have evolved out of sections of earlier trackways.

In the fields and hedgerows and along some of the roads, one finds in certain areas scores of prehistoric and historic monuments: here a megalithic tomb, there a Bronze Age barrow or stone circle, elsewhere an Iron Age camp or even a complete prehistoric village site, and stone wayside crosses by the dozen. There are few English counties with so rich a store of antiquities and so continuous a story to tell in such a visible form.

The pattern of tiny fields and dispersed settlements is more marked in Cornwall than in any other English county. Occasionally, however, large nucleated villages of the Anglo-Saxon type are found, more particularly in the east and north-east; and where the surrounding fields are long and narrow, strip-like in appearance, it is possible although by no means certain that the field pattern is of Anglo-Saxon origin. In other parts of the county much of the story of Cornwall unfolds itself through castles, churches, wayside chapels, mansions, farmhouses, fish cellars and bridges. Norman architecture in church and castle, medieval bridges, Elizabethan manor houses, nineteenth-century chapels, all in native stone, speak more eloquently than words of human activities long ago.

Cornwall has two unique landscapes in the mining and quarrying areas of the south-west. The skeletal remains of ancient tin and copper mining, and the white china-clay waste heaps, produce a scene quite unlike the normal industrial landscape of smoking tips and belching chimneys. Little is now left of the Cornish tin- and copper-mining industry, but it has left its mark on the county: acres of derelict land, of gorse and briar, of silent engine-houses and crumbling chimney stacks, now bear witness to the work of eighteenth- and nineteenth-century miners. The china-clay industry on the other hand continues to flourish, and the growing flat-topped mesa-like mounds of white scintillating silica-waste give an air of unreality to such areas as Hensbarrow Down near St Austell.

Cornwall is very largely a product of its own environment. Its own stone has been used in its farmhouses, cottages, churches and public buildings from time immemorial, and although this gives a greyness and certain sadness to many of the inland settlements, the buildings are in harmony with their surroundings. The architectural styles reflect the climate: slate-hung walls and cemented low-pitched roofs protect the granite and slate houses from strong winds and heavy rains, whilst solid, squat church towers stand four-square against Atlantic storms. Here in Cornwall we can see with a clarity perhaps greater than in any other county of England how the man-made landscape has evolved out of the natural landscape.

Richard Carew in his *Survey of Cornwall* of 1602 sums up the geographical individuality of Cornwall aptly when he describes how 'nature hath shouldered out Cornwall into the farthest part of the realm, and so beseiged it with the ocean that it forms a demi-island in an island'.

1. The face of the landscape

The structural basis. The form of the land.
The climatic factor. The skin of the land.
The mantle of vegetation.

IN AN EXPLANATION of the present scene one must not overlook the importance of the underlying factors of physical geography which have guided, influenced and in some cases determined the human utilisation of the natural landscape. To understand the stage and setting, we must first take note of certain basic facts of geology (Fig. 1) and geomorphology, and to appreciate the backcloth we must consider the essential elements of the climate, soils and vegetation.

The structural basis

Our story appropriately begins in the Lizard where we find some of the oldest rocks in Britain, dated by geologists as pre-Cambrian, i.e. at least 3,000 million years in age. Here most of the rocks are not sedimentary but rose into their present state in a molten fashion. Some remain as granite but other originally igneous rocks have been further altered or metamorphosed both chemically and physically by heat and pressure to form a range of schists, gneiss and serpentine unique in Britain. These rocks produce some of the most beautiful coastal scenery in Cornwall, although inland they give rise to unenclosed, treeless and windswept heaths, which whilst colourful with gorse in summer, can be cold and sodden with rushy, peaty hollows, bogs and standing water in winter. The serpentine is the basis of a small but flourishing ornamental-stone industry and the little workshops in Lizard, Cadgwith, Coverack and Mullion have by now supplied generations of visitors with souvenirs. The serpentine is, however, badly jointed and whilst this produces dramatic

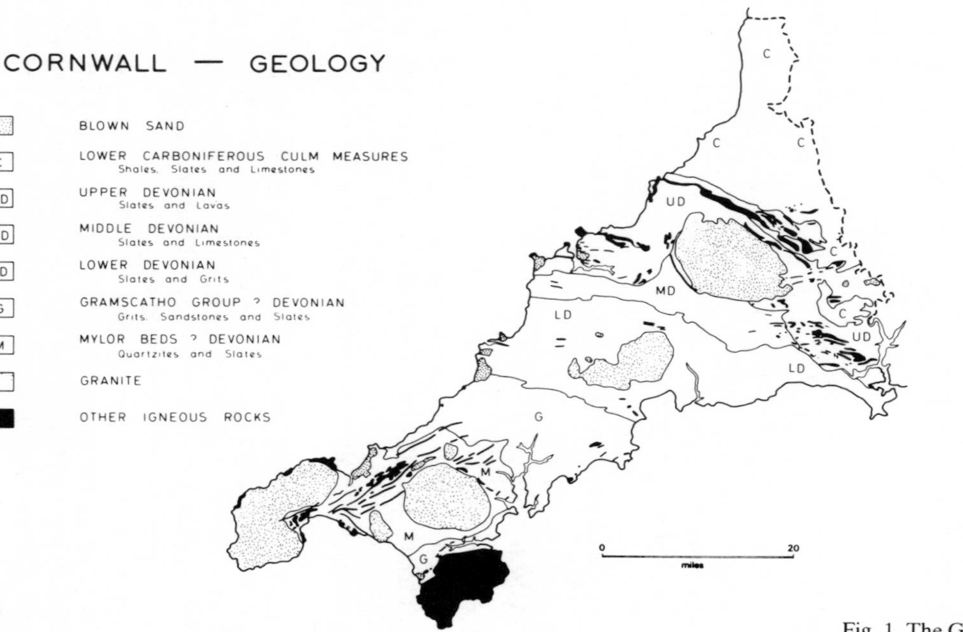

Fig. 1. The Geology of Cornwall (simplified). Based mainly on the quarter-inch maps of the Geological Survey.

coastal scenery it means that it cannot be used for building purposes like the granite.

The control of the serpentine on the landscape is clearly seen in the barren heaths of Goonhilly and Predannack Downs: where the outcrop ceases there is an immediate change to fertile farmed soils. Another landscape type is provided by the dark igneous gabbro of Crousa Downs which produces boulders of rocks (Plate 1) called 'crusairs' (from Crousa) originally scattered in their thousands upon the surface but now used to wall fields laboriously carved from the wasteland. The reward of this labour is a deep, rich, fertile yellow soil which gave rise to the appellation 'Garden of Cornwall' when the area once formed the main granary of the county. Another Lizard rock is the Kennack granite which is unique in being very close jointed. It does not produce the tors or the moorstone blocks of the normal granite and has no value as a building stone nor as a mineral source. To the north of the serpentine, gabbro and granites are schists – altered igneous and sedimentary rocks – forming the geologically intriguing Meneage suite and Breccia shatter belt, but from our point of view the significance is the resulting deep red fertile soil and the large number of roadstone quarries.

We are now passing into rocks of apparent Ordovician age, much folded and occurring in overthrust and shattered masses faulted against the Lizard rocks. Notable exposures can be seen at Manaccan, Veryan and Gorran Haven. Although limited in extent, these rocks supply evidence of the great Caledonian mountain-building episode, a remote phase in the geological history of the British Isles but of considerable significance in Cornwall, since it is from this event in the Silurian era that the peninsula owes its present dominant trend-line from north-east to south-west. This, the line of the Caledonian folding, was later to guide a series of granitic intrusions.

Before this occurred, however, the Caledonian mountains were worn away and the denuded stumps were submerged in a sea which allowed the accumulation of mudstones, thin limestones and grits of Devonian and Carboniferous age, later to form the basis of the killas country of Cornwall. Interspersed with these sedimentary deposits were occasional layers of lava, laid down under submarine conditions to give pillow forms, and at a later date there were intrusions of igneous rocks, such as greenstone dykes and sills.

These rocks developed more especially near the present-day St Minver. They are much more resistant than the surrounding killas and are now conspicuous in the landscape. Many small capes and headlands, such as Pentire Point and Trevose Head, are composed of varieties of volcanic and intrusive rock. These rocks are also often of economic importance for road metal.

All these deposits were in turn elevated into mountains during the Hercynian mountain-building episode of the late Carboniferous period. On this occasion the folding was mainly directed along east to west lines and since these were the last major mountain-building movements to affect the area, Cornwall, along with Devon, now consists structurally of a huge compound trough or syncline of pre-Cambrian, Ordovician, Devonian and Carboniferous rocks. Into this, but significantly along the lines of the Caledonian folds, there was intruded during the Hercynian episode a series of igneous rocks, largely granitic, which have been very important in the development of the natural and man-made landscape of Cornwall.

First and foremost amongst these intrusions are the granitic domes or bosses; of these the largest, Dartmoor, lies outside the county, but Cornwall claims the remaining four – Bodmin Moor, Hensbarrow or St Austell Moor, the Carnmenellis area west of Falmouth, and the Land's End or Penwith peninsula. The higher parts of the granite form extensive unreclaimed moorland strewn with weathered granitic blocks known as clitter or moorstone (Plate 2). These are bedded in loose granitic sand covered with heath of *Calluna* and *Erica* associations, and occasionally including ill-drained peat bogs. They afford a glimpse of the natural landscape from which early man wrested a precarious living, using clitter for his primitive dwellings, with dry-stone walls around his minute fields, ritual stone circles and huge slabs for his burial chambers. Looking at the size of the moorstones used, it is easy to explain the numerous legends that arose about giants that once lived in Cornwall. Just how prehistoric man handled these enormous blocks remains a mystery. Granite thus figures in the story of Cornwall right from early times down through the centuries to modern man.

The granite is usually jointed and this gives rise to the picturesque tors – piles of weathered slabs – which surmount the higher parts (Plate 3). These rounded blocks often rest precariously on top of one another, hence the name 'logan' (rocking) stone applied to many. At least two dozen tors over 1,000 feet high occur on Bodmin Moor; notably Brown Willy (1,375), Rough Tor (1,311), Kilmar Tor (1,296), the Cheesewring (1,250) and Caradon Hill (1,213). There are also smaller bosses of limited extent but equally significant in the natural and cultural landscape, such as Kit Hill near Callington, Castle an Dinas (with its Iron Age fort) near St Columb Major, Carn Brea (also with a castle) near Redruth, St Agnes Beacon near Perranporth, Cligga Head on the north coast, St Michael's Mount near Penzance, and the isolated archipelago of the Scilly Isles.

The overlying Devonian and Carboniferous rocks in immediate contact with the granitic intrusions were considerably altered as a result of the great heat and pressure, and we now find that the exposed granite bosses are surrounded by a metamorphic aureole of greater or less extent. Shales passed into phyllites, mudstones were compacted and hardened into slates, and famous varieties such as the Delabole blue were formed. It is a feature of the Cornish landscape that most old buildings are slate roofed and many are slate hung as a protection against the weather. In the slate areas walls, floors, lintels and sills as well as the roofs are constructed of slate.

The influence of the igneous intrusions had not yet ceased, however, for at a later date volatile substances in a liquid or gaseous condition rose through the granite and in places altered both the granite and the overlying sedimentary rocks. As these intrusions cooled, so ore bodies formed in the cavities and fissures, giving rise to tin, copper, silver, lead, zinc, wolfram and other mineral-bearing lodes and veins, which have been so significant in the history of Cornwall and so significant a factor in the present cultural landscape. The mineralised zone of Cornwall extends in a north-east-south-west line down the backbone of the county and is about eight miles in width. The lodes and veins also run north-east-south-west and the same trend-lines can be traced in the layout of the older lanes and streets in the Camborne-Redruth area: these, along with lines of old mine buildings, mineral railways and discarded material or 'deads' have been inherited from the time when the early miners followed the lodes.

Alterations in the granite also took place during these upheavals and the changes are of importance in the present study. In some areas the granite was tourmalinised, i.e. the felspars and micas were replaced by tourmaline and tough schorl rock resulted. Reef-like masses of this rock now resist erosion and form bold features in the landscape, as at Roche Rock on Hensbarrow Down (Plate 18), the Devil's Jump near Camelford, and Lanlavery Rock north of Bodmin Moor. The second type of alteration has been even more important in that some granite was kaolinised, i.e. the crystals of felspar were changed by carbon dioxide into kaolinite or china clay. With this kind of change the granite loses its coherence and disintegrates more easily. Whilst all the granite masses show some signs of kaolinisation, the Hensbarrow Down or St Austell mass has undergone the greatest change and an area of about thirty square miles now consists largely of china clay. The extraction of the clay forms an important industry and the white mounds of quartz and other rejected materials dominate this landscape. Once again, we may note that the change has taken place along fissures trending from north-east to south-west and the great pits have been opened up along these lines.

Finally, in some districts the granite has been changed in yet another way, resulting in the formation of china stone, a white, hard, resistant rock deriving much of its character from the introduction of fluorspar. It occurs most abundantly in the western part of the St Austell mass around Nanpean. Industrially it is important, after grinding down, as a base in the manufacture of porcelain.

The granitic sands of the flat-floored moorland valleys contain alluvial tin derived from the lodes within the granite. Stream tinners have been active in many areas since pre-Roman times, and more recently china clay has been extracted from the Hensbarrow Down and Bodmin Moor districts, whilst modern man has quarried the granite for building stones. These activities give each of the granite areas a strong individuality: Hensbarrow Down dominated by its china clay industry has almost entirely lost its moorland character, Carnmenellis is characterised by relics of a great mining past, the Penwith peninsula has antiquities scattered amongst small mixed farms, whilst Bodmin Moor, the highest and most remote of all the areas, is bleak and cold in winter, in contrast with the Scilly Isles, a land of mild winters and spring flowers.

Serpentine, gneiss, schists, slates, mudstones, phyllites, granite, china clay and intrusive veins of tin, copper, lead, silver, zinc and wolfram thus constitute the geological basis in Cornwall from which man has wrested a living and made his impress. But nature had first to provide the shape and form of the surface upon which human action could take place and it is to the geomorphologist that we must now turn for an explanation of the events which have produced the present-day physical landscape.

The form of the land

In attempting to explain the form of the ground, the geomorphologist must at times be concerned with past events for which little or no evidence is available. Thus in Cornwall we can only surmise that throughout the greater part of the 150-million-year geological era known as the Mesozoic, the areas uplifted by the Hercynian mountain building were gradually being reduced by erosion and that the granite intrusions were slowly emerging to form island-like masses rising above the surrounding less resistant rocks. Whilst it is probable that yet another marine submergence took place during the 65 million years of the Cretaceous period at the end of Mesozoic time, any associated deposits have long since been swept away in the continued erosion of the 70 million years of the Tertiary era. It does seem, however, that the present drainage pattern is inherited in part from that which probably existed in Cretaceous time and that it has been let down or superimposed upon the underlying Palaeozoic rocks from a Cretaceous cover. A hypothesis of this kind is necessary to account for the anomalous courses followed by some present-day rivers.

Another mountain-building episode, the Alpine, now intervened, but this had little effect on the Palaeozoic block of Cornwall. Subsequent earth movements associated with a marine transgression, however, led to the almost complete submergence of the county in post-Alpine time, such that only the summits of Bodmin Moor remained visible above the waves much as the Scilly Isles appear today. The ensuing re-emergence of the area from the sea appears to have taken place by discontinuous stages with the result that a series of old sea floors or planes of marine abrasion have been cut at successively lower levels into the pre-existing landscape of sub-aerial relief (Plate 4). These flatter surfaces now remain as narrow shelves eroded into the killas and the island-like masses associated with the granite. As the land re-emerged, so the rivers were lengthened and rejuvenated: where old valley lines were not followed, sharp V-shaped incisions were cut into the levels which had previously been the old sea floors. It is this sequence of events, more than anything else, that explains the present-day character of the inland scenery of Cornwall: a landscape which can be summed up in the statement that it is a region of deep, narrow, V-shaped valleys, alternating with flat-topped interfluves which rise in step-like formation inland from the surrounding coast. It is a theme which, in various guises, continually recurs in the geologic, topographic and literary descriptions of Cornwall throughout the last century and a half.

There are still some differences of opinion among geomorphologists as to the exact number, origin and age of the flatter areas or erosion surfaces, but these differences need not concern us here. Many of the features are unmistakable and comprise important elements in the physical landscape with clearly traceable repercussions in the cultural landscape. Of these, special mention should be made of the surface developed at about 1,000 feet which is well shown on Bodmin Moor and especially across the extensive locality known as Davidstow Moor. Here as elsewhere, the flatter areas are marked by broad, shallow valleys, often ill-drained and boggy and filled with peat and alluvium containing stream tin. The alluvial deposits have been turned over in both pre-Roman and medieval times in the search for tin, and the mounds and hollows left by the stream tinners, as for example on Withybrook Marsh, form a characteristic part of the moorland scene.

Below the 1,000-foot level, another flattening occurs between 750 and 800 feet which truncates all the hills of the Penwith peninsula and which can be traced shelf-like around Bodmin Moor and St Austell Moor. A further flattening from 550 to 675 feet is conspicuous on the southern border of Bodmin Moor and detectable in isolated fragments elsewhere. Below this occurs the very extensive and famous 300 to 430-foot platform which fringes much of the present Cornish coast and which is backed by an unmistakable bluff, marking the position of the old cliff line associated with this erosion surface. Both platform and bluff are especially well developed in the area from Boscastle to Trebarwith, along the coast west of Camborne, where from out of the plain rises St Agnes Beacon ringed with marine sands and clays. The platform continues along the coast from Land's End to St Ives and across the northern part of the Lizard peninsula.

The 300 to 430-foot surface merges into a lower surface from 200 to 250 feet which is important in the Newquay-Padstow area, in the southern part of the Lizard (where the ruler-straight skyline profile is most distinctive) and in the district around Falmouth. All these ancient marine surfaces and their associated cliff lines cut indiscriminately across the geological boundaries, and if later erosion has picked out a resistant member and left it upstanding, the top is normally relatively flat and truncated at one or other of the levels mentioned above.

On the basis of the few scattered marine sands and gravels, of which some are fossiliferous, found at St Erth, Polcrebo, St Agnes and on Crousa Common, the erosion surfaces have been dated as Pliocene to early Pleistocene. The lack of any general spread of marine deposits on the surfaces has been advanced by some as a serious weakness in the submarine origin interpretation. Recently, however, aqualung divers have shown that deposits on the west coast of Cornwall are confined to a very narrow beach zone and that a bare rock platform is soon reached. If past offshore conditions on the staircase of platforms resembled those of the present wave-cut abrasion platform, it is not difficult to account for the absence of deposits on the relatively narrow submarine shelves that are now exposed. It must be remembered that there was no large adjacent land mass in Cornwall upon which substantial debris-carrying rivers could arise.

The problem of the large shifts in sea level has also greatly exercised the minds of the geomorphologists, but coastal shelves of this magnitude are common in many other parts of the world, notably Portugal, California and the west coast of South America. The cataclysmic movements now associated with modern theories of mountain building as a result of the movement of crustal plates, might well provide a future answer to this problem.

The legacy of the glaciation of the Pleistocene period in Cornwall is largely confined to the accumulation of masses of frost-shattered rocks and solifluction material known as 'head' which now infills some of the valley bottoms. Accompanying this and associated with the increased rainfall and progressive denudation of the area, many minerals, especially tin, were redeposited in the upland valleys and this has spread the area worked over by the stream tinners. The delineation of the Ice-Age or Pleistocene coastline must have been very similar to the present coastline, for much of the latter is fringed by raised beach fragments of the glacial age. There was a further fall of sea level after the glacial episode and this allowed extensive over-deepening of the lower reaches of the major rivers. When the sea returned to its old level, probably in Neolithic times, the over-deepened parts were submerged and the ria-like branching estuaries of the Camel, Helford, Fal, Fowey, Looe and other valleys were created (Plate 5). These have been a mixed blessing to Cornwall, for whilst they have opened up a considerable area to the warm waters of the Gulf Stream, producing sheltered sub-tropical localities which encourage market gardening, flower growing and the tourist industry, they have also obstructed inland transport, necessitating many ferries, and making road and railway construction difficult; there are, for instance, thirty-four viaducts in the fifty-three miles of railway between Plymouth and Truro.

Much silting from tin streaming and china clay working has occurred in the upper parts of these estuaries and they are now much less extensive than when first formed. Tregony functioned as a port in the Middle Ages and barges were once able to reach Lostwithiel on the tide. Tresillian, Devoran and Point on the Fal have all declined. Gweek on the Helford, and Lelant on the Hayle river have shared the same fate.

Within historic time, a completely new type of natural landscape has been created on parts of the west coast with the accumulation of great masses of wind-blown sand piled into dunes or towans by the prevailing south-westerly winds. Whilst dunes are a common feature of nearly all the bay heads along the west coast, large complexes reaching heights of up to 200 feet and covering many square miles occur in localities such as Daymer Bay in the Camel estuary and along the coast near Perranporth and Gwithian. Proof of the relatively recent migration of the sand is afforded by the destruction and disappearance of oratories and chapels which must have been built originally on favourable sites. Most is known about the Perranporth district where the oratory of St Piran could have been founded in the sixth or seventh century by one of the Celtic saints. This little building, of which the walls still remain, had to be abandoned in the eleventh century because of the encroaching sand and a new church was built further inland. The medieval church in its turn was engulfed by the shifting sand and a third church was constructed in 1804 at Lamborne. Elsewhere the medieval chapel of St Constantine has been destroyed by the sands, the Norman church of St Enodoc near Daymer Bay was long buried in sand and was dug out and restored as recently as 1863, whilst the site of an oratory is also known at Gwithian, but this has again disappeared beneath the dunes and nothing is now visible. Historical records also reveal that much movement of the sand has taken place in the last few centuries; for example Leland found St Ives '. . . sore oppressed or over coverid with sandes . . .', whilst Norden records that St Minver was '. . . much annoyed with sea sand . . .'. More recently the planting of grasses has stabilised considerable areas: *Psamma arenaria* has been used extensively on the bare sand and this, when stabilisation occurs, is replaced by *Carex arenaria*. These areas now face a new threat with the over-use of the dunes in the summer holiday season.

Finally, particular mention must be made of the zone of interaction between the land and the sea wherein much of Cornwall's glory lies. There are some 268 miles of coastline in Cornwall and probably no county in Britain has such a diversity and beauty of coastal features as that possessed by the Principality. The charm undoubtedly lies in the fact that much if not most of the coastline is cliffed, but it is also interspersed with sheltered coves and warm and well-wooded creeks. The cliff forms are all directly related to the type of rock the marine forces are acting upon. The granites, greenstones, slates, serpentines and schists react in different ways, although all are highly resistant so that high and vertical cliffs are common, truncated by whatever erosion surface they are cut into.

The granite cliffs of the Land's End area achieve a splendour of their own through their battlemented appearance which is related to joint-controlled erosion (Plate 6). Other associated features include numerous caves, stacks, coves and 'zawns' or narrow gullies eroded along the joints. The greenstone is even more resistant to erosion than the granite and gives rise to some of the highest and least accessible cliffs in the Penwith peninsula, notably from Cape Cornwall to Pendeen and at Porth near St Ives. Zennor Head, Gurnard's Head and the Island at St Ives are also of greenstone.

In the killas country roughly parallel belts of shales, mudstones, slates and phyllites, which lie across the county from east to west, reach the north coast at right angles and this allows differential erosion by the fierce Atlantic breakers. Fine bays such as Trevone, Harlyn, Booby's, Constantine, Watergate, Perranporth and St Ives are cut in the softer slaty rocks. Demarcating the bays are numerous cliffed headlands of harder rock, such as the tough grit of Godrevy, the altered killas of St Agnes, the pillow lava of Pentire Point, and the greenstones of Park Head, Trevose Head, Stepper Point and the Rumps. There is even a chert (a flint-like quartz) headland in Beeny Cliff. On the south coast parallel outcrops of killas meet the coast at an angle and the pattern is broken by the extensive rias, but sandy bays such as Mount's, Gerrans, Mevagissey and Whitsand again characterise the softer sedimentaries with the headlands formed of igneous rocks, greenstones and granite. Only the Dodman (phyllite) and Rame Head (slate and gritstone) remain in the sedimentaries.

As might be expected, the Lizard has its own varied assortment of cliff forms in the serpentine, gabbro and schists. Here are found some of the best-known Cornish cliffs and coves – Kynance, Coverack, Kennack, Cadgwith and Carrick Luz to name but a few.

Whilst in general the cliffs are highly resistant to wave action, lines of weakness are eventually revealed and joints, faults, folds and bedding planes give the waves an opportunity to carve a splendid series of caves, blow holes, gullies, clefts or 'drangs', arches and stacks which add a spectacular variety to the coast. Merlin's Cave at Tintagel, the Banqueting Hall at Newquay, the Drawing Room at Kynance, and the blow holes at Holestrow and Lawarnick will be well known to many visitors.

The climatic factor

Whilst the geomorphological and geological characteristics set the stage for man, historically his options in terms of environmental utilisation are limited by the further conditions set by the climate, soils and vegetation. The climate of any area is broadly the result of its position relative to the patterns of the general circulation of the atmosphere, and the disposition of neighbouring land and sea masses. Over the British Isles the climate is dominated for much of the year by the mid-latitude westerlies whilst day-to-day weather variability arises from its marginal position between the Atlantic Ocean and the continent of Europe. Within this major meteorological complex Cornwall has a unique climate by virtue of its southerly latitude and projection westward into the Atlantic.

Maritime influences prevail and Cornwall has the most equable climate of the whole country. Yet it also exhibits some very marked local contrasts that can hardly be called pleasant. Winter temperatures in Cornwall are relatively high for Britain; averages of well above 5°C (41°F) are common on the south coast. The average January mean temperature in the Scilly Isles is 7.9°C (46.3°F). Along with this high winter figure are relatively low summer averages, often less than 16°C (59.8°F), which together with low diurnal ranges (4.2°C, 7.5°F in the Scillies) produce Britain's most equable temperature recordings. The maritime influence can also be seen in the lateness of the lowest and highest average temperature recordings. February usually reveals the lowest mean average temperature and August the highest. Averages can, of course, be misleading especially when the passage of a front with a steep thermal gradient can produce sudden temperature changes of 5–10°C (9–18°F). Cornwall also occasionally experiences air from the Continent when the westerly system breaks down. Both variations can produce extremes of heat and cold which are conveniently ignored by the guide books. Whilst it is true that severe frost is far from common it is by no means unknown and can be a hazard in low-lying situations subject to cold air drainage. Occasionally extreme minima well below freezing point may be recorded.

The rainfall is well distributed throughout the year with a small winter maximum, but the amount received over the county varies considerably, ranging from 35 inches on the coast to over 70 inches on the high moorland areas. There is a close correlation between rainfall and relief. The 40-inch annual rainfall line (isohyet) encircles the Land's End peninsula, the 50-inch Carnmenellis, Hensbarrow Down and Hartland, whilst the 50-, 60- and 70-inch isohyets parallel the contours on Bodmin Moor. Compared with much of the rest of England the precipitation would be considered heavy. Snow is rare, although occasional snow showers in winter may lie for a day or two on high ground. The frequency of the snow tends to diminish westwards and the quantity increases with altitude when, exceptionally, winter depressions skirting the edge of high pressure areas may deposit substantial amounts. The winters of 1928–9, 1946–7, 1962–3 and 1978–9 are particularly memorable in this respect. In a similar way, exceptionally heavy falls of rain have been absorbed into the folklore because of the damage caused. The downpour of

16th July, 1847 on Bodmin Moor destroyed most of the bridges on the Camel and Inny, and similar cloudbursts on 30th August, 1950 and 8th June, 1957 over Camelford caused further memorable floods. It is thought that the 8th June, 1957 rainfall over Rough Tor near Camelford, when between 6 and 7 inches fell in just over two hours was close to, if it did not exceed, the greatest hourly intensity ever experienced in Britain.

If Cornwall is somewhat wetter than the rest of England it is also considerably sunnier, apart from some selected stations in the south-east of England. The Scilly Isles average some 1,725 hours of sunshine per year and although the number falls inland with the increased cloudiness even here a drop below 1,500 hours is uncommon. June and July are the sunniest months followed by August. September is variable and there is a marked decline over the winter months. Sunshine correlates inversely with cloud and fog and it is the latter which also, paradoxically, characterises the Cornish climatic scene. Fog often blankets the land for days on end in winter – and sometimes in summer – and whilst this may produce picturesque sunsets and eerie effects with drifting shadows, it is another feature which is discreetly ignored by the holiday guide books. Advection fog arising from the cooling of moist tropical maritime air flowing over a relatively cold English Channel or cold land surface is the main culprit, but radiation fog can also occur.

Probably the most adverse factor is wind. Norden describes the 'fierce and furious wyndes' that 'sharply assayle the naked hills and dales' in Cornwall and modern records reveal that the county, thrust out into the Atlantic, has perhaps the most exposed position in England. Whilst Kew averages less than an hour a year with the wind above 40 m.p.h. many parts of Cornwall experience more than 200. Kew averages 60 hours per year with the wind above 25 m.p.h. whilst in Cornwall the average rises to 1,500 hours. Often the anemometers at Scilly, Lizard and Penzance record the strongest gusts for the year of all British stations: on 6th December, 1929 Scilly recorded gusts of 111 m.p.h.

Winds of this kind combined with the coasts of Cornwall have long formed a notorious death-trap for numerous ships.

It is quite likely that more wrecks have occurred in these waters than anywhere else in the British Isles. The many cliff-top burials bear mute witness to these disasters of the past. Even with modern sophisticated aids disasters occur; the Fastnet ocean yacht race of August 1979 resulted in the loss of fifteen lives and twenty-four yachts sunk or abandoned.

Shelter from the prevailing westerlies hence becomes of paramount importance and the climatic factor can be seen at work in the location of flower and vegetable fields, in the distribution of vegetation types, and in the construction and design of buildings. The winds also largely account for the contrast between the bare, open, plateau surfaces and the more thickly wooded valleys. Hedgerow trees in exposed places all lean to the north-east and have streamlined canopies (Plate 7), whilst in some areas the trees will not grow because even the heavy rainfall will not compensate for the excessive transpiration associated with the passage of a more-or-less continuous air-stream. In contrast, the sheltered southern valleys have locations where sub-tropical plants will survive; these have been introduced artificially and although they exist without much difficulty they cannot be said to thrive. Probably more significant is the fact that the temperature rarely falls below the critical point at which growth stops. Grass continues to grow throughout the winter and conditions are very favourable for the cultivation of early vegetables and flowers, such as cabbages, cauliflowers, potatoes, daffodils, narcissi etc..

Richard Carew in his 1602 *Survey* aptly summarises the climate when he states

> The spring visiteth not these quarters so timely as the eastern parts. Summer imparteth a very temperate heat, recompensing his slow fostering of the fruits with their kindly ripening. Autumn bringeth a somewhat late harvest. Winter by reason of the south's near neighbourhood and sea's warm breath, favoureth it with a milder cold than elsewhere, so as upon both coasts the frost and snow come very seldom, and make a speedy departure. This notwithstanding, the county is much subject to storms, which fetching a large course in the open sea, do from thence

Plate 1 Natural landscape on Crousa Down in St Keverne, showing residual blocks ('crusairs') of weathered gabbro.

Plate 2 The granite landscape of Bodmin Moor. Clitter covers the foreground and the slopes of Roughtor (1,311 feet) in the middle distance. Also seen is Fernacre Farm at 900 feet marking the limit of medieval and modern farming. Bronze Age hut circles lie just beyond the boundary of the farm.

Plate 3 The summit of Roughtor (1,311 feet) Bodmin Moor. Weathering along the joints in the granite produces 'tors' and 'logan' (rocking) stones.

Plate 4 Logan Rock, Porthcuno. A flat-topped coastal platform of marine abrasion cut in the granite near Land's End. Note also the lack of trees in this exposed position.

Plate 5 The river Fal estuary. An example of the drowned river valleys of the southern coastal zone. Note the wooded character of the steeper slopes of the valleys which dissect the exposed erosion surfaces.

Plate 6 Land's End. The combination of marine and sub-aerial erosion acting on jointed granite produces spectacular cliff forms.

Plate 7 Slades, Bodmin Moor. Wind-blown and desiccated trees. Strong winds both control and inhibit tree growth in exposed positions.

Plate 8 Halvana Forest, Altarnun. A Forestry Commission plantation on Bodmin Moor.

> violently assault the dwellers at land, and leave them uncovered houses, pared hedges and dwarf-grown trees as witness of their force and fury; yea, even the hard stones and iron bars of the windows do fret to be continually grated.

This brief sketch of the climate of Cornwall concentrates on the present-day characteristics. It must not be forgotten when considering the sequence of human occupation in the peninsula, that subtle and important changes in the climate have at times occurred and these have had profound effects on both man and his habitat. Attention will be drawn to these changes as the narrative unfolds.

The skin of the land

The soils of Cornwall are closely related to the interaction of the underlying geology with the climate, but the rocks are the major determinant and here we have several groups. On the granite much depends on whether areas are wet or dry and the extent to which vegetation enters the soil complex. The areas with high rainfall figures have peaty soils classified as either blanket or valley bog, or peaty gley soils (where the lower 'gley' horizon is grey and oxygen deficient). In badly drained areas, the peat may be very acid and several feet in depth. In better drained localities, a light black peaty loam may result, with a high fertility potential. Peaty ash-like soils known as podzols with a horizon of thin iron pan are found on uncultivated granite moorland carrying *Molinia* grass. At lower levels these pass into acid brown soils.

On the Devonian and Carboniferous grits, shales and slates, the soils contain numerous fragments of slate and are known in Cornish as shillet: these soils fall into the acid brown category, with free soil drainage and moderately fine textures, forming loams and clays which are heavily leached as a result of the high rainfall. Shale outcrops of the Culm Measures are notorious for their poor drainage and this may be aggravated by the flat plateau surfaces: these soils are boggy in winter which encourages the growth of reeds and rushes.

The texture of the soil is sometimes influenced by the

presence of wind-blown dust (loess) derived from the last phase of the Pleistocene period. This is particularly noticeable in the Lizard where several feet probably mantled the serpentine outcrop at one time. Locally, head deposits from the Pleistocene may have a considerable effect on soil formation.

The correlation between fertility, soil type and rock type in Cornwall was noted as early as 1842 by De la Beche. Lime, nitrogen and potash must be added to most Cornish soils if they are to be continuously productive. The beaches and sand dunes have traditionally supplied calcareous material and it is probable that some 70 per cent of the lime applied annually still comes from this source. Organic material lost through leaching has to be replaced by manure, seaweed or fertiliser.

The mantle of vegetation

Under natural conditions the vegetation would reflect the climatic and soil conditions. This would have been the case in Cornwall for the early part of the post-Pleistocene period until about 5,000 years ago when man first appeared in numbers on the natural landscape. A third factor of steadily-increasing importance was then introduced: today there are few natural plant communities in the Principality as a result of human deforestation, grazing and pasture changes. Man, having been subject himself to the effects of climatic and hence vegetation change, has in recent centuries been even more effective than climate in altering the natural scene.

Pollen analysis has given us a clear picture of the evolution of the vegetation pattern with the progressive amelioration of the climate following upon the glacial period. About 10000 B.C. birch trees and smaller pines characterised the initial cool phases of the post-glacial period, but after 7000 B.C. the warm, dry conditions of the Boreal climatic phase encouraged the spread of oak, elm, alder and hazel. About 5000 B.C. the climate changed to the cooler, wetter conditions of the Atlantic phase and the oak, elm and alder forests increased in altitudinal extent so that the whole landscape of Cornwall was probably covered with deciduous trees in this forest maximum. It is thought that the only trace of this cover now existing in Cornwall is the stunted oak wood at the Dizzard near Crackington Haven.

Subsequently, with the onset of even wetter oceanic conditions, the forests began to recede from the upland areas and blanket and valley bogs took their place. By 3000 B.C. man had begun to have an important impact on the landscape and the trend set by nature was accelerated by forest felling to provide land for pasture and cultivation. The grazing of domestic animals further prevented regeneration of the woodland and preserved a grass cover. Wood was also felled for constructional purposes and for fires.

Coppice cropping for charcoal and the harvesting of oak bark for local tanneries were common activities in historic time, so that it is little wonder that Cornwall now has but 5.76 per cent of its surface area under woods. Coupled with this man-mounted attack on the forests, there has also been the problem of the high casualty rate amongst trees at high altitudes as a result of the desiccation and exposure to the winds. Most of the woodland that now remains is located in sheltered valleys, is largely owned by the Duchy of Cornwall and consists of oak, beech, ash and sycamore.

One of the more attractive features of the limited Cornish woodland is the ground flora of the oak woods. Hazel, blackthorn, honeysuckle, holly, wood anemone, bluebells, primroses, ling, whortleberry, golden rod, and the huge pink and white flowers of the bastard balm add colour and variety in and out of season; but visitors will probably notice first and foremost the prolific fern growths; male fern, lady fern, golden scale and soft shield fern are all very common.

The eighteenth and nineteenth centuries saw the addition of patches of woodland and a considerable number of extensive gardens planted for scientific and amenity purposes. The woods include many introduced species, such as sweet chestnut, white poplar, Scots pine, Turkey pine and Monterey pine together with some magnificent stands of beech at places such as Boconnoc and Lanhydrock. A wide range of introduced shrubs often support the landscaped parks and gardens most of which are now in National Trust hands, forming an important part of the tourist industry. The gardens at Antony House, Cotehele House, Glendurgan, Lanhydrock House,

Penjerrick, Tregothnan, Trelissick, Trengwainton and Trewithen are particularly noteworthy. The twentieth century has witnessed additionally the activities of the Forestry Commission which has been responsible for a limited number of coniferous plantations (Plate 8). Glynn in the Fowey, Bodmin in the Camel, Herodsfoot in the Looe, and St Clement in the Allen valleys, together with two experimental exposure plantations on Wilsey Down and Croft Pascoe in the Lizard constitute the main holdings.

Moorland and heathland occupies over 100,000 acres of Cornwall (roughly one-eighth of the county) and it is largely, if not wholly, correlative with altitude: both moorland and heathland may also be sub-divided according to moisture content in the soil which in most cases determines the plants and dependent animal communities. With well-drained conditions heather moor occurs in the upland areas and purple heather or ling (*Calluna vulgaris*) dominates, although colourful patches of western gorse (*Ulex gallii*) and the crimson purple bell heather (*Erica cinera*) may add variety. Locally the whortleberry (*Vaccinium myrtillus*) is also found. If this type of heather moor is heavily grazed by sheep or rabbits, sheep's fescue (*Festuca ovina*) and fine bent (*Agrostis tenuis*) take over to form an upland grassland.

With increasing dampness the mat grass (*Nardus stricta*) and purple moor grass (*Molinia caerulea*) begin to dominate in an assemblage well shown to the north of Bodmin and on Bodmin Moor where purple moor grass is the main vegetative cover on the peat. Eventually this passes to a wet condition with standing or stagnant water on which *Sphagnum* moss and cotton grass (*Eriophorum angustifolium*) flourish. It is the continued growth of the *Sphagnum* moss which gives rise to the blanket and valley bogs. Exceptionally wet areas form the so-called piskie pits in which the moss, usually of a vivid emerald green, may reach depths of twelve feet or more. Extensive *Sphagnum* growth probably began on Bodmin Moor during the prehistoric wet Atlantic phase, and although the peat has not yet revealed any human remains, and few animal remains, it has preserved the pollen of former surrounding forests which enables us to build up a picture of the post-glacial evolution of the peninsula. For the keen botanist, the blanket bog areas also contain deer grass (*Trichophorum cespitosum*) which is rare in southern England, but the summer visitor to Cornwall is more likely to notice the cotton grass moor with its white cotton-covered fruits waving in the breeze. True valley bogs are now rare in Cornwall as so many were disturbed by the old stream tinners.

Large continuous stretches of moorland are found on the granite areas of Bodmin Moor, Hensbarrow Down and the Penwith peninsula although the edges have been nibbled away by pasture farms, a process which has gone right across Carnmenellis Moor. These moorlands exhibit the complete range of plants and conditions from dry to wet, with acid soils that may or may not be peat.

Heathland is normally associated with lowland where the soil has been leached after the removal of deciduous trees. Heath, also, can be wet or dry with differing results. The heathlands along the coastal strip of Cornwall, however, are now thought to be remnants of a natural vegetation cover only a few hundred yards wide which separated the cliff vegetation from the original forest cover, the dividing line being dependent on the penetration of salt spray. These heathlands have an oceanic flora not dissimilar from the Atlantic coasts of southern Europe and form the so-called Lusitanian element in the British flora. The western gorse *Ulex gallii* with its brilliant carpet of yellow flowers dominates in the summer months. Mining has, however, disturbed the natural habitat in many places.

Wet heaths are the lowland equivalent of the upland valley bogs. They develop in waterlogged acid soils along stream courses and were probably common in Cornwall until destroyed by the stream tinners. The Cornwall Naturalists' Trust has recently acquired a wet heath near Truro, known as Ventongimps Moor, which it is hoped to restore to a natural condition. This moor contains *Sphagnum* and a number of rare plants such as *Erica ciliaris* and *Pinguicula Lusitanica*. Also in this category and now within the keeping of the Cornwall Naturalists' Trust and the Nature Conservancy Council, is much of the famous Lizard heathland. These holdings plus the Goonhilly Downs satellite tracking station reservation, should ensure the preservation of the unique

Cornish heath of *Erica vagans*, found only in this part of England. It is the unique soil condition of the Lizard which explains the juxtaposition of species found in both acid and basic rich habitats. Other damp heathlands may be found on the Culm Measures of north Cornwall where there is frequently very poor drainage and rushes invade the pasture fields. This type of land often grades into rushy moors and then into cotton grass moors. On drier soils and near the limit of cultivation, pasture fields are frequently invaded by bracken (*Pteridium*). Elsewhere much of the heathland associated with Hensbarrow and Carnmenellis Downs has been disturbed by china clay and granite workings as well as by farming.

In north Cornwall various types of alluvial marsh exist. These areas are situated on the Devonian rocks near the sea, but they are not subject to flooding by salt or brackish water and they form a type of reedswamp. One such area near Polzeath contains *Cyperus longus* and *Sparganium erectus*. A further type of alluvial marsh is found higher up the rivers and farther from maritime influence: here *Juncus articulatus* is dominant and woody plants are beginning a process of colonisation.

A further conspicuous feature of the coastal zone is the extensive area of sand dunes already described. Many of the dunes are now stabilised with marram grass (*Psamma arenaria*), which is eventually replaced by *Carex arenaria* along with a mixed plant community which includes rest harrow (*Ononis repens*) and moss (*Tortula ruraliformis*).

Cornwall is also noted for its profusion of wild flowers. Throughout the county the banks and verges along the roads and the cliff edges, along with the remaining parts of the remoter areas, are gay with wild flowers during most of the year. More than 1,050 species of flowering plants and ferns have been recorded in Cornwall, of which approximately 20 per cent are aliens, casuals, garden escapes and introductions. About 130 of these can be classed as rare in Britain and many occur only in the south-west. This gives the Cornish flora a very distinctive character. The wild flowers on the coast are probably the most memorable. The most spectacular time is in May when the rocks and walls are ablaze with pink thrift, with flatter areas carpeted with blue scabious, whilst the dunes and cliff slopes are bright with yellow kidney vetch, and the salt marshes white with the flowers of the long-leaved scurvy-grass.

The car-bound tourist only too often fails to realise the superb walking country that he is in. Many footpaths traverse the woods, follow the rivers and estuaries, and ring the coast, whilst inland over sixty square miles of open moorland in the granite areas await exploration.

This, then, constitutes the scena or physical stage upon which Cornish men and women have been at work during the last 5,000 years, gradually reclaiming and altering, building and rebuilding endlessly, so that only a small part of the landscape can now be regarded as truly natural and even much of this bears the imprint of man. What we now examine in the following pages is the end result of some one hundred and fifty generations of never-ending alteration to the landscape: a dynamic process which will continue into the future, implying that our over-view is but a passing snapshot of conditions as they exist in the late twentieth century.

Select Bibliography

Balchin, W. G. V., 'The Erosion Surfaces of North Cornwall', *Geographical Journal*, Vol.90 (1937).
'The Geomorphology of the North Cornish Coast', *Trans. Roy.Geol.Soc.Cornwall,* Vol.17 (1946).
'The Denudation Chronology of South West England', *Roy.Geol.Soc.Cornwall*, 150th Anniversary Vol. (1964).

Barton, R. M., *An Introduction to the Geology of Cornwall* (1964).

Bere, Rennie, *The Nature of Cornwall* (1982).

Burrows, Roger, *The Naturalist in Devon and Cornwall* (1971).

Steers, J. A., *The Coastline of England and Wales* (1948).

Tansley, A. G., *The British Islands and their Vegetation* (1949).

2. The imprint of prehistoric man

The Neolithic period. The transitional Neolithic-Bronze Age period. The Bronze Age. The Iron Age.

THOUGH PALAEOLITHIC AND Mesolithic men roamed over Cornwall, they were few in number and were neither farmers nor builders. Their activities seem to have been confined to the open parts of the moors and coastal belt. Traces of their hearths and chipping floors have been found on the Penwith cliffs, Gwithian sands and on the north Cornish coast as well as near Dozmary Pool on Bodmin Moor. The evidence all points to a nomadic hunting economy. Their imprint on the landscape was therefore negligible.

In contrast, the Neolithic, Bronze and Iron Age peoples have all left their mark. Some of the Bronze Age invaders were exceptional in coming from the east, but all the rest gained entry by westerly landfalls. Sea-borne cultures have often altered Cornish history more significantly than land influences from England, and until recent time Cornwall's closest ties have been by sea with Brittany, Wales and Ireland. Even today the native Cornishman will talk of 'going to England'. It was Neolithic migration that initiated these early contacts, and it was then that, for the first time, man began to make an impression on the Cornish landscape.

The Neolithic period

The beginning of the Neolithic period in Cornwall, according to radiocarbon dating and tree-ring analysis, falls somewhere between 4000 and 3500 B.C. The most likely date seems to be about 3700 B.C. Cornwall at this time became a focal point in the midst of a colonising stream of peoples spreading along the west coast of Europe through Spain, Brittany and Cornwall, and on to Wales, Ireland and parts of Scotland.

Neolithic man was much better equipped than his predecessors as he had evolved a stone axe mounted on a wooden haft and could cope with forest clearance as a preliminary to the preparation of cultivated patches. Pollen analysis suggests that the upland areas at this time were wooded, although doubtless advantage would have been taken of any open patches on the plateau surfaces. Settlements now became permanent and it was Neolithic man who introduced the causewayed type found in many localities in southern Britain, but subsequently built over during later occupations and not now a conspicuous Neolithic landscape feature. In Cornwall, Carn Brea near Camborne is a noted example, although this has been modified by Iron Age activity.

The most striking visual testimony to Neolithic man's occupancy of the uplands is the presence of his remarkable megaliths and tombs which have inspired awe and attracted legends throughout the ages. The function of these constructions was undoubtedly as stone tombs for the dead and doubtless their appearance relates to the arrival in Cornwall of people with a new religious belief. Early Neolithic man seems to have had little regard for the dead, as no burial places have been identified. Communal tomb building in stone became characteristic of Neolithic culture throughout western Europe about 3000 B.C. and seems to have spread as a result of trading activities.

Archaeologists now distinguish four types of Neolithic tomb, three of which are represented in Cornwall. These are gallery graves, Penwith tombs, entrance graves and passage graves. Gallery graves originally consisted of a simple, rectangular, tomb chamber terminally situated in an oval mound or cairn. The cover material has often weathered away or has been removed by farming activities, so that the enormous uprights and table-like slabs on top have become visible. One may now walk within or beneath these erections and feel dwarfed. The most notable examples are at Pawton near Wadebridge, Lanivet near Bodmin, Lanyon Quoit in Madron (Plate 9), which collapsed and was re-erected in the nineteenth century, and Trethevy Quoit in St Cleer, which still looks exactly as Norden described it over 300 years ago:

'. . . a little howse raysed of mightie stones, standing on a little hill within a fielde'.

Restriction of entry to the original tomb was probably common either to keep spirits in or to keep raiders out. Devices for narrowing the entry seem to have included blocking stones, natural rock cleavage, and the so-called 'portholes' – round holes carved out of the rock used in the construction. Two of the latter have survived in Cornwall: the famous Men an Tol at Madron (Plate 10) and the Tolvaen at Gweek, both carved in granite. These holed stones have, however, been removed from their original locations as there is now no associated dolmen or quoit.

Penwith tombs are, as the name implies, a feature of the Penwith peninsula: they were originally up to forty feet in size and circular in shape, with a large capstone covering a small burial chamber which might have been used once only. Zennor Quoit is perhaps the best example although its capstone is now tilted owing to the removal of one of the supporting orthostats to make a nearby cartshed. The soil which would have covered the stones to make a cairn, has long since disappeared. Sperris Quoit in Zennor is another example and at least three other Penwith tombs may be found on the hills of the peninsula.

Entrance graves have no passage and the central chamber with a ceiling of flat slabs of stone is entered directly: the chambers would originally have been covered by a conical mound of earth, part of which may still exist. The size would have been up to twenty-five feet in diameter and ten feet in height. In Cornwall examples may be seen at Brane near Sancreed, Carn Gluze near St Just, Pennance near Zennor, and Treen near St Buryan, all in the Penwith peninsula. It is in the Scilly Isles in particular that entrance graves are found in profusion. Over forty graves are known here, whilst further remains are also found in Ireland, the Channel Islands and on the west coast of adjacent continental areas, indicating the widespread diffusion of these Neolithic peoples. Many of these graves have also yielded urns of Bronze Age date, indicating cremation rather than inhumation and of a continuing use of the burial chambers well after their Neolithic construction.

Passage graves constitute the fourth category but they have not been identified in Cornwall, although known in Devon at Broadsands, Paignton. As the name implies, the burial chamber is reached by means of a short passage.

The siting of these tombs is of considerable interest; whilst some are conspicuously crest sited, most are, in fact, inconspicuously placed in valleys or on the edges of erosion surfaces, which suggests that the location originally relates to easy accessibility from adjacent settlement sites.

The transitional Neolithic-Bronze Age period

More mysterious than the quoits or tombs and somewhat indeterminate in age are the stone circles and standing stones. These appear to span the late Neolithic and early Bronze Age periods. The stone circles certainly imply a ceremonial or religious use although suggestions of an astronomical function have also been made from time to time. Even with our present knowledge, we are probably no nearer the truth than Norden who could only say of one that '. . . this monumente seemeth to importe an intention of the memoriall of some matter . . . thowgh time have worne out the manner'.

Nine of these circles are to be found on Bodmin Moor with further examples in west Cornwall – Maxwell locates seven existing circles in west Penwith and suggests evidence for another ten now removed. The circles are not associated with any megalithic monuments and their exposed positions suggest that the majority probably had a religious function for the Bronze Age Beaker folk who are known to have occupied higher altitudes during better climatic conditions. The stones of the circles may be widely or closely spaced and vary in number from eight to seventy. The circles measure some seventy to eighty feet in diameter and the stones are usually four to six feet in height. The circles are often grouped in twos or threes, some of them being egg-shaped or flattened as at the Nine Maidens near Boscawen-un. There and at The Hurlers near the Cheesewring in the parish of St Cleer there is a single upright within the circle but not at the centre point.

Other notable circles include Stannon circle in St Breward, Tregaseal circle in St Just, the Merry Maidens near Rosemodress, Lamorna (Plate 11), and the Stripple Stones on Bodmin Moor. No direct dating evidence exists for the circles but associated early Bronze Age barrows with Beaker remains suggest that they were in use if not originated by the Beaker folk.

A somewhat similar mystery surrounds the standing stones. These are called *menhirs* in Cornish (*mên* = stone, *hîr* = long) and they usually occur either singly or in pairs. Though they cannot be dated with certainty, their proximity in many cases to the stone circles and dolmens suggests a contemporaneous origin: the few associated archaeological remains all date from the Bronze Age and recent archaeological opinion inclines to a Beaker folk origin for most. Their distribution during this period must have been widespread: Maxwell locates thirty-seven still existing standing stones in west Penwith alone and claims documentary evidence for a further fifty additional sites where stones are known to have existed.

Of the double stones, the Pipers at Boleigh in St Buryan are the most accessible whilst a further pair may be seen near The Hurlers in St Cleer. Dozens of single stones, varying in height from seven to fifteen feet, are scattered over the length and breadth of the county. The tallest seems to have been the Maen Pearn stone at Constantine which was twenty-four feet in height: sadly this was broken up in the eighteenth century. Others still standing may be seen at Try in Gulval parish, at Tresvennack in Paul, at Trelaw, Pridden and Tregiffian in St Buryan, at Trenuggo in Sancreed, at Kerrow in Zennor and at the Long Stone near St Austell.

The prehistoric standing stones must not be confused with the much smaller stones set up by farmers as rubbing posts for cattle. The latter are easy to distinguish from the true menhirs as they are usually much smaller and are normally located in the middle of the fields they occupy.

The Bronze Age

The Bronze Age in Britain began shortly after 2000 B.C. when the English plain was invaded from the east by the Beaker folk who brought with them a knowledge of the use of metal. Additionally, they brought new forms of agriculture which enabled more permanent settlements to be made, and also new burial customs. These changes constitute a significant cultural divide from their Neolithic predecessors.

Initially, settlement took place in open or lightly-wooded sites and although these people probably undertook little direct forest clearance, their continuing presence began a deforestation process which has profoundly altered the appearance of the English countryside. Their animals continually browsed on the seedlings of the woodland and so prevented natural regeneration. In the course of time, the existing trees died, the woodland evolved into parkland, and the parkland into open country, without the change being realised by the passing generations.

It is probable that the new technology diffused across country only slowly at first and a considerable time may have elapsed before it reached Cornwall. The evidence points to the period 1500 – 1300 B.C. as the formative period of the Bronze Age culture in the Principality, when there was a welding together of indigenous and immigrant people stimulated further by overseas trading contacts. There follows a period of relative stability from 1300 to 900 B.C. marked by a rise in the population density. From 900 B.C. onwards, however, a deterioration of the climate occurred as the warm, wet, sub-Atlantic phase set in. This made the higher moorland areas in Cornwall progressively less favourable for habitation, leading eventually to the growth of blanket peat bog, and by 450 B.C. the abandonment of many upper-settlement sites.

A considerable amount is known about the Bronze Age as numerous artefacts in pottery and metal have been found in burial sites and in excavations; the life of these people is well documented and museum illustration abounds. Our concern, however, is with the present-day visible remains of their handiwork on the landscape; stone circles and menhirs have already been mentioned as features of the transitional period, and in addition we have many traces of settlement sites, field patterns and features associated with their burial customs.

Tiny irregular walled enclosures testify to the miniature scale of this first permanent farming in Cornwall. Between the enclosures there is often a cluster of hut circles indicating the foundations of the small houses or huts in which the Bronze Age people dwelt. The stone walls of these houses must have been about four feet in height and the roofs were probably thatched. Their internal diameter was often no more than six or seven feet although exceptional examples up to thirty feet across have been found.

The present-day distinction between pastoral and arable farming seems to have emerged during this period, as both types of farming can be detected in the settlement remains. Pastoral areas are marked by nucleated settlements of from five to thirty round huts with associated stock pens. Arable settlements, on the other hand, are open with the huts grouped on the edge of the fields. Two to four huts with six to eight fields would constitute a small settlement, probably related to a family holding. Fields were small, rarely more than a third to half an acre in size and were edged with boulders cleared from the surface before cultivation. Evidence that ploughs were in use has come from Gwithian where actual plough marks have been preserved by blown sand; these reveal a system of cross ploughing.

The remains of these settlements are common on the western side of Bodmin Moor especially by the bank of the De Lank river, on Garrow Tor, and on the slopes of Rough Tor which also carries traces of a stone fortress. A similar concentration occurs around the Cheesewring near Liskeard. All these areas indicate a relatively dense population in the middle Bronze Age. Less profuse remains are found on the moors of the Penwith peninsula and the Lizard promontory. We probably owe the preservation of many of these Bronze Age habitation sites to the abandonment of the moorland areas during the climatic deterioration of sub-Atlantic time. Unfortunately, a great number have probably been demolished at lower levels within historic time for the making of walls and roads.

While the huts of the Bronze Age people are now mere traces and not always immediately obvious in the heather, their burial mounds form conspicuous features in the present landscape. Centuries of farming have undoubtedly removed great numbers of barrows but they still remain numerous and widespread on the hills, moors and cliffs of Cornwall. Maxwell locates 171 existing barrows in the Penwith peninsula and identifies in the same area the sites of 124 which have now disappeared. The Ordnance Survey maps reveal at least 875 specific barrows, the distribution reflecting the well-known improvement of the climate in sub-Boreal time which allowed colonisation on the heavier soils at higher altitudes.

Although in Cornwall barrow building was probably confined, as will be seen, to the middle Bronze Age, the number of barrows still extant is an indication of the relatively dense population of the time. Clearly the majority of folk were consigned, after cremation, to simple graves, and barrows reserved for the more important. The siting of the barrows in conspicuous locations (summits of hills seem to be especially favoured) indicate a regard for the dead and some form of ancestor worship: the important deceased were certainly set apart from the settlement areas and the occasional grouping of the mounds suggest the emergence of recognised burial grounds.

The size of the barrows varies greatly, ranging from a few feet in diameter to well over a hundred. The largest in Cornwall, and probably in Britain, is the great tumulus at Carne in Veryan (Plate 12), whilst others are found near Newquay and on Goonhilly Downs near the Lizard. Most mounds were built of stones, earth or turf and as such have been vulnerable to both weather and later farming practices. Their centres usually contain a burial urn filled with ashes resulting from a cremation: occasionally multiple interments have been found with up to five, six or seven urns.

The archaeological evidence from the barrows which have been opened in Cornwall indicates that there was no complete uniformity in barrow construction or burial practices. Variety within the context of a burial mound seems to have been the order of the day. There is, however, an association of barrows with the earlier form of ribbon-handled urns which date from about 1400 B.C., i.e. middle Bronze Age. This correlates with the known later settlement in Cornwall by Bronze Age peoples. It would seem that barrow building began to decline thereafter and by 900 B.C. may well have died out as hardly any barrows contain pottery that can be ascribed to the late Bronze Age.

The Bronze Age also sees the emergence of Cornwall as a source of tin. The manufacture of bronze requires a mixture of copper with up to 10 per cent of tin. Ireland had an ample supply of copper and gold in the Wicklow and Kerry Hills, but her merchant smiths had to turn to Cornwall for tin. The discovery of Irish gold collars (*lunulae*) and Irish axes of Bronze Age date in Cornwall indicates a trade between the two areas with the Cornish contribution taking the form of tin. Cornish tin was also moving east to the people of Wessex for the manufacture of ogival daggers, and by the middle Bronze Age trade was also being carried on with the Mediterranean as is evidenced by finds of blue faience beads at Carn Creis in Penwith.

The late Bronze Age from 900 to 450 B.C. is marked by the introduction of new kinds of bronze tools and weapons ranging from swords, palstaves, socketed axes and knives, to gouges and chisels, all of which increasingly appear in archaeological finds in the rest of England. These are, however, few in number in Cornwall which then appears to be outside the main stream of continental connections, although trade with Ireland and Brittany was maintained as is evidenced by finds of Irish gold bracelets at Morvah in the Penwith peninsula and Breton square-socketed axes at Gwinear and Carn Brea near Redruth.

The Iron Age

The traditional view of the Iron Age in Britain is a period marked by new invasions from the Continent; successive groups of Celtic peoples arriving from France and Belgium and settling in strength in southern England (e.g. C.F.C. Hawkes). Three main phases have been distinguished: Iron Age A which appears in the seventh and sixth centuries B.C. towards the end of the continental Hallstatt culture period; this is poorly represented in Cornwall. Iron Age B appears in the fourth and third centuries B.C. during which there appears to have been a massive movement along the Atlantic seaboard from Spain through France and Brittany into Cornwall; this correlates with the continental La Tène culture. Finally, Iron Age C arrives in southern England in the late second to

Plate 9 Lanyon Quoit in Madron. The remains of a Neolithic gallery grave.

Plate 10 The Men an Tol at Madron. A 'porthole' stone thought to be part of the entrance to a Neolithic tomb, but now removed from its original site.

Plate 11 The Merry Maidens, Rosemodress, Lamorna. A prehistoric stone circle dating from the Neolithic-Bronze Age transitional period.

Plate 12 The tumulus at Carne in Veryan. Believed to be the biggest barrow in Britain. Note the size relative to the scale factor.

Plate 13 Rumps Point in St Minver. An Iron Age cliff castle with the ramparts clearly visible in the narrow neck joining the point to the headland.

Plate 14 Trencrom Hill in Lelant. An Iron Age hill fort with summit ramparts.

Plate 15 Chysauster in Gulval prehistoric village site. An Iron Age courtyard community living in kraal-like huts based on dry-stone walling.

Plate 16 The granite boundary wall of a prehistoric (Bronze or Iron Age) field, showing the method of construction with small stones on top of great granite boulders (grounders) and the whole surmounted by a layer of turf.

mid-first century B.C. with an influx of Belgic tribes from Gaul into Kent and the Thames valley.

This interpretation has more recently been challenged by some archaeologists (e.g. B. Cunliffe) who have argued that the known historic invasions of the Romans need not necessarily be the pattern of prehistoric time. Migration and diffusion rather than invasion and conquest might be the key, and a broad cultural continuum might have existed with evolutionary change rather than cataclysmic change brought about by invasion and conquest. The known regionalisation of Iron Age groups might reflect difficulties of communication rather than different invading groups. Similarly hill forts could just as easily arise as a result of indigenous differences rather than as a response to the appearance of invaders. Either way, the fusing of these Celtic peoples in Cornwall with the Bronze Age survivors produced by the end of the Iron Age the *Dumnonii*.

Celtic society differed greatly from Bronze Age society. The population was organised in tribes under chieftans and in tribal confederations under kings. Struggles for land holdings produced a bellicose people and warfare was a major occupation. Much labour was employed in building fortifications and numerous hill forts appeared in the landscape. Although iron was the predominant metal, the Cornish tin trade appears to have flourished under the *Dumnonii*, Gallic merchants acting as middlemen for the Mediterranean market. Written records of the trade become available in the *History* of Diodorus Siculus. Agriculture, however, was the basis of the economy, with stock rearing as the most important activity.

The most spectacular contribution of the Iron Age people to the present Cornish landscape is undoubtedly the chain of fortifications spread throughout the Principality. We may distinguish two main types, the cliff castle and the hill fort. Cornwall's precipitous headlands offered admirable sites for fortification: all that was needed was a ditch and rampart across the neck of the promontory. Practically every important headland was converted in this fashion and the traces of at least twenty-two cliff castles can still be seen. Apart from Mayon Castle in Sennen, which has a stone wall, they all follow the same plan of one or more bank and ditch. Porth

Island in St Columb Minor is probably the most elaborate, and excellent examples are also found in Willapark Head near Tintagel, Rumps Point in St Minver (Plate 13), Cape Cornwall in St Just, the Dodman in Gorran, and Rame Head near Plymouth. There are rarely any signs of permanent habitation in these cliff castles and they were probably only used in time of trouble.

Altogether different in type are the hill forts. At least twenty-seven Cornish hills are crowned with these Iron Age earthworks, most dating from the Iron Age B period. Castle-an-Dinas in Ludgvan has a triple rampart of stone, and Caer Bran in Sancreed a triple rampart of earth, whilst the finest and best preserved of all the Cornish hill castles, that at Castle-an-Dinas in St Columb, also has three circles of defence.

Associated with the cliff castles and hill forts are a number of small forts defended by a single rampart which are known as *rounds* in Cornwall. These are circular or oval enclosures about an acre in extent and they represent defended kin-group homesteads rather than tribal hill forts. Some examples include Trevinnick (St Kew), Castle Gotha (St Austell) and Trevisker Round (St Eval). Rounds are more common in mid- and north-east Cornwall. At the time they were occupied they must have been numerous, since Maxwell has located at least sixty-three sites in west Penwith alone. Nowadays the passage of time has subdued them as a feature in the landscape and place-name evidence (*castel, din* and *ker*) is more often a quicker clue to their probable existence.

Certain of the hill forts contained permanent habitations. Trencrom Hill in Lelant (Plate 14) and Chûn Castle in Morvah both have hut circles and stone walls within the ramparts. But in general Iron Age man lived in small village communities outside and a little below his fortress. The ruins of many such villages still exist and enable us to reconstruct their mode of life. Some of the buildings were kraal-like structures, with huts linked together to form a ring fence. Hirst located no fewer than twenty-three of these sites in the Land's End area, whilst more recently Maxwell lists thirty-nine sites in west Penwith. The most remarkable village is that at Chysauster in Gulval (Plate 15), where dry-stone walls of local granite have remained standing for over 2,000 years to the present day. A series of large houses is arranged in pairs along a 'street', with each house being constructed around a central courtyard on to which the rooms open. Other cluster-type villages occur at Crofto in Morvah and Bosullow in Madron, and numerous sites are found on the moors near Rough Tor, Blisland, Fernacre and Trewortha Marsh; and on Goonhilly Downs, Godolphin Hill and the south-western slopes of Mulfra Hill in Madron.

Associated with the courtyard settlements are a number of underground chambers known in Cornwall as *fougous*. The most notable are located at Carn Euny in Sancreed and at Chysauster. These have given rise to a variety of stories in Cornish folklore but it is now almost certain that they were nothing more than underground storage chambers for food, perhaps acting as communal cellars or cold stores. It should perhaps be noted that some archaeologists incline to the view that the courtyard house villages are of Romano-British age as some of the walling may be later than the Iron Age. There seems little doubt, however, that the original siting is Iron Age and we simply have an example of continuous habitation.

In addition to the forts and the settlement sites, the Iron Age peoples modified the landscape both agriculturally and by mining. Their great agricultural innovation was the wheeled plough which accelerated the intake of land for cultivation. Lynchets appeared, terracing the slopes around their villages, particularly on Bodmin Moor and on the south-western slopes of Mulfra Hill. Tiny fields were also wrested from the moorland, and the boulders cleared from each patch were piled into dry-stone hedges (Plate 16). It is now almost impossible to say with certainty that any particular hedge is of Iron Age date because of later repairs, but a virtually certain index of Celtic origin is the small size and squarish pattern of many fields on the moorlands and in the Penwith peninsula. Unlike the enclosures of the Bronze Age, many of these Celtic fields are still in cultivation. The reason for this may be sought in the climatic deterioration of the sub-Atlantic phase at the end of the Bronze Age. The higher parts of the moorland used by the Bronze Age farmers became too bleak and raw for agriculture and were slowly abandoned. At the same time, the forest and marsh of the valleys were also inhospitable, with the result that the later Bronze Age and Iron Age peoples sought out the erosion surfaces that lay between the moorlands and the valley-bottoms for their fields and villages. Not since that time have these areas become unsuitable for cultivation, so that an unbroken occupancy has continued down to the present day with the field boundaries in many areas remaining unaltered for over 2,000 years.

The tin trade, which had begun in the Bronze Age, flourished and grew in the succeeding centuries. Reference to it in classical writings are numerous and, although some authorities consider a Phoenician contact improbable, it is generally agreed that the *History* by Diodorus Siculus in the second century B.C. is proof of a substantial trade between the Greeks and the Cornish centre of St Michael's Mount shortly before the Christian era. The extraction was achieved by means of 'streaming', the tin being washed out of the alluvial deposits in open workings. Shaft mining does not make its appearance for many centuries – probably not until the fifteenth century.

The Celtic peoples also re-introduced inhumation burial in place of the Bronze Age cremation. One of the most spectacular finds in this respect was the Harlyn Bay cemetery found beneath blown sand in the early twentieth century. The dead had been buried in foetal positions in slate cists or coffins. This cemetery yielded a great number of valuable grave goods which enable a picture of the life of these people to be pieced together. Other Iron Age graves have been found at Trevone near Padstow, Trelan Bahow in St Keverne and Poynters Garden in the Scilly Isles.

The Iron Age peoples further brought with them the Brythonic branch of the Celtic language, which survived in Cornwall in the spoken form until the eighteenth century and is still with us today in the place names of the county. Although Celtic place-names are not a visible element in the landscape, they are conspicuous on the map, and are an invaluable source of information. A glance at any of the Ordnance Survey sheets of the county will reveal their wide distribution and some of the oldest include the elements *caer*, *castel* and *din* in their derivatives. Each implies a fortress or a defensive site, Gover instances well over two hundred examples throughout the county.

By piecing together the archaeological and place-name evidence we are able to obtain a reasonably accurate portrait of conditions in Cornwall immediately preceding the Roman period. There must have been a considerable number of hill-top forts, which may have been tribal centres as well as citadels, surrounded by villages, huts and subsidiary settlements at slightly lower levels on the middle erosion surfaces. Tiny fields were making inroads into moorland and woodland, patches of bright green in a sombre landscape, and tin-streaming waste had begun to litter the river valleys in raw heaps. This is the scene which persisted with but slight modifications right through the Roman era and on into the Dark Ages. For although the Romans were interested in the Cornish tin trade, they made little or no attempt to absorb the county into their political framework. In contrast with their permanent imprint upon the English landscape as a whole, the Roman influence in Cornwall was negligible. They left little that is readily visible, reminding us once again, only this time in the negative sense, of the remoteness and distinctiveness of Cornwall.

Select Bibliography

Crawford, O. G. S., 'The Work of Giants', *Antiquity*, Vol. X (1936).
Fox, Aileen, *South-West England* (1973).
Hencken, H. O'Neill, *Archaeology of Cornwall and Scilly* (1932).
Hirst, F. C., 'Courtyard House sites in West Cornwall', *Journ. British Archaeological Assoc.*, Vol. II (1937).
Maxwell, I. S., 'The Location of Ictis', *Journ. Royal Institution of Cornwall,* Vol.VI (1972).
Historical Atlas of West Penwith (1976).
Ravenhill, W. L. D., 'The Settlement of Cornwall during the Celtic Period', *Geography,* Vol. XI (1955).
Woolf, Charles, *Archaeology of Cornwall* (1970).

3. The rural landscape

The Celtic foundation and Roman contribution. The Anglo-Saxon settlement. The Domesday Survey. The later Middle Ages. Field patterns. Hedges and walls. Churches and chapels. Wayside crosses. Castles. Manor houses. Parks and gardens. Other buildings.

The Celtic foundation and Roman contribution

LITTLE IS KNOWN for certain about Cornwall during the period which immediately followed the Roman occupation of Britain. Occasional references in the Anglo-Saxon Chronicle, the *Lives* of the saints, and writers such as Nennius, Gildas and the twelfth-century Giraldus Cambrensis are the only literary sources. In Cornwall the lack of information is particularly unfortunate since much of the present-day settlement pattern was determined at this time. The rebuilding which has taken place on continuously-occupied sites has destroyed much archaeological information, and only place-names now throw light on a most obscure period. The county entered a long phase during which the maritime contacts associated with the tin trade declined and the main influences were landward from the east. The only literary clue to a continuation of the tin trade is an isolated reference in the life of John the Almsgiver to a sixth-century sailing from Alexandria to Britain of a ship laden with corn and returning with a cargo of Cornish tin. It is clear that Cornwall had once again become relatively isolated.

The Roman contribution to the present-day landscape in Cornwall, unlike the rest of England, is very limited. Although the *Dumnonii* were probably brought under Roman control by A.D. 48 and were administered from *Isca Dumnoniorum* (Exeter), there appears to have been no real Roman presence in Cornwall until a second offensive was launched against the *Dumnonii* in Nero's time. After the Romans had advanced into mid-Cornwall, they established a two-acre fort at Nanstallon on the river Camel west of Bodmin. This was occupied until A.D. 75–80. No other Roman fort has been found in Cornwall. Similarly only one Roman-style building has been located. This is a rather poorly constructed small country house at Magor near Camborne dating from the mid-second century.

Similarly no Roman roads have been identified with certainty in Cornwall although their existence in some form or other is indicated by the discovery of five milestones dating from the mid-third and early fourth centuries. Evidence of road links in both north and south comes from milestones found at Tintagel and Boscastle, and at St Hilary and Breage: whilst a further milestone at Gwennap Pit near Redruth suggests the possibility of a spine road following the length of the peninsula. The discovery of Roman coins on at least twenty-seven sites in west Penwith is a further clear indication of a Roman presence and trading activities.

It is likely that communications in Cornwall during the early Roman period were maintained more by sea than by land and were limited because of the decline of the tin trade. The Romans had a plentiful supply of tin from their Spanish mines until these became exhausted in the mid-third century A.D. after which a revival of the Cornish tin trade took place.

Hence for the majority of the *Dumnonii*, the Roman occupation of Britain led to little change in their mode of life apart from some rebuilding of settlements on existing sites. In the fifth and sixth centuries A.D. after the departure of the Romans, there were even migrations of Britons across the English Channel to Armorica (Brittany) where the district name of Cornuaille preserves the memory of a mysterious movement. At the same time a number of tribal kingdoms seem to have emerged in Cornwall, probably based upon the hill-top capitals. The evidence for this development is provided by excavations of some hill forts, especially Castle Dore. This had been deserted in the first century A.D. but was later re-occupied during the fifth and sixth centuries. A large rectangular timber hall was then erected within the original rampart post-holes of the fort: the size and general layout of the buildings suggests the palace of a Cornish Celtic 'king'. Similar evidence of the re-occupation of a hill-fort site comes from Chûn in Penwith. Adjacent to Castle Dore is an inscribed stone which possibly commemorates Drustranus, son of Cunomorus, who has been identified with the King Mark of the Tristan legend. There are a number of stones with Latin inscriptions scattered over the Cornish landscape which appear to date from the fifth and sixth centuries, and which tie in with the period of Aurelianus and the King Mark, Tristan and King Arthur legends. The limited facts all point to Cornwall, as part of *Dumnonia*, having become a repository of a Christian Romano-British civilisation in the face of strong Anglo-Saxon heathen pressure.

North-east Cornwall is haunted by memories of King Arthur. Quite apart from the castle at Tintagel with Merlin's Cave beneath, there is King Arthur's Hall on Bodmin Moor and Dozmary Pool into which Bedivere supposedly threw the sword Excalibur, whilst Camelford claims to be Camelot and Slaughter Bridge nearby contends for the site of Arthur's last battle. Although we may be fairly certain that there was a sixth-century British leader of this name who may well have lived in Cornwall for part of his life, it is very doubtful if his existence was anything like the romantic figure of the Arthurian legends. Other parts of Cornwall, as well as Wales and Somerset, also claim Arthurian associations.

It was into this society that Irish and Welsh incursions later occurred. The main motive was probably missionary zeal which has been important in influencing the present-day distribution of churches and the foundation of many settlements. Our story goes back to the fourth century A.D. when the Gaelic Celts of Ireland were complicating life for the Romans by raiding the western coasts of Britain. Somewhere about A.D. 405 they carried off to Ireland the young son of a Roman-British priest as a slave: he subsequently escaped but his experience had given him a vision of converting the Irish to Christianity. The young man was St Patrick and in A.D. 431 he returned to Ireland to organise the Christian Church there. It was not long before Irish missionaries were migrating to Wales and south-west England to support the British Church then threatened by the heathen Saxons. By the sixth and seventh centuries Irish saints were all over Wales, Cornwall and Brittany. They left a record of their activities in their *Lives* but unfortunately much of this information was destroyed during the Reformation. Enough has remained, however, to give us an insight into what was happening at this time.

In the semi-darkness of the period one can detect the beginnings of a new pattern of settlement which has in places been handed down to the present day. Before this time, the Cornish people had lived in entrenched communities on the higher ground, or in hut-clusters closely associated with the hill-top forts. Several centuries later this pattern had disappeared, being replaced by wider and more dispersed settlement at lower levels, in smaller groups, and in isolated homesteads or *trevs*.

There appear to have been a number of underlying causes for this movement. There was first of all the natural pressure of an increasing population upon the available land. Secondly, there was another climatic change, and thirdly there was the example being set by the Celtic saints. The importance of the latter is clearly seen today in the vast number of saint names scattered over the Cornish landscape. Most of these names derive from monastic foundations: Aileen Fox records that 174 of the 212 ancient parishes of Cornwall are dedicated to a western saint. These foundations lacked the magnificence of the great monasteries of late medieval England. They were nothing more than a few simple huts built around a small church or chapel with no regular plan. We have an example of an early chapel in the oratory of St Piran at Perranporth, for long buried beneath the sands; this dates from the sixth to eighth centuries and probably exhibits the earliest church remains still in existence in south-west England. The remains of one of these communities has also been excavated on the headland at Tintagel, revealing a series of tiny rooms with earthen floors and walls of turf.

E.G. Bowen has demonstrated that most of the settlement sites established by the Celtic saints in Cornwall were carefully chosen in relation to the topography and water supply. Many were tucked away in the landscape so that they would not be readily visible to any sea-borne marauders. This is well illustrated by the location of known settlements of the Celtic saints in the Fal estuary. St Gluvias, Mylor, St Kea, St Clement, Lamorran, Ruan Lanihorne, St Just-in-Roseland, St Mawes and St Anthony ring the estuary, but are by no means obvious from the sea. It must also be remembered that probably more movement took place by sea than by land during this period. Cornwall, with its heavily indented ria coastline, provided excellent facilities for small-boat navigation.

After A.D. 500 the climate became warmer and drier and many of the upland sites were probably untenable for lack of water. The importance of an adequate water supply is very evident from the *Lives* of the Celtic saints. Natural springs were regarded with a great deal of veneration at this time and nearly a hundred wells in Cornwall are still recorded as 'holy' wells.

It can also be seen from the *Lives* that a further factor in the movement was the increasing importance of agriculture in the economy, and the consequent search for deeper and more productive soils. We read in the *Life of St Brioc* how 'all gird themselves to work, they cut down trees, root up bushes, tear up brambles and tangled thorns, and soon convert a dense wood into an open clearing . . . then the soil was worked carefully with light hoes, and being ploughed with very small furrows, its various produce was placed in due time on the threshing floors . . .'

Another source of information lies in the distribution of a number of inconspicuous inscribed stones carrying the curious Morse-like Ogham script (e.g. at St Kew and St Clement) which are known to be of Irish origin. Most of these are located in the north-east of the county.

Together with the incursions from Ireland there were also movements of people from Wales. Some of these were probably unwelcome and this may explain the mysterious 'Giant's Hedge', an earthen rampart and ditch which can be traced from Lerryn to West Looe, apparently linking the estuaries of the Fowey and the West Looe. No doubt it represents a tribal boundary of the period but no precise date can be given to it. F.E. Halliday suggests that it might represent the boundary of the territory held by the semi-historical King Mark of Cornwall whose 'kingdom' appears to have been based on Castle Dore.

The spread of settlement can also be seen in the distribution of certain Celtic place-name elements. The occurrence of *din*, *caer* or *castel*, usually associated with older fortifications, is thought to imply settlements of Iron Age origin. Henderson further suggested that *ty, lis* (or *les*) and *lan* are very old and are closely followed in date by prefixes such as *Bos, Bod* and *Tre. Lan* was used to describe an enclosure (which when associated with a saint's name must have been monastic), and also a woodland clearing. *Bos* and *ty* imply a house and *tre* means a homestead or small hamlet. A glance at the Ordnance Survey maps of Cornwall will show the widespread distribution of these place-name elements.

The remains of one of these early settlements, long buried in the towans of Gwithian, has been excavated. Adjacent to the already-known chapel of Gwithian, and similarly buried near the Hayle river, the site reveals a set of fifth-century huts which were replaced in the sixth century. The inhabitants kept sheep, cows, pigs, horses and dogs; they were eaters of fish, especially limpets, mussels and oysters, and they worked in iron. They made pottery initially in the Roman style but subsequently copied Irish productions.

The Anglo-Saxon settlement

The Romans during their 400 years of occupation in Britain seem to have paid little attention to Cornwall and after their withdrawal another 400 years were to pass before the next major invasion took place. Although during this 800 years (approaching half of historic time for Cornwall) much of the present-day settlement pattern was laid down, the next phase was also to add a substantial contribution to the landscape.

The Anglo-Saxon conquest and colonisation of southern Britain had been spreading slowly westwards. Hoskins has shown that the whole of Devon had fallen into English hands by the end of the seventh century, and whilst there may have been some infiltration across the Tamar in the eighth century, it was another hundred years before the Saxons, no doubt deterred by the wild upland areas of Dartmoor and Exmoor, were ready to move in a large way still further west.

When the Anglo-Saxon invasion came, however, it seems to have been in earnest. In A.D. 814 Egbert invaded *Dumnonia* and 'laid waste the land from east to west', compelling all to do homage to him. In A.D. 825 the Cornish rebelled but were defeated in battle at Gafulford, which is thought to be Camelford, where Slaughter Bridge probably commemorates Egbert's battle rather than King Arthur's. The Cornish tried again in A.D. 838 when a Danish fleet appeared off the coast and they joined forces with the Norsemen in an attempt to expel the Saxons. But Egbert put paid to this attempt at the battle of Hingston Down and this marked the end of Cornish resistance. It also ushered in a period of relative peace because, oddly, Cornwall never suffered from any Norse settlement such as took place extensively in Ireland, along the Welsh coast and also in France where they gave their name to Normandy. Even coastal raids appear to have been few, the most notorious being in A.D. 981 when Petrocs stow (Padstow) was sacked. It was as a result of this raid that the monastery moved to Bodmin (Plate 17).

Actual Anglo-Saxon settlement in Cornwall, however, appears to have been a slow process and it is not until after A.D. 900 that we find an increasing number of places, significantly in east Cornwall, listed in the Anglo-Saxon land-books. The conquest of the peninsula remained largely political, Cornish isolation preserving the ancient customs, habits and language. In this respect the Celtic tradition lived on. The Saxons took over the local government, substituting their feudal system for the Celtic clan system. The county was divided into six hundreds, later increased to nine, and then subdivided into manors. Old tribal centres became new manors and we can see where this happened where the suffix *tun* (later *ton*) was added to old Celtic names such as Binner and Winnian (Fig.2).

The area of effective Anglo-Saxon settlement in Cornwall emerges from a study of the place-names. Some 200 true English names occur in two main groups in the east, one to the north and another in the south; those in both areas show close affinities with those across the border in Devon. Names such as Stratton, Week St Mary and Poundstock are pure English.

The distribution suggests two colonising streams. Elsewhere the English influence is revealed by the occasional name which combines both Celtic and English elements, such as Morwenstow and Kilkhampton (Fig.3). One finds this as far west as Helston which was originally the Cornish *henlis* – 'old court or old hall' – to which the old English *tun* was added. Here it was not only a matter of a change of name. The Saxons planted a large nucleated village in a landscape of hamlets and farmsteads, as can be seen from early editions of the Ordnance Survey maps (Fig.4). Twentieth-century development has regrettably eliminated many of these features. Further evidence of Saxon influence on the landscape is revealed in a number of *trev* names which are compounded with old English personal names, such as Treboy and Trehawke.

During the ninth and tenth centuries, then, the Saxons were moving in and settling alongside the indigenous Cornish, producing a secondary-settlement pattern. On the one hand were the older isolated farmsteads and *trevs* of the Celts, surrounded by tiny vegetable fields and larger pasture areas for their stock. On the other hand, there were small Saxon villages with a few cottages clustered around a manor or a church.

There is further evidence which suggests that although land was parcelled out to Saxon landowners, many were probably absentee landlords, the Cornish peasantry continuing to farm in the traditional manner. This situation may be deduced from the manumissions (freeing of slaves) recorded in the tenth-century Bodmin Gospels. The names of the slaves and those of the witnesses are mainly Cornish, whilst those of the manumittors are mainly Anglo-Saxon.

The Domesday Survey

The difficulties encountered in reconstructing earlier landscapes can be overcome for the eleventh century as the Domesday Survey of 1086 is available for analysis. There are two Domesday descriptions for Cornwall: the Exchequer folio, which is a summary, and the more detailed earlier account, usually known as the Exeter Domesday, forming part of the *Liber Exoniensis* which has been in the custody of

CALLINGTON U.D.
Lady Ashburton Mine
(Copper & Silver, Disused)
Old Shaft
Old Shaft
Old Shaft
L.B
B.M.514·
G.P
L.B
B.M.488·3
461
Smithy
Pengelly
Springs
Chapel
Valentine Row
Gas Works
Tors View
B.M.582·9
589
G.P
School
B.M.467·4
B.M.543·9
Chap.
Ch.
FORE STREET
Police Station
Meth. Ch.
B.M. 505·0
Spring
Spring
W
503·7
Chapel
NEW ROAD
School
CALLINGTON
513
CATTLE MARKET
SALTASH ROAD
F.P.
Stone
541
G.P
Temperance Hotel
CALLINGTON
G.P
520
571
Acres 2531·372
0
1000
2000
3000
4000
5000
3280 Feet
0
¼
½
¾
1 Mile

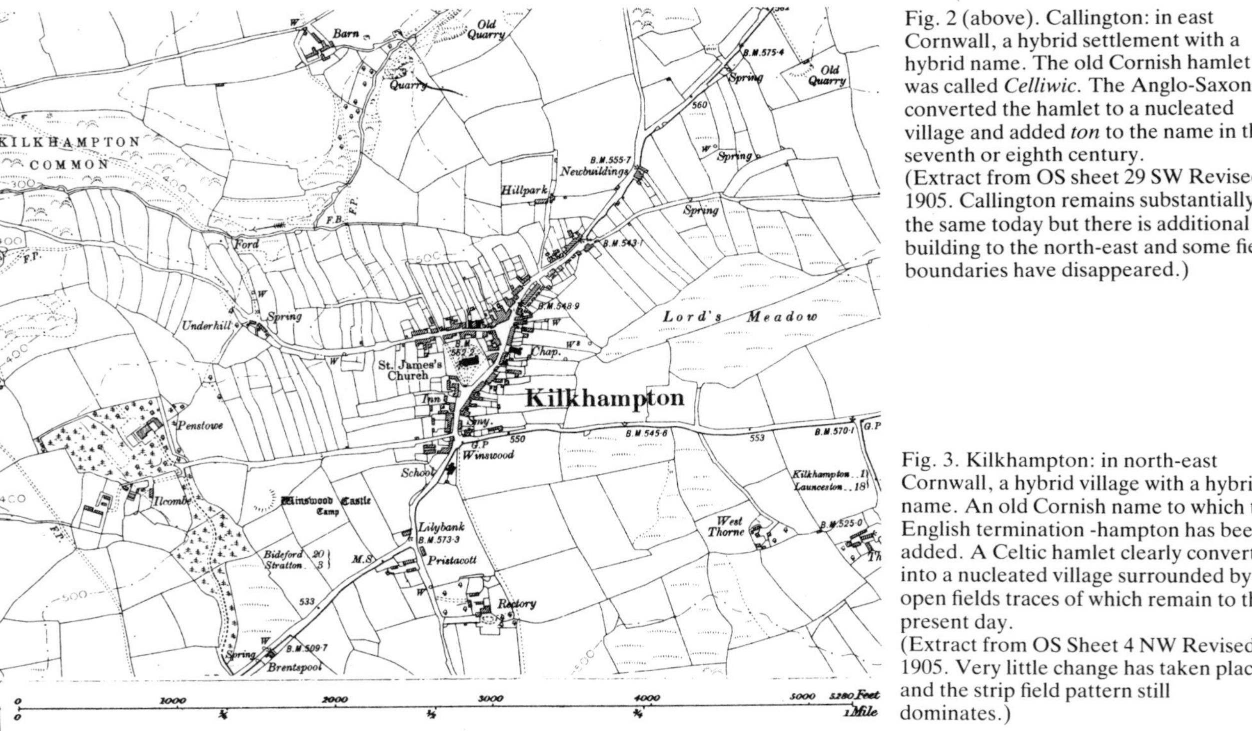

Fig. 2 (above). Callington: in east Cornwall, a hybrid settlement with a hybrid name. The old Cornish hamlet was called *Celliwic*. The Anglo-Saxons converted the hamlet to a nucleated village and added *ton* to the name in the seventh or eighth century.
(Extract from OS sheet 29 SW Revised 1905. Callington remains substantially the same today but there is additional building to the north-east and some field boundaries have disappeared.)

Fig. 3. Kilkhampton: in north-east Cornwall, a hybrid village with a hybrid name. An old Cornish name to which the English termination -hampton has been added. A Celtic hamlet clearly converted into a nucleated village surrounded by open fields traces of which remain to the present day.
(Extract from OS Sheet 4 NW Revised 1905. Very little change has taken place and the strip field pattern still dominates.)

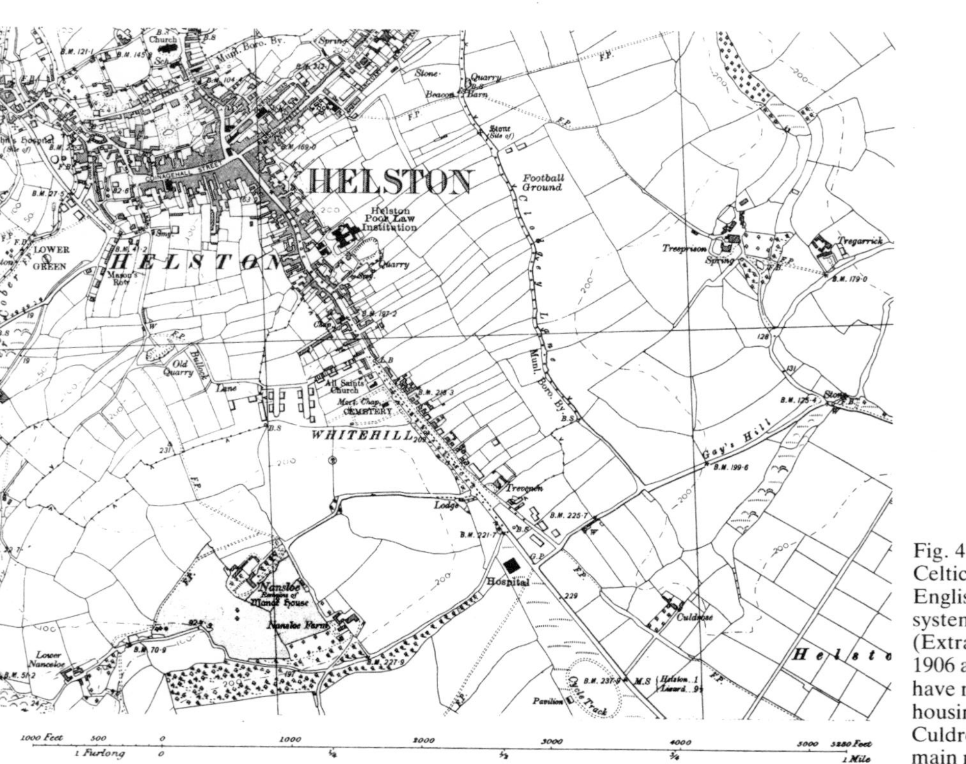

Fig. 4. Helston: a further example of a Celtic settlement taken over by the Old English and possibly given an open-field system, well shown on this early OS map. (Extract from OS Sheet 76 SW Revised in 1906 and 1945. Almost all the strip fields have now disappeared under extensive housing estates arising from the adjacent Culdrose airfield. Clodgey Lane is now a main road by-passing the town.)

Exeter Cathedral since the eleventh century. The *Liber Exoniensis* also includes a number of other documents which provide valuable information. Among these are the *Terrae Occupatae* and the Geld Rolls or Geld Accounts together with lists of hundreds which supply much additional data.

The Domesday Survey has long been an information quarry for historians, notably F.W. Maitland and L.F. Salzman, but subsequently geographers, working under H.C. Darby, have converted the Domesday fiscal data into map form to produce a fairly accurate picture of the geography of the period. This exercise was carried out for Cornwall by W.L.D. Ravenhill. It was not an easy task, for although most villages, farms and hamlets can be identified and located there are many difficulties of interpretation. As in other parts of the country, manors do not always coincide with either village or parish: two or more manors might also make up a single hamlet whilst, conversely, several vills and isolated settlements might form a single manor. Further complications ensue as a result of the changing county boundary with Devon. The existence of the Exchequer account along with the supplementary texts produce complications as there are many disagreements in detail. The Exeter account usually distinguishes between the hidage (area) of the demesne and that of the peasantry, whereas the Exchequer account does this only for the royal manors. The Exeter account also enumerates the demesne livestock and provides information about ownership.

Despite these difficulties the survey of settlement sites, population, plough-land and plough-teams along with a great deal of incidental information relating to livestock, woodland, meadow, pasture, waste, mills, churches, markets, castles, salt pans, fisheries and urban life does enable a fairly accurate picture of eleventh-century Cornwall to be reconstructed.

At least 330 separate named places are mentioned in the Cornish Domesday but there were certainly more unrecorded settlements as we know that some manors were composite, containing several sites. The county is unusual amongst the Domesday accounts in that as many as four-fifths of its place-names emerge today not as parish names but as those of hamlets or individual farms and houses. Cornwall also now has a large number of parishes which do not find a mention in Domesday.

The analysis of the names reveals clear traces of two separate agricultural systems existing side by side, reflecting the English and Celtic settlements which together made up the human scene. Characteristic Celtic names incorporating *pen, lan* and *tre* elements locate isolated homesteads and small hamlets, and are correlated with pastoral activities without plough-land. Complementary to this pattern there are Anglo-Saxon names incorporating *ton* with recorded data indicating substantial villages similar to those of the English plain. The overall distribution reveals a preponderance of Celtic influence in the west of the county and English influence in the east, with large unoccupied stretches of upland moorland where the granite outcrops. It is quite obvious that by the eleventh century settlement was concentrated in the lowland areas of the Devonian and Carboniferous slates, shales and grits.

The large vills in particular stand out in the account: these were situated mainly in the east, in the river valleys and at their heads, and with twenty or more plough-teams must have been typical English settlements. They carry names such as Henliston (now Helston), Trewinton, Gluston and Carneton. Occasionally a large manor, e.g. Pawton, is recorded in the west of the county. Some of these large manors undoubtedly included without specific mention a considerable number of *trevs* or hamlets with an independent existence.

In contrast to the large manors is the second type of entry, representative of very small settlements of Celtic origin. In some cases no plough-team at all is mentioned, and a pastoral economy is clearly implied. Such a farmstead is that of Trevelyan in the parish of St Veep. It lies about a quarter of a mile east of the head of Penpoll Creek, an arm of the Fowey estuary, and is the ancient home of the Trevelyan family, the farm from which they take their name. It is of unknown age, a Celtic *trev* or homestead originating perhaps during the downward movement of settlement from the uplands in the Dark Ages. It was, therefore, already ancient when Domesday recorded: 'The count (of Mortain) has a manor called

Trevillein which Alric held in the time of King Edward. Therein is one ferling of land and it rendered geld for half a ferling. One team can plough this. Rainold holds this of the count and there Rainold has two slaves. And it is worth three shillings yearly, and when the count received it it was worth the same amount.' Although its area was expressed by saying that one team could plough it – probably about a hundred acres or rather more – there was in fact no plough upon it. What we have is a small pasture run by two slaves. It is not known when the Trevelyans appeared on the scene – most probably in the twelfth or early thirteenth century, if we may go by many other West-Country families of similar origin. Here, among the Cornish lanes, is a farmstead which has certainly been continuously occupied for a thousand years, and possibly much longer.

Domesday gives other examples of this type, where there are no ploughs and no plough-oxen. On five such 'manors' there is a total population of only seven cottagers and three slaves. Obviously they are scattered homesteads. For those who wish to track them down in their solitude they are (besides Trevelyan), Landare in Duloe, Ellbridge in Landulph, Lanjore in St Germans, and either Hele in Jacobstow or Hele in Stratton. There are, of course, a great number of small arable farms also recorded in the Domesday Book for Cornwall, such as Killigorrick and Brodbane, both in the parish of Duloe. There are just over a hundred manors with two plough-lands or less. It is clear that these entries can only refer to small hamlets or *trevs* which had no relation to an open-field system, quite apart from the fact that the names in themselves are strikingly un-English. When we visit such farmsteads we may be quite certain that the hedgebanks that lie near the dwelling are at least of pre-Conquest date. To find these farms one needs the 1:25,000 Pathfinder Ordnance Survey map for the district as many are not marked on the smaller scale maps. Walking with the Ordnance Survey Pathfinder maps in search of remote farmsteads recorded in Domesday is a revelation, even to those who think they know the county well. To spend a long day exploring a parish in such a search is to see the real Cornwall, of which neither the beach-addict nor the motorist careering along the inland main roads is in the least degree aware. What one additionally needs for such an exploration are a copy of Ravenhill's analysis of the Domesday Survey for Cornwall and a volume on the place-names of the county. Armed with these tools and an enquiring mind, the explorer of the Cornish landscape will find enough pleasure to last him for years as he walks around, from farm to farm, and parish to parish, and he will see things that have never been seen before in that light.

Even by the end of the eleventh century the natural landscape of Cornwall had been tamed only to a limited extent. We can deduce this from the Domesday Survey in two ways. Entries such as that for the great royal manor of Winnington in Gunwalloe, where we are told there was land for sixty plough-teams but only twenty-six ploughs, are frequent in all parts of the county, and indicate that much land within the manorial boundaries still remained unused. Altogether in Cornwall, Ravenhill records 2,562 plough-lands but only 1,217⅝ plough-teams. Though this statement is capable of more than one interpretation, and not all historians and geographers are agreed about it, it does look as if less than one-half of the potentially usable land had been rescued from the natural waste by 1086, and to this we must add the large areas of moorland and some woodland which also existed. Much of the county must still have remained in its natural state: we should certainly be safe in saying at least a half, taking all things into account, and very probably more. There was still a vast amount of colonisation to be done by the medieval peasantry.

We may also see, by a second test, that of population, how much remained to be accomplished. The Survey lists the number of bordars, villeins and serfs in each settlement and if we add all these together along with the burgesses of Bodmin and a small number of coliberts and *cervisarii*, we arrive at a total of 5,528 recorded individuals for Cornwall. This figure is actually more representative of households than individuals and must be multiplied by a factor of four or five in order to obtain the actual population. This means that the total population of the county in 1086 was probably somewhere between 20,000 and 25,000 – fewer than the population of either Penzance or St Austell today. A distribution map of the recorded population reveals densities of 5.8 per square mile in the east, falling to 2.4 in the west. Few counties appear to have been as thinly populated as Cornwall – only Yorkshire, Staffordshire and Cheshire have lower figures and these areas might have been wasted by the war. It is once again clear that much of the peninsula must have been in a natural condition.

We find the densest settlement in the north-eastern hundred of Stratton, and between the Lynher and the Tamar in the south-east, perhaps because these were the parts most heavily occupied by the Saxon farmers, as the place-names show. It may well be that the agricultural technique of the Saxons was more advanced than that of the Cornish and that they made better use of the land, so that their farmsteads were more thickly strewn over the landscape. By contrast, the far west of the county was very thinly peopled, except in the lowland neck between Marazion and Hayle, and rather surprisingly in the Lizard peninsula. This difference between east and west may have been partly due to the poorer soils in the west, though much of the land taken over by the Saxons in the north-east of the county on the heavy and unrewarding clays of the Culm Measures was itself poor. On the whole, it would appear to be mainly a matter of a more advanced Saxon farming technique.

Domesday also gives us a glimpse of a number of other interesting aspects relative to the landscape. Two types of woodland are recorded – wood and underwood – usually in acres. Although this information is by no means complete, it is clear when the data is plotted on a map that much of Cornwall was without wood. Exposure to the salt-laden Atlantic gales and the poor granitic soils seem to account for large treeless areas on the west and north coasts and in the interior. Only the sheltered south coast valleys record wood and underwood in any quantity.

Domesday also mentions relatively few meadows in Cornwall: only forty-two entries are to be found and these are mainly in the east, all are small, measuring only one or two acres in extent. With pasture recorded for over 90 per cent of the settlements, the lack of meadows suggests a climatic explanation – the mild winters obviated the need for winter hay. Livestock statistics indicate an emphasis on sheep; flocks of many hundred were frequently recorded and were well distributed throughout the county, giving a total of over 13,000 *oves* compared with a few hundred each of *caprae* (goats), *equae* (mares), *vaccae* (cows) and *porci* (swine).

The only urban settlement in Cornwall at the time of the Domesday Survey appears to have been Bodmin, and the Exchequer entry for this makes interesting reading: 'The church of St Petrock holds Bodmin. There is one hide of land which never paid geld. There is land for 4 plough-teams. There, 5 villeins have 2 plough-teams with 6 bordars. There (are) 30 acres of pasture and 6 acres of underwood. There St Petrock has 68 houses and one market. The whole is worth 25s.' Obviously Bodmin must have been a small market centre with an agricultural and religious flavour. Its recorded population of 79 implies a total population approaching 400. Whereas Somerset could produce nine 'boroughs' and Devon five 'boroughs' Cornwall could only muster one at the time of the Survey.

Churches as such are not enumerated, but we may deduce that they were numerous from the prolific distribution of Celtic saints' names which normally implies a church foundation. Only two castles, those at Dunheved (Launceston) and Trematon are mentioned. Mills are recorded for only five places with Launceston claiming two of these. Markets are recorded for only five places and an annual fair for one place. Taken together, these supplementary data point to a general backwardness in the development of the peninsula, compared to other parts of England.

The later Middle Ages

In contrast to the time of the Norman Conquest and the Domesday Survey, the later Middle Ages is a period of limited landscape data so far as Cornwall is concerned. We must revert to reading the landscape once again rather than reading any written record. It was, however, an important formative time for the county for there was initially a growth in the population which led, on the one hand, to increased land reclamation and, on the other hand, according to a number of historical geographers (Baker, Butlin, Fox etc.) to the emergence of the open-field system and strip cultivation which was to affect later field boundaries (q.v.).

This surge of colonisation was characteristic of many parts of lowland Britain as well as Cornwall in the thirteenth and early fourteenth centuries. It has been well demonstrated for west Penwith by Maxwell. But the movement was reversed later in the fourteenth and fifteenth centuries as a result of a succession of plagues (more especially the Black Death of 1348) and consequential economic adjustments. The fourteenth century in particular was marked by the abandonment of many settlements in lowland Britain so that deserted medieval village sites are now a well-known feature of the lowland landscape. Cornwall, however, seems to have escaped this disastrous transformation: whereas most English counties can list deserted villages by the hundred, a mere handful have so far been identified in Cornwall.

Most of the Cornish sites are located on Bodmin Moor (Garrow, Carwether, Temple, Tresibbet and Trewortha in particular) with other isolated occurrences at Lanyon (Penwith peninsula), Porthillie (near Polzeath) and Treworld (Boscastle). Deserted medieval villages do not appear to be a feature of the landscape of Cornwall as they are in other English counties: but this is an area of potential future research which might yield additional sites, for Cornwall so far has not been intensively worked over as have most other parts of the country.

Field patterns

Much of the character of the rural scene in any part of England depends to a large extent on the size, arrangement and appearance of the fields. We often find the oldest parts of the cultural landscape in the field patterns, for houses eventually need replacement whilst hedges and walls only require maintenance. However, any explanation of the evolution of the field pattern is likely to run into a labyrinth of problems which, whilst providing the basis for a fascinating detective story for the historical geographer, greatly complicates any attempt at generalisation.

The standard reference, Gray's *English Field Systems*, of

1915, has now been superseded by many detailed studies in various parts of the country and the realisation that progress in the study of field systems can only be made by combining field-work with an examination of medieval extents, deeds, court rolls, *compoti*, estate maps, manorial surveys, probate inventories and tithe maps. Gray devotes few pages to Cornwall in his original account but he does enumerate three types of field system in the county. He distinguishes 'open' fields with intermixed parcels which might more accurately be described as subdivided, others where cultivation took place in undivided enclosures, and a third on the borders of the waste where field systems had emerged from a plentiful supply of grazing land and which resembled the historic infield-outfield system.

Much of the subsequent argument revolves around the extent and the age of the 'open' field. Gray thought that there were few open fields in Cornwall and that they differed in function from the open fields of the Midland villages with their two- and three-field systems. Subsequent investigations have modified this view. Henderson, for example, advanced in 1935 evidence for open fields round many of the Cornish boroughs and Rowse in 1941 demonstrates their presence on a number of rural manors. As regards the age of the 'open' fields, Henderson in 1935 and Hoskins in 1955 with others have favoured Anglo-Saxon origins, but more recently work by Baker and Butlin in 1973 and others has cast doubt on the whole thesis of the Anglo-Saxon origins of the open-field system. The situation is complicated in the case of Cornwall by the paucity of documentary records and by the variety of the patterns that can be distinguished in a landscape which probably has more hedges per square mile than any other county in England. In the present survey, we can only hint at the possibilities that may exist for the detailed explanation of any particular area and caution the reader against deductions drawn from limited evidence, whether of a cartographic, bibliographic or field-survey kind. A thorough search of all sources of information for a particular locality is a necessity to ascertain the true facts.

The contribution of Bronze Age and Iron Age man to the cultural landscape of the moorland area has already been noted. The small fields, often quite clearly lyncheted, and the small gardens or enclosures which were constructed near their rounded huts, are traceable upon Bodmin Moor even after 2,000 years of decay. But prehistoric man also inhabited areas which were subsequently not abandoned and in these the fields he made have sometimes come down to us almost intact. Crawford has drawn particular attention to the small and irregularly patterned fields occurring in the Penwith peninsula. Some especially good examples are to be seen in the neighbourhood of Zennor (Fig.5). The boundary walls are built of huge granite boulders or grounders surmounted by smaller stones, all undoubtedly removed laboriously from the natural moorland to clear the ground for agriculture. Once built they would not be readily removed. Taking into consideration the small size of the fields and their irregular pattern plus their association with prehistoric sites, there seems little doubt that the fields also date from prehistoric times. Additional evidence is afforded by place-names and occasionally archaeological finds such as a Bronze Age hoard in a field bank (as at Amalveor in Towednack) which removes all doubt as to the age.

Originally groups of small fields must have existed as islands in the natural landscape; there could not have been any continuous chequerboard pattern such as we now know. Settlements must have been widely spaced and would have consisted of small collections of homesteads, or even single farmsteads, around which lay the fields. This would have produced a pattern similar to the infield-outfield system. The infield lay in the immediate vicinity of the homestead and was permanently cultivated: beyond this lay the outfield appurtenant to the farm, but broken up and cultivated in small patches at a time, a change being made to a new spot when fertility was temporarily exhausted. Cattle pens or folds would also be constructed and taken in from the waste. Crawford has drawn attention to the field boundaries which sweep in continuous broad curves across some parts of the Cornish landscape and which probably mark phases in the development of the outfield and cattle management. The far western parish of Towednack at Amalveor has a succession of long, continuous, curved field boundaries, strongly sugges-

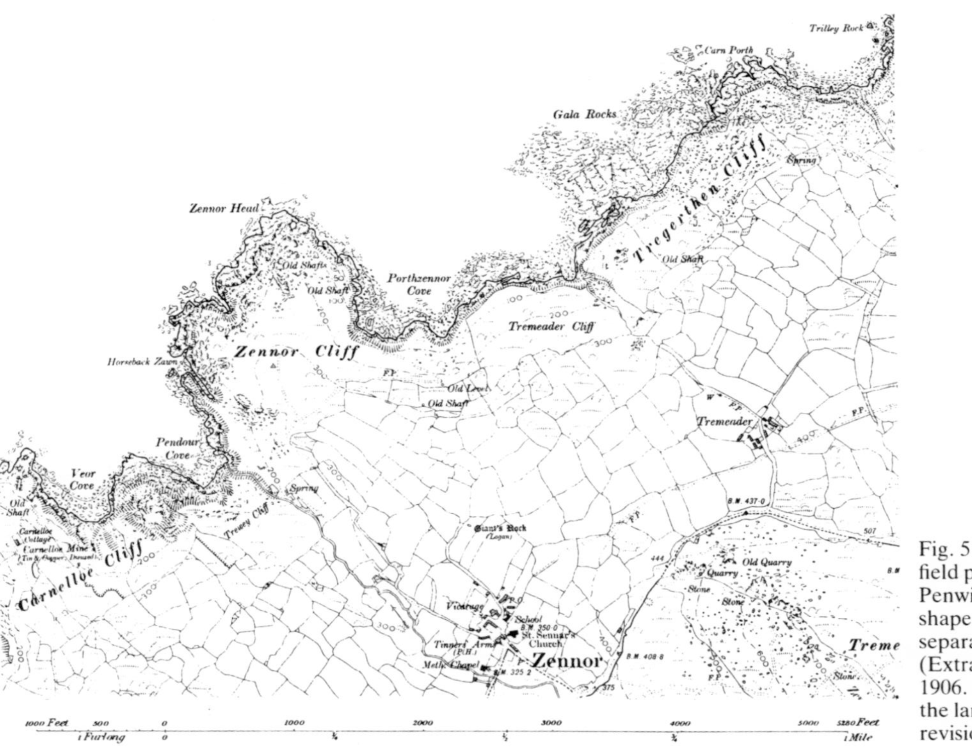

Fig. 5. Zennor: a characteristic Iron Age field pattern in Zennor parish in the Penwith peninsula: tiny fields of irregular shape, but often roughly square, are separated by walls of granite boulders. (Extract from OS Sheet 61 SW Revised 1906. Hardly any change has occurred in the landscape of this area since the revision of 1906.)

tive of prehistoric developing outfields (Fig.6), whilst a prehistoric cattlefield is likely at Castallack in Paul parish (Fig.7).

Henderson states that near the original homestead there is usually a field called 'the *Gew*', a name implying 'the hedged-in place' and representing the first piece of land to be secured against intrusion. Adjacent to this is a *Parc* (or Park) also implying an enclosed field, and then the *Gweal* which is a much larger 'open' field representing the old outfield. Subdivisions of the outfield may have occurred at a later date, as does the enclosure of the intervening waste, and it is by this process continuing slowly but surely through the centuries that the present scene has emerged.

Thus far for Cornwall the experts seem to agree, but with the advent of the Dark Ages a divergence of opinion has more recently taken place. It was originally thought that into this land of scattered homesteads and hamlets working the infield-outfield system, the Anglo-Saxons burst with a totally different agricultural pattern, that of the open field with strip cultivation and a more communal organisation based on the nucleated village. That the 'open' field did exist in Cornwall is clear from certain records: Henderson says of Helston that 'Gweal Hellis on the north side of the town is Cornish for the open field of Henlis, or Helston, and takes us back to the time when the town was surrounded after the Anglo-Saxon fashion by great open common fields in which each burgess had a number of strips or stitches. Nearly all the Cornish towns of the Middle Ages had such fields surrounding them.' Rowse similarly draws attention to examples of the open field in surveys of the Cornish manors of the Earl of Devon, and mentions that on the manor of Tinten in North Cornwall the fields have only recently been enclosed.

Studies of field systems by Baker and Butlin, however, challenge the concept of the Anglo-Saxon origin of the open field: they point out the lack of any documentary evidence for this system in the early part of the Dark Ages, together with increasing references to the system in the later Middle Ages. The thesis is advanced that the open field and strip cultivation emerged in the Middle Ages as a response to increased population pressure. We certainly know of a great surge of colonisation in Cornwall and the rest of England during the

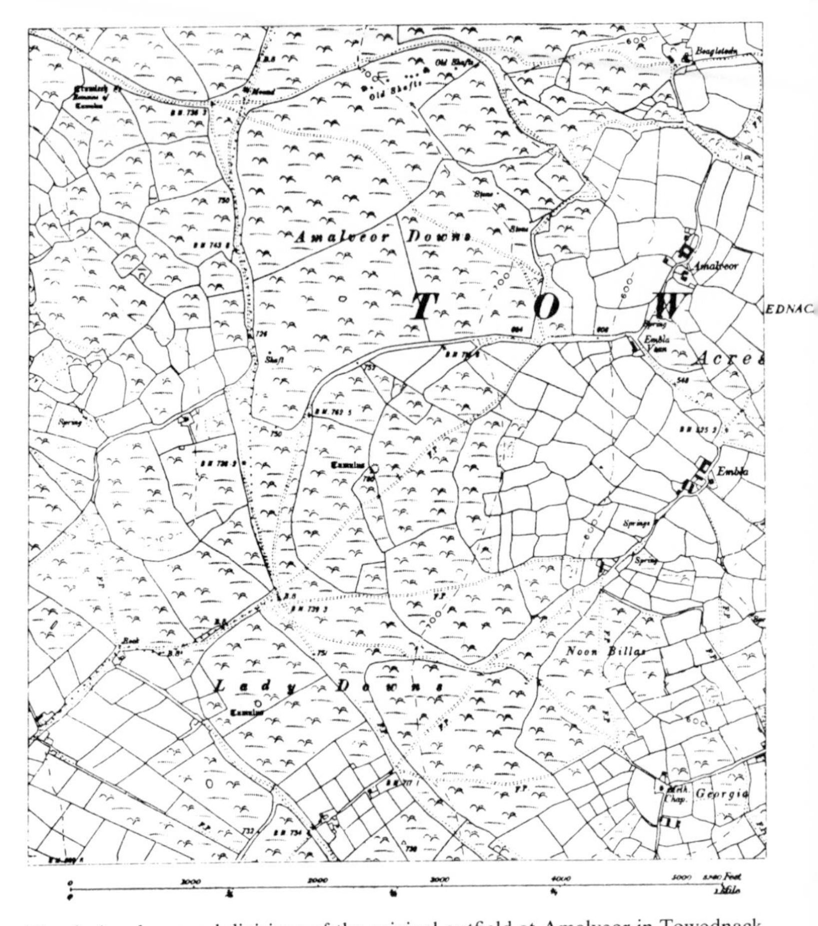

Fig. 6. Amalveor: subdivisions of the original outfield at Amalveor in Towednack parish. The boundaries of the outfield are indicated by broad sweeping curves of walling inside which a multitude of small enclosures were later made.
(Extract from OS Sheet 68 NW Revised 1906. Little change has taken place in this landscape since 1906.)

twelfth and thirteenth centuries and all existing settlements must have been under considerable pressure. Fox in a more recent study of the field systems in Cornwall also argues for the emergence of strip fields in Cornwall to be associated with population growth and the practice of communal assarting: he finds no evidence for the operation of partible inheritance. The transition from the prehistoric infield-outfield system through the open field to the modern field pattern will probably remain clouded in mystery for a long time to come in Cornwall. Currently it seems that the prehistoric infield-outfield pattern was typical for longer than was originally thought and probably remained until the medieval population explosion forced a more intensive agricultural system. Eventually the open-field system was itself overtaken by enclosure, a process which is well documented as we move into more recent time.

Fairly definite evidence that enclosure of the open field was proceeding in the sixteenth century is provided by Richard Carew's *Survey of Cornwall* which was written in the 1590s. Speaking of pasture he says, 'But since the grounds began to receive enclosure and dressing for tillage the nature of the soil hath altered to a better grain'. Later, in discussing the husbandmen, he writes, 'These in times not past the remembrance of some living rubbed forth their estate in the poorest plight, their grounds lay all in common, or only divided by stitch-meal'. Some of the Cornish hedge-banks must therefore date from the sixteenth century.

Cornwall can also offer its own special type of field pattern in what used to be the principal tin- and copper-mining districts – a pattern of hundreds of small squarish fields of roughly the same size (Fig.8). The origin of this type is well explained by Lysons in *Magna Britannia*, Vol. III, Cornwall. Writing in 1814 he states, 'Much of the dreary wasteland in the mining district has been greatly improved in appearance and value by the good policy of the land-holders, who have granted leases to the labouring miners, for ninety-nine years determinable on three lives, of portions of the wasteland, each consisting of three acres, at an annual rent of ten shillings, on condition of building a cottage and cultivating the land.' The writer of *Cornwall Illustrated*, 1831, adds that 'this

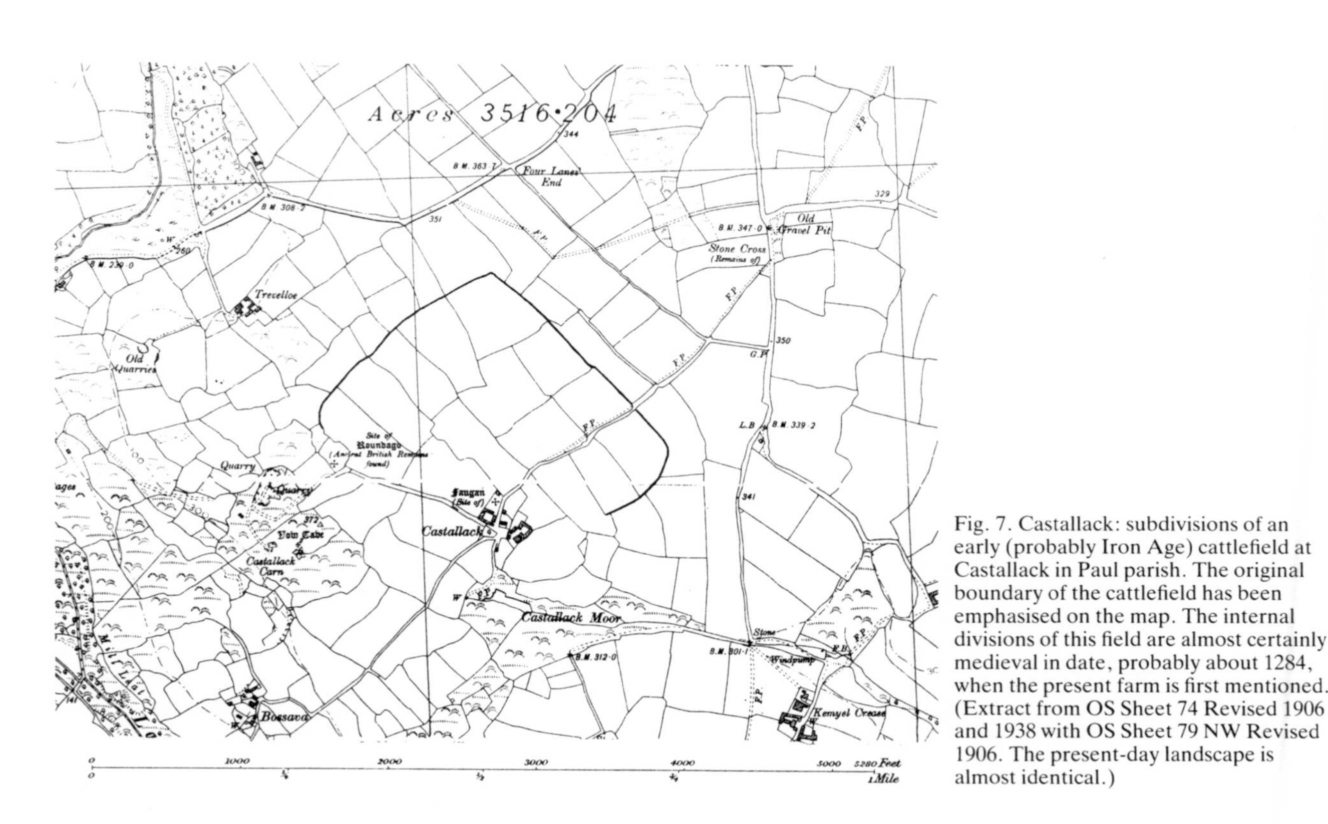

Fig. 7. Castallack: subdivisions of an early (probably Iron Age) cattlefield at Castallack in Paul parish. The original boundary of the cattlefield has been emphasised on the map. The internal divisions of this field are almost certainly medieval in date, probably about 1284, when the present farm is first mentioned. (Extract from OS Sheet 74 Revised 1906 and 1938 with OS Sheet 79 NW Revised 1906. The present-day landscape is almost identical.)

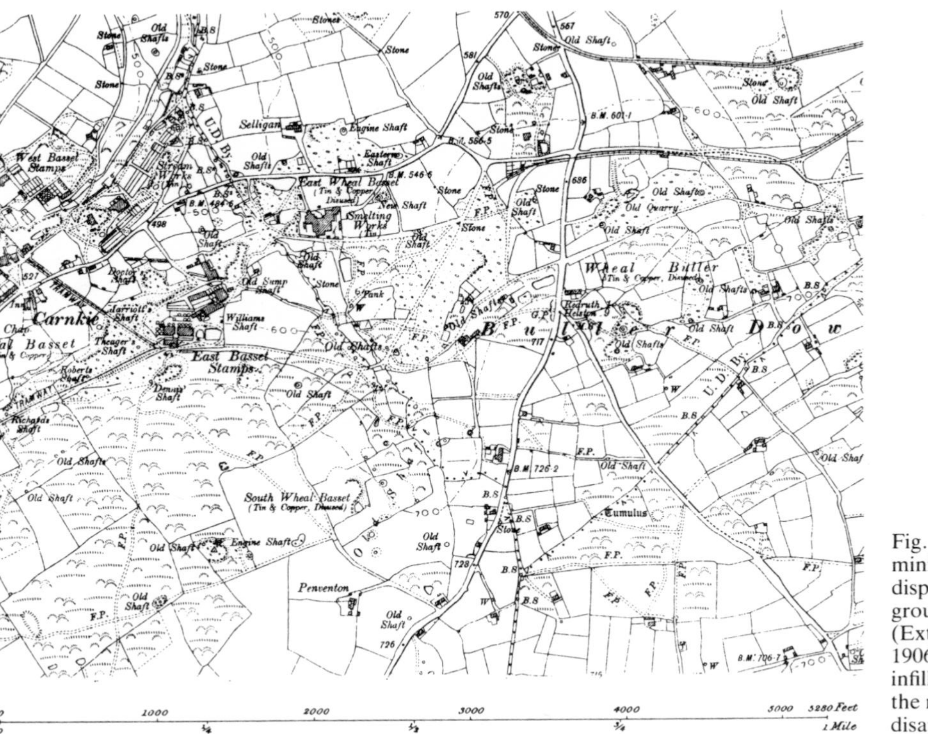

Fig. 8. Redruth: the landscape of tin mining, small rectangular fields, dispersed settlement and worked-over ground.
(Extract from OS Sheet 63 SE Revised 1906. More recently there has been infilling with houses on some plots and the railway lines have largely disappeared.)

practice has tended to improve the appearance and condition of the country, whilst the industrious miner is materially benefited in health, in moral habits, and in property, and the landed proprietor enhances his rent roll.' 'At the expense of the industrious' further adds a subsequent reader of my copy, who pencils a footnote that 'This infamous system was abolished the latter end of the nineteenth century.' Whether infamous or not, it made its own characteristic mark on the Cornish landscape and the pattern of small square fields and dispersed settlement of many of the mining areas is there to be seen to the present day.

More recent enclosure is usually marked by straight hedges with larger square or rectangular fields and some good examples may be found on Connor Downs in Gwithian (Fig.9). Regrettably Cornwall is not immune from barbed-wire fencing, but this method of demarcation cannot be said to be permanent, and being so well endowed with massive hedgebanks and small fields the county has but limited need of this twentieth-century eyesore.

Enclosure of the limited open field and both ancient and more recent enclosure from the waste thus combine with the original Celtic field boundaries and miners' fields to produce the present-day field patterns. Scattered settlements and hamlets are now spread very uniformly throughout the county. The hamlets are usually found at cross-roads (Fig.10) and less frequently round a parish church (Fig.11). Elsewhere the units are made up of a farmhouse, outbuildings, and perhaps one or two labourers' cottages. The distance between each is remarkably constant and the number of homesteads per square mile rarely falls below eight or rises above twelve. Farm holdings, therefore, average between fifty and eighty acres.

The moorland remaining today is found on the granite of Bodmin Moor, Hensbarrow Downs and the Penwith peninsula. A further area on Goonhilly Downs is related to the serpentine of the Lizard. Elsewhere, the moorland is less extensive and in process of disappearance with gradual enclosure. Carnmenellis Moor is now but a name and much has been reclaimed on the Penwith peninsula and on Hensbarrow Down. But the advance is not always in the same direction, as

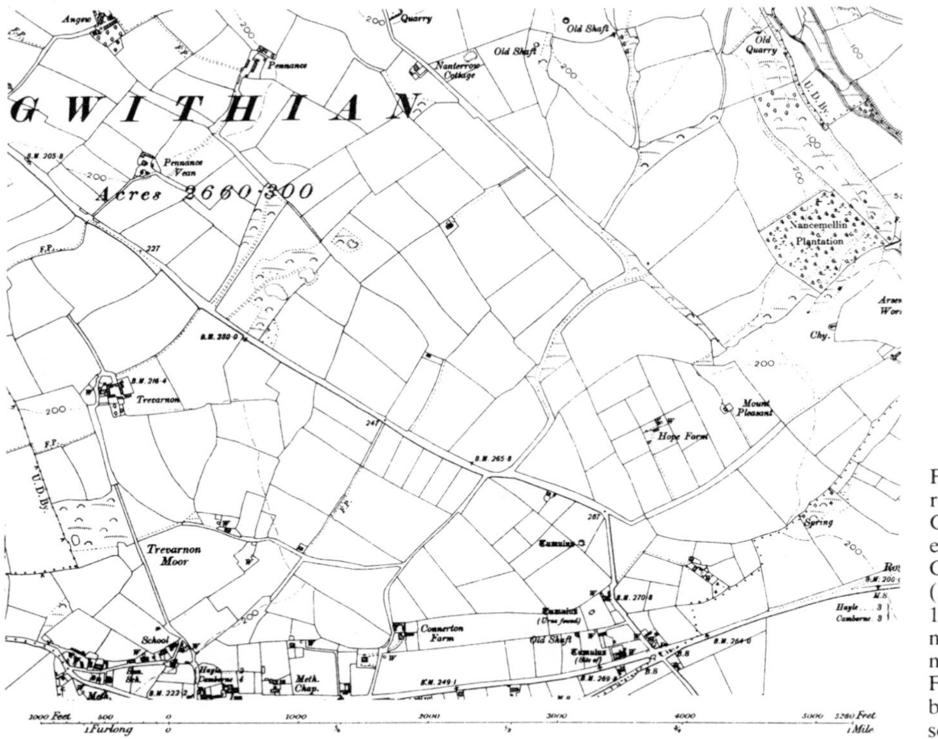

Fig. 9. Gwithian: the field pattern of recent enclosure on Connor Downs in Gwithian, square or rectangular enclosures, much larger than those of Celtic or medieval origin.
(Extract from OS Sheet 62 SE Revised 1906. A 1980 ground check revealed a number of hedge disappearances in the north-west of the area and around Hope Farm. There has also been additional building along the main road to the south.)

will be seen if comparisons are made between Greenwood's map of 1826–7 (which closely resembles the first edition of the one-inch map of the Ordnance Survey) and the twentieth-century Land Utilisation Survey map of 1932–8. In most areas of sedimentary rock there has been a reduction of moorland, but in the serpentine Lizard and around the edges of the granitic Bodmin massif the moor has increased. The frontiers of cultivation are very sensitive to minor climatic and economic fluctuations and examples of enclosures that have been allowed to revert to moorland are common. In an evening light, one may often see the outlines of a whole group of fields now completely overwhelmed by bracken.

In any examination of the field patterns, either on the ground or on the map, we must be prepared for a considerable mixture of types and origins. We may begin with the tiny, irregular, prehistoric 'Celtic' fields well illustrated near Zennor (Fig.5). Then there are the larger but still irregular fields produced by the original outfields with their subsequent subdivisions, illustrated so neatly at Amalveor (Fig.6). Or there may be medieval subdivisions of prehistoric cattle pounds as at Castallack (Fig.7). Elsewhere we may find elongated and more regular fields produced by enclosure of strips from open fields as at Kilkhampton (Fig.3) or small squarish fields typical of the mining areas (Fig.8) contrasting with larger rectangular fields of more recent enclosure (Fig.9).

Field patterns, of course, are not necessarily static: some hedge boundaries were lost during the landscape gardening of the eighteenth and nineteenth centuries and further inroads were made during the construction of airfields in the twentieth century. Since the Second World War some of the more enterprising farmers, endeavouring to adjust to modern techniques, have removed still more field boundaries. In Cornwall, however, the massive size of the hedgebanks and granite boulders are a great deterrent to removal even with modern mechanised earth-moving equipment, with the result that the greater part of the historic pattern still remains. The casual visitor, indeed, might well gain the impression that little or no change has taken place, but this is soon dispelled if a comparison is made beween the Ordnance Survey's original six-inch

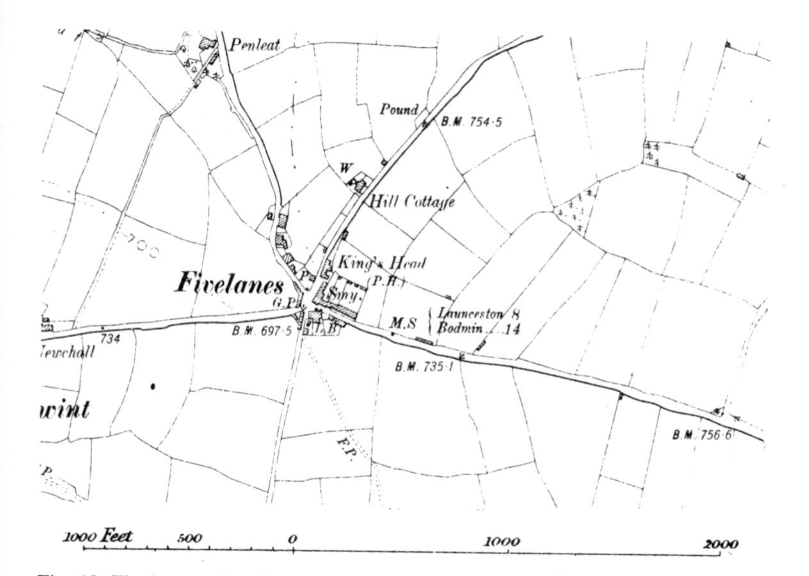

Fig. 10. Fivelanes: a hamlet at a cross-roads containing a smithy and an inn but no church at the time of the survey in 1905.
(Extract from OS Sheet 15 SE Revised 1905. Fivelanes found itself on the main A30 road but has now been by-passed. A cattle market and school have been added recently but the field boundaries remain the same.)

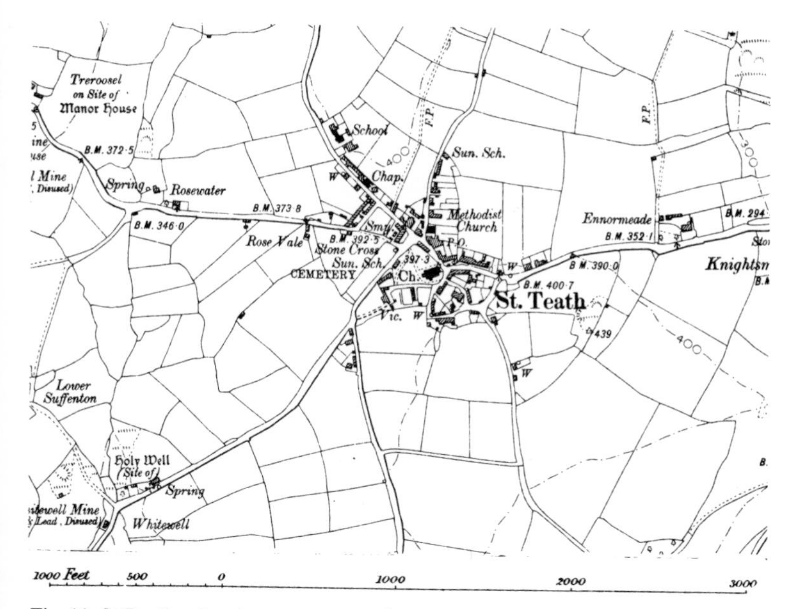

Fig. 11. St Teath: a hamlet at a cross-roads and also the site of the parish church. The present building contains Norman fragments indicating that a church existed here in the twelfth century.
(Extract from OS Sheet 20 NW Revised 1905. The present landscape remains almost identical apart from several new houses north-west of the village centre.)

(1:10,560) maps which largely date from 1875–85 (revised in 1905–6) and the modern 1:10,000 maps (mainly surveyed and revised from 1960–80). Many fields have been enlarged and a surprising number of hedges have disappeared, although the resulting landscape change is nothing like that which has taken place in East Anglia.

Hedges and walls

Combined with the field patterns, and of equal if not greater importance in the appearance of the landscape, are the field boundaries. Man rarely moves his hedging materials more than a short distance and most field boundaries faithfully reflect the underlying geology. In Cornwall, therefore, the traditional boundary is either a granite dry-stone wall or a slate-faced hedge-bank.

In the granite areas, dry-stone walling has been practised from the Bronze Age onwards. One of the first steps in the reclamation of the 'waste' would have been the removal of the moorstone which littered the surface. This was used as grounders or foundation stones for the hedging in the new fields. On top of the grounders smaller stones were placed (Plate 16). Other methods were also tried and sometimes one finds the stone walls reinforced by a kind of daub or mixture of earth which has set, but true mortar rarely occurs. By now, many of these dry-stone walls have become well covered with lichens but they support little else other than the odd wind-sculptured hawthorn or blackthorn bush. At these high altitudes, their situation is too exposed to the fierce winds which sweep across the peninsula to support much in the way of vegetation.

In the slate areas a different method has been employed. Here, the field boundaries are traditionally thick earthen walls with a slate facing, the stones being obtained from shallow excavations in the immediate vicinity. The slates may be laid horizontally, vertically or sometimes in herring-bone courses, and the top of the bank is usually turfed. Fortunately it is County Council policy to continue with the traditional hedging techniques and recently widened or new sections of road are always hedged with the brown or grey slate-faced earthen banks.

These walls and banks with their innumerable niches and readily-accessible interior earth enable plant life to flourish in profusion. The range of plants is a botanical feast in the mild climate of the south-west and often over a hundred different species can be found in a few hundred yards of hedge. Some plants will occasionally dominate and produce seasonal splashes of colour which make Cornwall so memorable: the pink thrift (*Armeria maritima*), red valerian (*Centranthus ruber*), white sea campion (*Silene maritima*), pink and white English stonecrop (*Sedum anglicum*), and primrose (*Primula vulgaris*), are notable examples but more often the hedge-banks consist of a mixture of these plants along with foxglove (*Digitalis purpurea*), golden rod (*Solidago virgaurea*), wall pennywort (*Umbilicus rupestria*), golden saxifrage (*Chrysosplenium oppositifolium*), wild thyme (*Thymus drucei*), and gorse (*Ulex europaeus*), along with a mass of intricate green tracery of ferns. In spring and early summer the brightly coloured hedges give to parts of Cornwall a special delight of their own. In sheltered areas some of the hedgebanks are topped by blackthorn and hawthorn bushes, but as soon as these are subject to the slightest exposure their growth is distorted and their form stunted. Wind-sculptured trees are a common sight especially on the more exposed western and northern coasts.

These two types of hedge, with their minor variations, account for the greater part of the field boundaries in the county: but local anomalies, usually of a much more recent age, also exist. These may range from cast-iron railings and concrete posts on the one hand, to slabs of slate set up vertically, tombstone fashion, on the other hand. Inevitably also the odd barbed-wire fence and electric fence has made its appearance, but these are normally transient and generally Cornwall has not suffered seriously in this respect: the ancient crafts of walling and hedging, begun in the Bronze Age, still go on in much the same way and dominate the hedgerow scene.

Churches and Chapels

With the gradual colonisation of the natural landscape characteristic buildings were added to the scene. Few traces of the earliest domestic buildings now remain for rising standards have inevitably led to much demolition and replacement. But when our ancestors erected their churches and built in stone more permanent structures resulted and these are often the oldest buildings still in day-to-day use.

The earliest ecclesiastical buildings in Cornwall are associated with the Irish saints. The remains are now scanty but the work of these missionaries is important as they have in many instances determined the original sites of existing churches. There seems to have been a fertile field in Cornwall for Irish missionary zeal in the fifth to seventh centuries and the story is recorded in a colourful way in *The Coming of the Saints*. Irish Christianity, influenced by Egypt and Syria rather than by Rome, had by this time evolved along monastic lines and the saints erected stone cells or chapels in holy places. The latter were often determined by the availability of water so that spring points were favourite sites.

Few of these cells now remain but there is a fine example in Cornwall north of Perranporth where the cell or oratory of St Piran is located. This is undoubtedly the oldest and earliest extant chapel in south-west England and it gives us a good idea of the nature of these ancient foundations. Although there is some doubt as to the exact age, most authorities favour the sixth or seventh centuries: it is constructed of slate and granite rubble with coarse clay in place of mortar, and measures twenty-nine and a half by sixteen by nineteen feet. Inside, stone seats face a small altar and the illumination is provided by one small window. The chapel has been preserved only because encroaching wind-blown sand buried it before the great rebuilding of so many Cornish churches began in the twelfth century. It subsequently reappeared after several hundred years beneath the sands and is now protected by a concrete shelter.

Many of these oratories or chapels must have been built in Cornwall as is witnessed by the dedications of present-day churches to a whole host of saints with the strangest of names – St Petrock, St Adwenna, St Buriena, St Breaca to name but a few of several hundred. The sites of other chapels may be indicated by some of the Celtic crosses still surviving and also by certain place-names. As well as the classic oratory of St Piran, another is known to exist in the sands at Gwithian near Hayle, having been excavated in the nineteenth century. The ground plan of a cell has also been found on Tintagel Island. These, with the addition of a small number of inconspicuous inscribed stones carrying Ogham script (e.g. at St Kew and St Clement) are proven examples of original Irish work in Cornwall.

From the seventh to the eleventh centuries, churches were established in England by the Anglo-Saxons, but Cornwall, not absorbed until the eighth century, was little affected. The choice of St Germans, an old Celtic site, as the centre of Saxon religion in the far west in A.D. 936 reflects the isolation of the peninsula from the rest of England.

Whilst the Irish saints had a profound effect on the choice of church sites, it is to the Normans that we owe the first permanent structures. No fewer than 140 of the present 220 parish churches in Cornwall show traces of Norman work to some degree or other. Most of the traces are indeed slight and one can only enjoy them as architecture in churches such as St Germans, Morwenstow, St Michael Caerhays and Egloskerry, but to the student of landscape history these traces are good evidence of the tremendous century of church building that followed the Norman Conquest, reflecting in turn the generations of colonisation among the woods, along the hillsides, and up on the moors that preceded the Conquest. For the parish church was the ultimate seal of this intense secular activity, the recognition that a new human community had come into being and now called for spiritual sustenance.

Partly because of the existence of the venerated and holy sites inherited from the Irish saints and partly because of the scattered Celtic settlement pattern, not all the churches were neatly placed with respect to their parishioners. Isolated churches remain a peculiar feature of the Cornish landscape to this day. Many towns (e.g. Wadebridge, Launceston, Callington and Looe) had no parish church within their boundaries until late in the Middle Ages. The town of Camelford had no church of its own until well into the nineteenth century, Lanteglos serving as its parish church.

Most pre-Conquest churches were simple rectangular buildings consisting of little more than a sanctuary and a nave. The Normans introduced a new design – the cruciform – with north and south transepts dividing off the altar/sanctuary from the nave. Towers were also added in various places – for example at the head of the north transept in Bodmin, and central to the cruciform at Tintagel, Crantock and St Enodoc, whilst the western end of St Germans acquired the famous twin towers.

Cornish granite was rarely used by the Normans in their church construction as it was too hard and crystalline to allow of manipulation with the simple pick and axe. Softer free-stones were quarried from Ventergan in Warbstow parish (now worked out), from Tartan Down in Landrake parish, from Polyphant – a most beautiful dove-grey stone – in Lewannick parish near Launceston; and the Hicks Grey Mill stone from the same parish. Pentuan near St Austell was another favourite quarry and in the west the serpentine of the Lizard cliffs was used. In the north, cliffstone was employed, most notably at Morwenstow, at Tintagel, and the dark blue Catacleuse cliffstone at Padstow. In the east of the county towards the Tamar, the builders occasionally used the green volcanic ash from Hurdwick near Tavistock in Devon, just as the Devon builders occasionally, but all too rarely, drew upon the Cornish Polyphant. It is interesting to reflect when standing in these now empty and overgrown quarries upon the buildings that have come out of them in bygone centuries. These local stones were also supplemented by the import of the more easily carved Caen stone from Normandy, a good example being the parish church of St Anthony-in-Roseland.

The Normans built their walls on average some three feet thick and the low structures give them a ponderous but powerful ethos which doubtless accounts for J.D. Sedding writing in 1884 that

> there is in the older Cornish churches an indefinable something which makes them seem more identified with the local surroundings than is the case with church architecture in

> other parts of England. These simple structures seem to be part of the simple nature of the moor and down which surround them, they have what painters call 'quality' or tone about them: they are essentially human, and eloquent of the character of the men who reared them.

They have generally neither grace nor beauty: they have a 'strong salt flavour' and are 'wild, rustic and moorish'.

These scores of Norman churches, some with a simple nave and sanctuary plan, others with the more elaborate cruciform plan, must have been a conspicuous element in the wild medieval landscape before the newly-dug stone had been darkened by beating rain and by age.

Responding to both increasing population and increasing wealth, a second great building period opened in the fifteenth century after 200 years in which only minor new work was contributed. A period of rebuilding and enlargement in the Perpendicular style then began and lasted for about a hundred years. Most churches lost their cruciform plan by the addition of aisles which absorbed the earlier transepts, and nearly all had square towers raised at their west ends. The towers are usually in two, three or four stages with battlements and pinnacles at the top. Buttresses if present are very slim. Probus is usually regarded as the most magnificent tower in Cornwall but those at Ludgvan, Constantine and St Columb Minor are also very beautiful. East of the Cornish tower a long nave is usually flanked by two aisles almost as wide and as long as the nave, and the nave and aisles are often each surmounted by a wagon or cradle roof.

Skills and tools had improved steadily over the centuries and the Cornish granite, which gives such a tremendous character to the churches today, was used extensively in the great building period of the fifteenth and sixteenth centuries. But even then the granite was rarely quarried, being picked up and rough hewn on the moors where it lay about in massive blocks. No wonder that these granite monolithic piers, crude and intractable still to the carver, have such a powerful quality: they are the living rock of the moors that lie around them.

It is the contrast between the upright square block of the

tower and the low horizontal blocks of the nave and aisles which characterises the special contribution of the church to the rural landscape. Departures from this standard pattern often imply rebuilding earlier than the fifteenth century. There are, for instance, a few churches with spires and these ante-date the fashion for square towers, e.g. at Lostwithiel, St Enodoc, St Gerrans, St Minver, Cubert and Rame. Some of these spires might have been built as landmarks for mariners if the church was near the sea; St Eval's tower, for instance, was rebuilt in 1727 at the expense of Bristol merchants for precisely this purpose. The Early English style can be seen most effectively at St Anthony-in-Roseland whilst fourteenth-century work occurs at St Ives, Sheviock and North Hill. Elsewhere the Perpendicular style, with its square tower and three aisles, is repeated with almost unfailing regularity.

The fifteenth-century masons had better tools than the Norman builders for we no longer find the softer Catacleuse and Polyphant stone monopolising the carved work. As well as the use of granite, there is an increasing use of other locally quarried stone. By the early sixteenth century, considerable decoration was added both inside and outside many buildings. On the exterior much decoration was incorporated in the walls as at St Neot, Bodmin and St Mary Truro (now part of the cathedral). Launceston is the most remarkable example of all. Internally beautiful rood screens, carved bench ends, and cradle roofs appeared. But the interior work did not remain for long for almost at the height of the decorative phase the Reformation arrived.

The Reformation commences in 1535 when Henry VIII became Supreme Head of the Church of England and the rift with Rome began. The retaliatory measures taken against Roman Catholicism affected Cornwall as much as the rest of the country. The monasteries were suppressed, bringing about the collapse of the great religious centres at St Germans and Bodmin, many associated chapels were destroyed (e.g. St Thomas of Canterbury at Bodmin) and the interiors of most churches were stripped of their rood screens, images, pictures, stained glass, plate and jewels. In the seventeenth century, yet another wave of 'purification' accompanied the Puritan movement and what little that had survived the phase of the Reformation was swept away in a second attack on the interiors. Needless to say, there was no enthusiasm for church building through these troubled centuries so that by the nineteenth century the parish churches of Cornwall were in a sorry state. Religious enthusiasm had shifted to the Wesley brothers and it was Methodist chapels that then began to form a new element in the Cornish scene.

The nineteenth century eventually saw a movement to 'restore' churches in Cornwall along Gothic lines. The results were often disastrous and some authorities have maintained that Cornwall suffered more than most other English counties in this restoration phase. However, there were many cases where the change was beneficial, e.g. Lanreath, Creed and Blisland. The middle of the century also saw the addition of many new churches in the mining areas and then in 1880 the building of Truro Cathedral, the pride of Cornwall, began.

Truro Cathedral took thirty years to construct and is unique in many respects. It was the first cathedral to be built in England since St Paul's in London, and the first cathedral to exist in Cornwall since the loss of the St Germans bishopric over 800 years previously. The architect, J. L. Pearson, modelled the cathedral on the Early English style and its siting in crowded, narrow streets produces vistas reminiscent of some towns in northern France. Cornwall's traditional links with Brittany might well have been in Pearson's mind at the design stage. The cathedral actually incorporates part of the sixteenth-century church of St Mary and fittingly the choir stalls have dedications to the Cornish saints who came from Ireland, Wales and Brittany.

The Reformation also swept away many private chapels and oratories which had become a special and endearing feature of the south-western landscape. These had been licensed in Cornwall by the bishops of Exeter from the thirteenth century onwards. The earliest licensed in Cornwall was at Trusehara (1272), followed by Boswythgy (1283), and an increasing number appeared in the fourteenth and fifteenth centuries. Some still exist in a ruined state – for instance St Julitta's Chapel in Tintagel Castle, and St Michael's Chapel on Roche Rock (Plate 18). Bosence Chapel in Sancreed and Incework near Millbrook are further examples. Others have been variously employed as houses (Chapel Idne in Sennen Cove) or as stables (as at Hall Barton near Bodinnick, and at Earth Barton near Saltash). The best surviving example in all Cornwall is the chapel at Trecarrel near Launceston, a perfect example of its kind which was licensed in 1405. The existing structure represents a building of about a century later. The observant visitor will also notice fragments of window tracery in some of the larger farmhouses, which frequently mark the position of an ancient private oratory incorporated from the beginning into the house itself.

One picturesque feature of the Cornish village scene fortunately survived the Reformation in many localities. Nearly every parish had had its holy well from early Christian days, and when the rebuilding of the churches took place in the fifteenth and early sixteenth centuries a large number of holy wells had little structures raised above them. Many have survived to this day, notably those at St Cleer near Liskeard (Plate 19), St Ruan's well in Grade, St Cyr's well near Luxulyan, Menacuddle well near St Austell, the holy well at Morwenstow, and Dupath well near Callington. Many others will be found in the villages of Cornwall, although sadly some of the attractive little overbuildings are neglected and occasionally in a ruinous condition.

Wayside crosses

Crosses exist in other parts of the western British Isles but nowhere in such large numbers or in so widespread a variety as in Cornwall. Taking the inscribed stones together with crosses, Langdon reports, in his notable survey of 1896, the existence of over 400. Since that time others have come to light and Henderson mentions an additional fifty. More recently Maxwell lists seventy-three in west Penwith alone and produces evidence for 118 that have disappeared.

Although we rarely have definite literary evidence to date any of these monuments, it seems probable that the forty or so inscribed stones all precede the true crosses and are of Celtic-Christian origin. The crosses differ from the pagan sepulchral stones in that many have distinctive Christian names or characters incribed upon them. Some of the best examples are found at Cardinham (in the churchyard – Plate 20), at Menabilly near Fowey (the Castle Dôr stone) and at Mawgan in Meneage (the village centre). The magnificent Cardinham cross was found embedded in the east wall of the chancel. The fact that the fifteenth-century church builders had no reverence for it is proof of its great age. The Castle Dôr stone has a Latin inscription on its front and a T-cross on the back and could date from the sixth century. The Mawgan cross has Hiberno-Saxon letters and is probably of tenth-century origin.

The 'normal' crosses probably developed from the inscribed stones and their erection seem to have become common in the later Middle Ages. Their distribution, even now, is ubiquitous although there is plenty of evidence to indicate that many have been moved, often into a churchyard or the church itself, for safety. Many still remain by the wayside or are scattered over the bleak moors, suggesting a function as route markers. Isolated crosses may have been erected for devotional purposes similar to the wayside crucifix still found in Catholic countries overseas. Yet others were doubtless boundary stones whilst the inscriptions which some carry clearly indicate memorial stones.

The crosses may be grouped into several types. There is the simple wheel or round-headed type with the cross inscribed within the head such as is found in Penzance, Boskenna (several), St Buryan, Crows-an-Wra, Brunion and Rosemorran. A more complicated design is the four-holed decorated Celtic type such as the specimens in the churchyards at Phillack and Sancreed. Others have Christ figures in relief on the cross as in the churchyards at Sancreed, Paul, St Just in Penwith, Madron and St Levan, whilst another variant is the simple Latin cross as at Trereife, Kerris, Kemyel Drea, Tremethic, Newlyn and Ludgvan. A completely different type is the square-headed Lantern cross found in St Ives churchyard, at St Erth and on St Michael's Mount.

While many places are named after a cross which still stands in the vicinity, other localities such as Parc-an-Growse, Grouse, and Rose-an-Grous have lost their crosses. With so much movement having taken place, it is now hazardous to attempt any detailed interpretation based on the geographical distribution of the crosses, unless one assumes that migrations have only been over short distances. Actually the distribution shows no marked characteristics apart from an increasing concentration westwards. The crosses diminish eastwards and northwards, with the extreme north-east where the English settled being devoid of crosses. It is generally assumed (although this is a debatable point) that the decorated crosses are later than the simple crosses and that most fall within the period A.D. 700–1100. Few can be dated precisely and added interest is perhaps attached to those for which a date can be indicated. Henderson has shown that the conspicuous cross in the sands near St Piran's Church at Perranporth must be older than A.D. 960. Professor Macalister has dated the well-known wheel-headed cross in Morrab Gardens, Penzance, as earlier than A.D. 924, whilst at St Cleer there is an inscribed cross carrying the name Doniert, who has tentatively been identified with Dumgarth, King of Cornwall, who died about A.D. 878. Some crosses are richly decorated, notably at Lanherne in Mawgan and at Cardinham; whilst the largest, some seventeen feet in length, stands in the churchyard at Mylor near Falmouth. More recently Maxwell, as a result of a detailed study of west Penwith, has advanced the theory that most crosses appear to have been used to mark the paths between individual homesteads and the parish church.

It is significant that practically every village and town in Cornwall now has a modern Cornish cross, usually of the wheel-headed Celtic pattern, as a basis for the local war memorial. Here is an example of continuity of cultural traits extending over many generations: for we can look beyond the medieval cross to the inscribed stone and even further back to the prehistoric menhir, and yet bring the custom right up-to-date with the twentieth-century war memorial.

Castles

Another addition to the medieval landscape was the castle, of which Cornwall still retains some examples. Of the smaller castles originally in the hands of the Barons of Cornwall only earthworks now remain, as at Cardinham, Week St Mary and Kilkhampton. Cardinham Castle commands the steep valleys of the south-west edge of Bodmin Moor and is still conspicuous on the ground; the motte and bailey west of Kilkhampton occupies a similarly commanding position, but the remains at Week St Mary are adjacent to the parish church and are less conspicuous.

The castles owned by the Earls of Cornwall which passed to the Dukes of Cornwall in 1336 and so to the present Duchy of Cornwall were more substantial buildings and three of the four still existing retain much of their original form. Of these Tintagel Castle with its romantic literary associations is the best known and the most dramatic.

Little now remains of this island castle and it must have fallen into ruin at an early date for Leland says of it about 1538 'the residue of the buildings of this castle be sore weather beaten . . . Belike it had three wards but two be torn away by the gulphing in of the sea insomuch that it has made almost an isle . . .' Recent excavation on the island has revealed an early Roman farmstead dating from the fourth century A.D. followed by a Celtic monastery of the sixth century probably founded by St Juliot. Although still in the hands of the Celtic Church in the eleventh century, there is no mention of the monastery in the Domesday return. The castle was built by Reginald, Earl of Cornwall, in the middle of the twelfth century, enlarged by Earl Richard, brother of Henry III, in the thirteenth century, and modified by the Black Prince in the fourteenth century. There is no evidence to connect this castle with King Arthur who in any case lived several centuries earlier; the association probably arises from the fertile imagination of the chronicler, Geoffrey de Monmouth, who was a contemporary of Earl Reginald. Although historic research has removed the romantic element, the remains of the castle will be found both intriguing and beautiful whether seen in the scintillating sunshine of summer or the windswept wetness of winter.

Whilst little now remains of Tintagel Castle, the castles at Trematon, Launceston and Restormel still retain much of their original form. All of these are broadly of the same design, namely a large shell keep with a single bailey. Trematon was built by Robert de Mortain, half-brother of William the Conqueror, in the eleventh century, but after two centuries it went into decline until Benjamin Tucker, Surveyor-General of the Duchy of Cornwall, constructed a Georgian mansion within the bailey in 1807. Part of the curtain wall was removed to open up a view of the Lynher estuary and also to provide material for the house. The western and eastern parapeted curtain walls remain largely untouched along with the shell keep.

Possibly more dramatic than Trematon is Restormel Castle set on a natural hillock in the valley of the river Fowey north of Lostwithiel (Plate 21): it dominates the surrounding countryside and forms a conspicuous landmark. It probably began as a wooden fort in the eleventh century and appears as a castle of the de Cardinan family in the twelfth century, eventually passing to the Dukes of Cornwall in the fourteenth century. The unbroken imposing battlemented shell keep is some 125 feet in diameter and contains considerable remains of the original living quarters and chapel all dating from the twelfth and thirteenth centuries. With its surrounding moat, the castle exhibits some of the finest military architecture in Cornwall and of its kind is one of the best in England.

The fourth castle of the Earls of Cornwall was at Launceston, originally known as Dunheved. Shortly after the Norman Conquest an ancient fort on the present castle hill was acquired by Richard de Mortain and a wooden palisade and tower with protective earthworks constructed. This became de Mortain's principal seat from which all Cornwall was controlled. By the early thirteenth century, the wooden fort had been replaced by a stone shell keep. Further additions included a tower, a moat, and curtain walls within which were many buildings. The later Middle Ages saw a period of decline and the castle gradually became more ruinous, despite its use as a prison. About 1540 Leland wrote that the hall and chapel 'were quite level with the ground'. The parts which have survived to the present day include the bailey, the keep and two gates. The castle once sustained Launceston as the most important town of Cornwall; indeed it remained the county town until as late as 1835 although the importance of the castle had long since declined.

Although the need for castles passed before the end of the Middle Ages, the custom of fortifying large houses continued for a time. Cotehele House near Calstock, which derives its name from Hilaria de Cotehele, a fourteenth-century ward of the Earl of Cornwall, is one of the most notable. The manor and the house passed into the possession of the Edgcumbe family where it remained until it became National Trust property in 1947. Today it ranks as one of the finest and least altered early Tudor mansions in the West Country, various additions having been made between 1485 and 1627 to the original manor house of the fourteenth century.

Ince Castle on the north shore of the river Lynher in south-east Cornwall is another sixteenth-century example, originally constructed as a square fortified manor house with a castellated tower at each corner. The house has associations with the notorious Killigrews of Falmouth, one of whom is reputed to have kept a wife in each tower. It was 'modernised' in the Georgian style early in the nineteenth century.

Place House in Fowey was the seat of the Treffrys for over 500 years. Built in the fifteenth century, its castellated towers rise above the roofs of the ancient town of Fowey and dominate the view of the town as seen from the river. Again there has been substantial nineteenth-century alteration so that Georgian and Victorian Gothic now intermingle with the Medieval.

Caerhays Castle on the shores of Veryan Bay four miles south-east of Tregony might at first glance appear to be yet another example, but this highly ornate Gothic 'castle', battlemented and turreted, was built in 1808 by John Nash for the Trevanion family. It is, in fact, one of the most recent of the 'historic' castles and houses of Cornwall.

Coastal scenery is occasionally enriched by castles and towers built for the defence of harbours and the most impressive amongst these are the two castles at the entrance to Falmouth Harbour, Pendennis and St Mawes. These were erected by Henry VIII between 1540 and 1546 and remain in an almost perfect state of preservation. Their plan is based on interesting semi-circular variations of the keep and curtain wall. The original castle at Pendennis was enclosed later by vast Elizabethan earthworks whilst the walls and dry ditch were a reaction to the Spanish threat of the seventeenth century. St Mawes Castle, by contrast, is much as Henry VIII left it and, having seen little if any action, is in an excellent state of preservation.

The earlier castles are generally built of local stone but towards the end of the Middle Ages the economy was able to bear the cost of transporting more durable materials from a distance, and, as these coastal castles illustrate, an increasing use was made of granite.

Manor houses

Church and State thus supply some of the oldest buildings in the Cornish rural scene, but with the passing of the Middle Ages there was an increasing amount of domestic architecture which has survived to the present day. The Old Post Office in Tintagel is in fact a small fourteenth-century manor house, but the most notable surviving examples in Cornwall are manor houses dating drom between 1550 and 1650. The political stability and economic prosperity of the sixteenth century led to what Hoskins has called 'the Great Rebuild of Rural England' as the homes of people at almost all levels of society were built or rebuilt to higher standards of comfort and convenience (Plate 22). In Cornwall the wealth of a hard-working class of small gentry of farmers and traders now found expression in new manor houses, dozens of which went up all over the county.

The manor house in Cornwall, as elsewhere in England, evolved from the hall which, with its outbuildings, surrounded a square courtyard. It was originally planned for defence but by Tudor days the need for this had gone and the courtyard emerges as a pleasure garden with a decorative gateway for entry. Buttery and kitchen were divided from the hall by a screened passage and above was a solar or drawing-room. Those acquainted with the Oxford and Cambridge colleges will immediately recognise the plan. Whilst this arrangement was fundamental and can be traced throughout Cornwall, many alterations have been made since the initial construction and the original plan is not always obvious. The changes are largely due to the absorption of small estates into larger units and the consequent letting off of the lesser manor houses to tenant farmers who have modified the older buildings to suit their needs.

Of these manor houses particular interest is attached to Arwenack House in Falmouth, once the home of the Killigrews; Keigwin House in Mousehole, now the Keigwin Arms; Trerice House in Pydar, undoubtedly the finest Elizabethan house in Cornwall; Place House in Padstow, the home of the Prideaux family; Lanhydrock House near Lostwithiel, noted for its long gallery; and finally beautiful Cotehele House (Plate 23), nestling in the hills above the gorge of the Tamar and once the home of the Edgcumbes. Almost a hundred lesser ancient manor houses from this period now enrich the Cornish rural scene, but very few are still in the possession of the families that built them. The ravages of death duties in the twentieth century have paradoxically impoverished the families but enriched the tourist, for most of the important properties have passed to the National Trust and are now open to the public for a modest fee.

Of particular interest to the student of the landscape is Cotehele House which was developed between 1485 and 1627, and then virtually deserted by the Edgcumbes in favour of Mount Edgcumbe overlooking the Tamar estuary. This is perhaps the least altered of the manor houses. Another great architectural treasure is Trerice House some three miles south-east of Newquay. Set among ancient elms and green lawns it was long associated with the Arundell family and is undoubtedly an Elizabethan gem. Its construction saw the introduction of completely new and 'foreign' architectural ideas into the then traditional Cornish styles. Lanhydrock House, three miles south-east of Bodmin, should also be visited for its unique great gallery which alone survived the great fire of 1881. The rebuilt house, however, recreates the original plan, and the magnificence of Baron Robartes' seventeenth-century house is readily appreciated.

While the greater part of the rebuilding took place within the hundred years from 1550 to 1650, the movement had by no means expended itself and the next hundred years saw the addition of at least another twenty-five houses. Defoe in the early eighteenth century was much impressed by the 'many pleasant seats of the Cornish gentry, who are indeed very numerous'. Dating from this later period is Antony House (1710–21) two miles west of Torpoint. The estate is mentioned in Domesday and became the home of the Carews in the fifteenth century. The most notable member of the family was Richard Carew, author of the classic *Survey of Cornwall* published in 1602, but nothing now remains of the house in which he worked. The present Antony House is attributed to Sir William Carew. This house and the estate have also passed to the National Trust. Almost within the same period Tregenna Castle near St Ives was constructed as a castellated residence for John Stephens in 1774. It has now been converted into a hotel and the additional building hides much of the original.

Largely as a result of the mineral wealth of Cornwall, the nineteenth century saw the addition of further houses and the rebuilding of some earlier structures. New houses appeared in selected sites and mansions began to dot the Fal, Fowey and other protected estuaries of the mild south coast. Many of these have so far escaped the rapacious tax man and remain in private occupation, but their gardens are frequently in the hands of the National Trust or are open to the public. Trelissick House on the Fal was built in the Grecian style in 1825 and is perhaps best known for its gardens which fall to the river at the King Harry ferry. In this sheltered spot are found magnificent displays of azaleas, camellias, magnolias, rhododendrons, tree ferns, Chinese fan palms, bamboos and gunnera.

The romantic castellated mansion of the Earls of Falmouth at Tregothnan in the woody peninsula between the Truro, Tresillian and Fal rivers also dates from the early nineteenth century (1816–18). The architect was William Wilkins who built the National Gallery in London. The house is surrounded by magnificent natural and man-made woodlands and gardens which are at their best in spring.

The picturesque Caerhays Castle near Mevagissey also belongs to this period. A battlemented neo-Gothic edifice, it dates from 1808 and was constructed by John Nash for the Trevanion family; it subsequently passed to the Williams family. Here again there are magnificent gardens with camellias, rhododendrons and azaleas.

Less well known is the house of the Eliot family at St Germans which was rebuilt by Sir John Soane in 1802–6. The house, a castellated mansion of simple design, is also supported by gardens laid out by Repton and both can be seen from near St Germans' Church.

Parks and Gardens

The rise of the true country house in the sixteenth century, and its aggrandisement during the next 300 years, introduced a new element into the landscape of Cornwall – the park. The great rolling and timbered park is not, indeed, so prominent an element in the Cornish scene as in the Midland counties or the country nearer London. But there are nevertheless some notable Cornish parks, the creation of which profoundly modified the immediate landscape.

The earliest parks were simply large enclosures for hunting, probably a piece of open woodland country surrounded by a ditch and high bank, or a palisade. 'The true deer park,' says Henderson, 'is an enclosure of some hundreds of acres, surrounded by a venerable dike or palisade, lying perhaps a mile or more from the lord's residence, and containing a stream of water with numerous groves of trees.' The Bishop of Exeter in the middle of the thirteenth century enclosed the woodland of two of his Cornish manors (Pawton and Lanner) to make such deer parks, and his successor later made another at Penryn. By the middle of the fifteenth century, the bishops ceased to visit their Cornish deer parks: they were disparked, split up into smaller units, and let to tenants as farmland. At Pawton, some fields still bear the name of Deer Park; and at Penryn, West Wood is one of the few remaining groves of the former park. There were several other medieval deer parks, but the only one to survive to the present day is that of Boconnoc, high up above the west bank of the Lerryn river and about three miles east of Lostwithiel. Here one may still see the ancient dike that shut it off from the outer world, and the gnarled oak trees, a rare surviving fragment of a medieval landscape.

With the appearance of the true country house, built for the pleasure of living and with no thought of defence, we have also the beginnings of parks as we understand the word. But Cornish estates were generally small and the Cornish gentry preferred to let their lands as farmlands or to farm it themselves, rather than to make an ostentatious display of wasted acres. Most were content with little walled gardens round their houses, an orchard, a bowling green, and 'the Walk' overlooking some favourite view. The Edgcumbes at Mount Edgcumbe, far wealthier than most of their fellows, had certainly made a pleasure-park overlooking the mouth of the Tamar by 1698 when Celia Fiennes passed this way. They had had a deer park since Elizabethan times, but this was something more: 'a hill all bedeck'd with woods, which are divided into several rows of trees in walks . . .' But elsewhere in Cornwall she finds no parks worth commenting upon, and it is unlikely there were any.

Such considerable parks as there are today owe their appearance to the landscape gardening of the second half of the eighteenth century, when men like Repton laid out Port Eliot (1792–3) and Catchfrench, not far away. 'Gardens which had previously been pent up inside walls were thrown open, and it was the ambition of every landowner to extend his park or demesnes as far as the eye could reach.' At Port Eliot, 'trees were planted, hedges removed, cottages and church towers pressed into service as picturesque objects' (Henderson). Werrington Park near Launceston was in all probability laid out by William Kent about 1740. Here the grand scheme involved demolishing the little medieval church, which stood in the way of a vista, and rebuilding it elsewhere. Most of the Cornish parks are small by Midland standards – Werrington is only 350 acres – but they are usually exceedingly beautiful.

The nineteenth century saw the addition of many extensive ornamental gardens, some of which have now passed into the keeping of the National Trust and they are therefore open to visitors in season. Cornish gardens, as might be expected, are noted for their displays of tropical and sub-tropical flora as well as the native temperate trees and shrubs. Magnolias, camellias, rhododendrons, azaleas, hydrangeas, tree ferns, fan palms and many other exotic species will be found in most gardens, which in nearly all cases are at their best in spring.

One of the most beautiful gardens is Trengwainton two miles north-west of Penzance, surrounding a house which was once a home of the Arundell family. It was the Bolitho family, however, who created the present-day gardens in the mid-nineteenth century. South-west of Falmouth are the two gardens of Glendurgan and Penjerrick, both attributable to the activities of the Fox family, Quakers from Falmouth. Glendurgan, which has an appropriately decorated entrance, is noted for its laurel maze and magnolias. Penjerrick has extensive shrubberies and a great variety of sub-tropical plants. Trewithen, one mile east of Probus, is another extensive garden at its best in spring. Pencarrow House near Bodmin, the home of the Molesworth-St Aubyn family, has also recently opened its gardens and house to the public. Most of the manor houses described in the preceding section also have extensive gardens, notably Trelissick, Lanhydrock, Cotehele and Tregothnan, and all deserve the tourist's attention.

Other buildings

Far more numerous than the castles, manor houses and country houses in the rural scene are the farmhouses scattered over the landscape. Most of them occupy very ancient sites – many foundations go back to Celtic times and few are later than the medieval period – but the visible structures that we see today are mainly post-medieval in age. The casual visitor to Cornwall is more than likely to be impressed by the great profusion of twentieth-century building and the old farmhouses have to be sought out at the end of narrow farm lanes or remote tracks in the less frequented upland areas.

There are two distinct categories of site occupied by the older farmhouses. One is the so-called platform site often found at elevations between 200 and 300 feet on fertile soil, sheltered by trees, and with access to water from a nearby stream. Many of these are ancient Celtic sites subsequently settled by peoples from Iron Age camps. The prefix *tre* (homestead) frequently occurs in the name. A second category of settlement site is found located near to the edges of the coastal plateaux or high up on the inland moors in relatively exposed positions. These mark the colonisation moves of the early and middle medieval periods.

The archaeological evidence shows that early thatched rubble huts were replaced in the medieval period by two basic house types: the long-house of the peasantry and the hall-house of the gentry. Both were based on the medieval architectural plan of a long building divided into a series of rooms. This concept had developed from the earlier idea of a homestead consisting of one building – the hall or house place – supported by other secondary building which reflected the activities of the occupants. The main difference between the hall-house and the long-house was in the use of the end or lower room. In the hall-house this was a service room but in the long-house the lower end was for cattle, and men and beasts both used the same doorway and passage. Both house types were single storeyed.

These farmhouses were superseded during the great rebuild by houses with two storeys for the yeomen and the lower gentry, with a parlour wing additionally attached for the gentry. It is the modified form of these houses that is now found in so many locations. Richard Carew in his *Survey* of 1602 tells us a good deal about the transformation which took place during the rebuilding period. The low-built, dark houses with thick walls, small windows, earth floors, open hearths and thatched roofs were gradually replaced by taller buildings rising two or even three storeys in height, equipped with larger glassed windows, closed fireplaces and slated roofs. There is ample evidence that many new architectural ideas were entering the county during this period and also new techniques were being tried with building materials. The traditional wattle and daub, turf and thatch were being replaced by granite, slate and wood (Plate 24).

Examples which still carry traces of the medieval peasant house include Trewitten and Treforda in Minster parish above the coast road from Boscastle to Tintagel; and a long-house now converted to two cottages at Trebarwith near Tintagel. At Truthall in Sithney parish near Helston there is a medieval hall-house now part of the farm outbuildings but still in a good state of preservation, while at Methrose near the Luxulyan valley there is a medieval hall-house still surviving as a dwelling house. The design of the Methrose house resembles that of the Old Post Office in Tintagel. At Trevear in St Stephen-in-Brannel there is an early seventeenth-century house with a parlour wing.

In the later seventeenth and eighteenth centuries there gradually evolved larger, more comfortable farmhouses along with cottages for the farm workers. The break-up of some large farm units also led to the appearance of smaller family farmhouses.

For those who wish to delve deeper into the art of deciphering the evolution of the Cornish house reference should be made to the book by V.M. and F.J. Chesher. It is a fascinating although complicated story, for few houses conveniently spell out the date of their construction like the farmhouse at Trerithick near Altarnun which carries the inscription 1585 over its entrance door.

Cornish almshouses of the same period also make attractive vistas at times. The picturesque Moyles group at St Germans with projecting gables and separate ground-floor and first-floor flats is well known, as are the Rashleigh almshouses in Fowey which were erected in 1631. All these charitable foundations, and the rebuilding of the farmhouses throughout the county, reflect the great prosperity of these two or three generations.

Although the wind is so great an element in the Cornish weather, the windmill has never been a conspicuous feature in the landscape. Celia Fiennes records that she saw not a single windmill in Cornwall or Devon. There were indeed a few in each county but they were largely confined, like the old mill above Fowey, to high land near the coast. Some were of great age: one on the Lizard, for instance, is shown as disused on a seventeenth-century map.

The remains of an ancient water-mill hidden in a valley bottom is the more usual type one is likely to find at the present day. As a source of power we can distinguish four main categories: corn-mills, tucking-mills, mining water-wheels and a miscellaneous group covering wood sawing, paper manufacture and bone crushing. Hardly any of these are in operation today but, although the demand for scrap metal has led to the disappearance of most of the wheels and machinery, many of the stone buildings, dams, leats and roadways can be readily detected in the present landscape.

The mining, woodworking and paper-mills have largely gone and often further building has taken place on the same site but the tucking-mills and corn-mills have mainly been abandoned without any redevelopment and their remains are more readily traceable. Homespun cloth was cleaned, dipped and dressed in the medieval period by machinery driven by water-wheels and fulling- or tucking-mills were widespread in the West Country. The earliest recorded fulling-mills in Cornwall were at Sheepstall near Ruan and at Talgarrek in Camborne both of which were in existence by 1260. The name 'tucking-mill' is applied to a number of cottages today which reveal by their construction the original function of the building. By the fifteenth century Tregony had become an important centre for this industry. Charles Henderson located over sixty sites but all had ceased working by the mid-nineteenth century.

It was the corn-mill, however, that was at one time ubiquitous in the Cornish landscape. Although introduced into Britain by the Romans the corn-mill was slow to penetrate into the county: only six mills are recorded in the Domesday Book – at Connerton, Cargoll (in Newlyn), Trevisquite (on the Camel), Liskeard and Launceston (where there were two). Assuming that these mills were corn-mills this is a remarkably small number compared with ninety-eight in Devon and 371 in Somerset. Probably the primitive hand quern was still used extensively in Cornwall for grinding corn. The coming of the Normans, however, saw the introduction of the manorial mill and, as a result, there was a big increase in the number of corn-mills. It has been suggested that over the centuries Cornwall may have had as many as three thousand corn-mills in operation. The deeply dissected topography and the plentiful water supply certainly facilitated their construction. As a result, the term 'mill' commonly appears in place-names. In addition, tidal-mills were possible in a number of estuaries. The eighteenth and early nineteenth centuries saw the heyday of the water-mill but a decline then began with the introduction of the more efficient steam-mill.

Despite the technological advance of the steam-mill, water-mills were still being constructed as late as 1922 (Trelowarren near Helston). The twentieth-century rise of the milling combines concentrated flour milling in the big seaports and eventually put an end to most local corn-mills and only three were known to be operational during the preparation of this book. These were Hingham Mill (Wadebridge), Trewoofe Mill (Lamorna) and Town Mills (Grampound).

The present-day interest in industrial archaeology and concern for preservation has led to the rehabilitation of a few other water-mills notably Morden Mill (on the Cotehele estate) and Addicroft Mill (on the river Lynher). Other historic mills, all recorded before 1500, include Treen Mill (Porthcuno, operational until 1910), Nanjulian Mill (St Just, operational until 1927), Lamorna Mill (Lamorna Cove, operational until 1919), Gweek Mill (Helston, operational until 1920).

No account of the buildings of Cornwall would be complete without a mention of the place of the inn in the county. In an area of scattered settlement and late development of towns, it is perhaps not surprising that few ancient foundations can be traced. The Punch Bowl at Lanreath, the Bush Inn at Morwenstow and the Pandora Inn at Restronguet Creek all claim a thirteenth-century origin. The Carpenter's Arms at Metherell, Callington, and the Sloop Inn, St Ives, are probably of fourteenth-century ancestry whilst the Bull's Head, Callington, and Severn Stars, Penryn, have a fifteenth-century origin. Some notable houses from the sixteenth century include the Victory Inn, Towan Cross, Mount Hawke and the Old Inn at Mullion and Finneygook Inn at Crafthole.

But, in general, facilities for travellers and local refreshment were few and far between until the seventeenth century. Ale and beer were for long brewed on a domestic basis and small hop gardens and barley fields were then a feature of the Cornish countryside. The rarity of accommodation is shown by the returns made by the Justices of the Peace in response to an Order in Council of 1577 requiring an account of all the inns, taverns and ale-houses in the kingdom. In the four western hundreds of Cornwall there were only thirty-nine wine taverns and 132 ale-houses returned. Both John Norden in 1584 and Richard Carew in 1602 had good reason to complain of the low standards of the few inns that did exist.

From the seventeenth century onwards there is a considerable increase in the number of licensed premises. The seventeenth-century expansion was largely based on increased numbers of ale-houses and beer-houses, the eighteenth century saw the rise of the gin palace and brandy shop (accompanying the smuggling of brandy, tea and tobacco), whilst the nineteenth century experienced a big increase in beer-houses as a result of the Goulburn Act of 1830.

Many of the licensed premises from these three centuries have now vanished but some notable seventeenth-century inns include the Port Gaverne near Port Isaac, Driftwood Spars at St Agnes, the Plume of Feathers at Penhallow and the Old Success Inn at Sennen Cove. During the eighteenth century the improved roads which came with the Turnpike Trust era of 1760–75 and the Royal Mail routes encouraged the appearance of many coaching inns catering for both men and horses. Some notable old coaching inns still functioning include the Norway Inn at Perran-ar-Worthal (Plate 42), Jamaica Inn on Bodmin Moor, the Coach and Horses Tavern at Rosudgeon, and the King's Head Hotel, Five Lanes, Launceston. Old coaching inns are easily recognised by a frontal gateway leading to a central courtyard.

By all accounts the seventeenth to nineteenth centuries were rumbustious, hard-drinking days in Cornwall, accompanied by a great deal of drunkenness. The special conditions of the mining and fishing areas aggravated what was a national weakness of the time and the problem was made worse by the Goulburn Act of 1830 which removed the tax on beer and cider and threw open the retail sale to anyone on payment of a two-guinea fee for a licence from the excise officer. This was a negation of all the legislation relating to the sale of alcoholic liquor from the sixteenth century onwards and it produced a disastrous demarcation between the respectable fully-licensed house, providing service and accommodation, and the simple drinking den – hundreds of which sprang up all over Cornwall, particularly in the mining areas.

The reaction to all this was the nineteenth-century Temperance Movement and a revival of Methodism. The damage of the 1830 Act was not repaired until an Act of 1869 took the beer licensing away from the excise and gave it to the magistrates. There has since been a steady reduction of licences to a figure more in keeping with actual needs.

The twentieth century has seen the updating and conversion of many inns and taverns to meet the needs of the tourist and a large number of fascinating ports of call now exist in Cornwall for the discerning visitor.

The nineteenth century saw further characteristic features added to the Cornish countryside. Numerous nonconformist chapels date from the early part of this period. When the Wesley brothers began their missionary visits to Cornwall in 1743 they came as ordained clergymen of the Church of England and were welcomed by many of the parish clergy. Later a rift appeared between the Church authorities and the followers of Wesley (by then known as the Methodists), and this forced the nonconformists to erect their own chapels. With but a small number of worshippers and limited resources at their disposal, only tiny and simple meeting places could be constructed. Roseworthy Chapel, near Camborne, dating from the close of the eighteenth century, illustrated this simplicity before its demise in recent years. Earlier and still in active use is the attractive and simple Friends Meeting House of 1710 at Come-to-Good near Feock, a delightful little thatched and whitewashed building.

Expanding town populations later necessitated the rebuilding of many of these simple early structures, and the architects sometimes made unfortunate excursions into ecclesiastical architecture. In the country, however, the simple chapel has remained, and it will be found in nearly every hamlet and settlement, occasionally in an isolated position yet central to scattered farms. Improved communications have in recent years reduced the need for many of the smaller isolated chapels, and they have been converted to a variety of uses, ranging from workshops and wool-storage barns to dwelling houses and recreational halls. The latter part of the century also saw the addition of the board-schools to many hamlets in Cornwall. Although a new architectural note was struck, local building stones were employed, and in most cases the results have by now merged into the landscape.

Most of the buildings considered so far were built of local materials. Granite and slate account for nearly everything; brickwork is almost entirely absent. Apart from the scarcity of brick-earth, Carew himself gives us an additional reason: 'As for Brick and Lath walles, they can hardly brooke the Cornish weather: and the use thereof being put in triall by some, was found so unprofitable, as it is not continued by any.' The use of cob walls in building was possible only by protecting them with slates hung vertically, and this custom has been handed on in the wetter parts. Slate-hung walls may now be seen accompanying both granite and slate stone buildings; Bodmin and Liskeard are profuse in examples. Slate roofs have also been extensively cemented as a protection against high winds on the coast and high rainfall in the interior. These silvery roofs are almost peculiarly Cornish. The materials available and the prevailing climatic conditions have thus been of great importance in shaping the buildings, and largely account for the essential character and colour of the traditional architecture. Early efforts resulted in simple straightforward buildings, without undue embellishment, and satisfying primary needs. These have long since merged into harmony with the environment so that 'they appear to have grown out of the land and they form an integral part of the Cornish landscape' (Thompson).

Local materials continued in general use well into the nineteenth century and only minor ideas, such as stucco-work, filtered in along the coach routes. But the coming of the railway opened the way to cheaper building materials from more distant parts of the country, and in areas where Cornish granite and slate once reigned supreme, machine-made bricks from the clay lands of England, purple slates from Wales, and bright red tiles from the Midlands began to appear. This catastrophe has gone one stage further in the present century, for in addition to these materials we now find Dutch bricks and tiles, foreign cements, Canadian and Scandinavian woods, Belgian slates, and a final horror of pink asbestos. The late Victorian era is further marked by a phase of decoration and ornamentation, and to many of the older and simpler structures, storm porches, red-tiled roof ridges, and half-timbering have been added. This activity manifests itself at its worst in the coastal 'beauty' spots; here the speculative builder has often completely ruined the local character with his scatter of holiday bungalows, wooden shacks and temporary structures. The two world wars also added their quota of derelict buildings, abandoned camps, and Nissen huts: but fortunately the last few years have seen efforts to remove these eyesores.

Thus, what might be called 'the second English invasion' of the last hundred years has had regrettable results, and it is only recently that efforts have been made to arrest the decline by stricter control and by a return to local building materials. New possibilities have emerged in the use of china-clay waste and slate waste as aggregates for concrete. Some very attractive new houses, well proportioned and modelled on traditional lines, are now appearing in rural areas and on the outskirts of the towns.

Select Bibliography

Benney, D. E., *Cornish Water Mills* (1972).

Beresford, M. and Hurst, J. G., eds., *Deserted Medieval Villages* (1971).

Chesher, V. M. and F. J., *The Cornishman's House* (1968).

Darby, H. C. and Finn, R. Welldon, eds., *The Domesday Geography of South West England* (1967).

Daniell, S. V., *Cornwall's Churches* (Tor Mark).

Delderfield, E. R., *West Country Historic Houses and their Families* (1968).

Dexter, T. F. G., *Cornish Crosses, Christian and Pagan* (1938).

Doble, G. H., *Cornish Saints* (a series of forty booklets) (1933).

Douch, H. L., *Old Cornish Inns* (1966). *Cornish Windmills.*

Fox, H. S. A., *A geographical study of the field systems of Devon and Cornwall* (Cambridge Ph.D., 1970–1).

Gover, J. B., 'Cornish Place Names', *Antiquity*, Vol.ii (1928).

Henderson, Charles, *Cornish Church Guide* (1925).

Langdon, A. G., *Old Cornish Crosses* (1896).

Rawe, Donald R., *Cornish Villages* (1978).

Rowe, Laura, *Granite Crosses of West Cornwall* (1973).

Sedding, E. H., *Norman Architecture in Cornwall* (1909).

4. The urban landscape

Medieval boroughs. The ports of Cornwall. The tourist towns.

Medieval boroughs

THE CORNISH NEVER took kindly to town life. At the time of the Domesday Survey only Bodmin showed any of the signs of being a 'town'. In the main *descriptio* of Bodmin it is noted that there are sixty-eight houses, which ties in neatly with a later entry where St Petrock is described as housing sixty-eight burgesses. Since St Petrock held Bodmin there is little doubt that the burgesses lived in the houses. Bodmin ('dwelling by the sanctuary') is thus probably the oldest town in the county. Lying in a gap which looks north-west to the Camel estuary and south to the Fowey estuary, the site must have been of significance even in prehistoric times. It was to this spot that the monastery of St Petrock migrated from the coast at Padstow in the Dark Ages; within the protection of the monastery it is likely that a market flourished in late Saxon times (Plate 17).

Bodmin is the only place in Cornwall where the Domesday Book assigns burgesses but there were other sites in the Duchy where markets or fairs are known to have existed and these might have functioned as urban areas even though they had no burghal status in the record. In the eleventh century, Robert Count of Mortain is known to have granted or held market rights at St Michael's Mount, Liskeard and Trematon, whilst in the north of the county there is evidence that, in the tenth century, 'Lanscavetona' was a mint or coinage town on a par with Exeter, Totnes, Barnstaple and Lydford in Devon. In 1066, the canons of St Stephen's at Lanscavetona had a market in their manor but this was removed by the Count of Mortain and placed in his castle at Dunheved around which emerged the present Launceston (Plate 25).

Two other settlements were probably functioning as early 'towns'. Domesday has references to forty *cervisarii* at Helston and whilst it is unlikely that there were forty 'brewers' in Helston there could have been forty burgesses who held their tenements in return for a rent of ale to the lord of the manor. Similarly the existence of ten saltpans at Stratton suggests a settlement larger than a mere agricultural vill. At the most, there can have been no more than seven incipient urban sites in Cornwall at the time of the Domesday Survey.

The Norman Conquest linked England with the Continent and trade expanded as the economy was stimulated. Cornwall shared with the rest of England the prosperity of the twelfth and thirteenth centuries which led to the founding of many boroughs by kings and barons. With a rising population and a developing internal and external trade, ecclesiastical and lay landowners were quick to realise that permanent market centres could be a profitable source of income through market tolls, urban rents and the tolls of fairs. The stage had also been reached where a lord could convert a settlement into a borough and his *villani* into burgesses. The king welcomed the money which the burgesses were prepared to pay for their privileges, which were formalised by the grant of a charter. The feudal lords, both ecclesiastical and lay, further realised the value of urban centres as sources of larger income than that produced by agricultural communities.

Hence many towns were deliberately founded as optimistic speculations in real estate. A large number of places in Cornwall can trace their origins as towns to a seignorial charter given in the closing years of the twelfth century or during the thirteenth century. An old law specified that no new market should be established within six and two-thirds of a mile from any existing legal market; taking into account the difficult terrain and the slowness of medieval transport on pack horse, this distance reflected a reasonable sphere of market influence for the time. An early seventeenth-century survey of the manor of St Austell significantly complains, 'There is neither markett or faire within the manor, but the towne is fitt for both especially being so remote from markett townes. The nearest markett townes are Lotwithiel 6 myles, Tregny 6 and Grampound 6 myles.'

Many charters in Cornwall were granted to the lord who held jurisdiction over the town rather than to the burgesses of the town. It was often the lord who took the initiative to negotiate the charter which might be obtained either from the king or from the Earls of Cornwall exercising their quasi-palatine powers. Not all of these speculations succeeded. Their initial artificial nature (Henderson calls them 'plants of exotic growth') is revealed by the tax assessments of 1327 which show that the original inhabitants of these new boroughs were to a large extent 'foreigners'. At Penryn the burgesses were half Cornish and half 'foreign' while at Tregony and Grampound the 'foreign' element predominated. Some time had yet to elapse before the independent Cornish people took to living in the towns. Nevertheless, by the middle of the fourteenth century the number of boroughs and market places had grown from the handful of the Domesday Survey to nearly forty, although only half of these attained sufficient importance to acquire a mayor instead of a portreeve (Fig.12).

With so many drowned estuaries penetrating the land one is seldom far from the sea in Cornwall so that it is not surprising to find that many of the market places also emerged as seaports. This was a marked feature of medieval time rather than later since the estuaries were then more navigable. Vast quantities of sand and gravel have since been transported by the rivers into the estuaries, both naturally and also as a result of tin-streaming, with the result that many have gradually silted up. Thus Tregony, formerly a port and the home of the Norman baronial family De la Pomeroy and a borough for taxation purposes in 1306, had lost its maritime role by 1600. It is now difficult to visualise the place as a busy medieval port, but such it was until the silting of the river Fal gradually converted it into an inland town some miles from the sea. It returned two members to the Westminster Parliament from 1294 and managed to retain this privilege until 1832. Lostwithiel and Helston were similar casualties.

Geographical factors seem to have influenced the siting of many of the markets. Grampound (Grandpont, Plate 26) had a bridge over the Fal, Camelford and Mitchell (Plate 27) were key points on the communication network, as also were

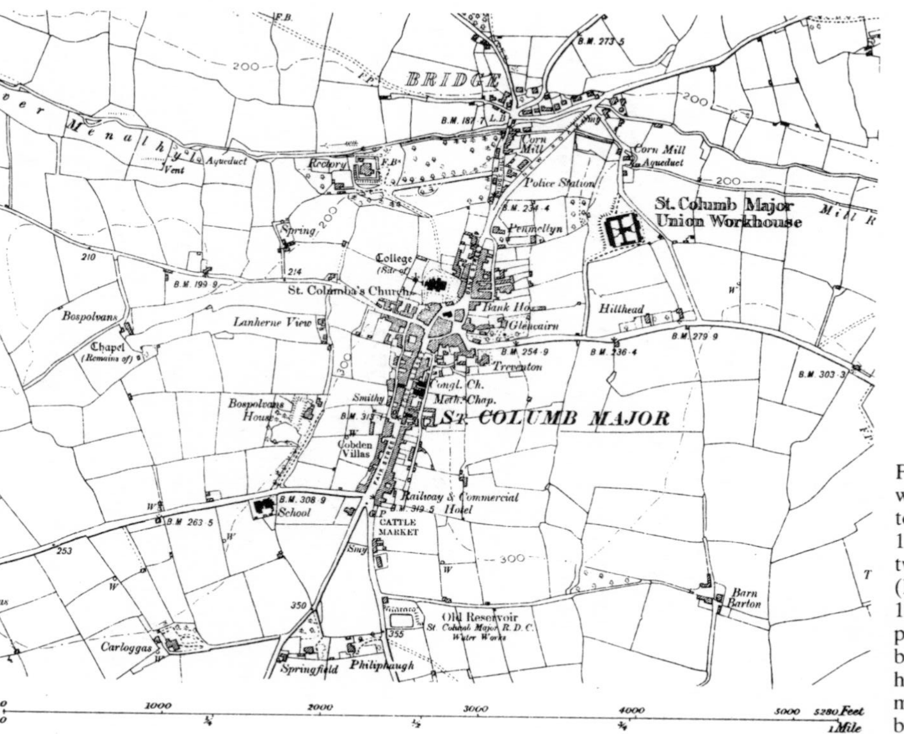

Fig. 12. St Columb Major: a hamlet which developed into a medieval market town. A market and fair were granted in 1333. Later there were two markets and two fairs.
(Extract from OS Sheet 32 SE Revised 1905–6. Substantial change has taken place recently. There is now a major N–S by-pass to the east of the town, new housing has appeared west of the cattle market and a large sewage works has been added west of the rectory.)

Kilkhampton (Fig.3) and Week St Mary at the junction of ridge roads. However, to survive and grow trade was necessary and many early foundations failed to meet the hopes of their sponsors. Many were to become the rotten boroughs of the eighteenth century. By the end of the medieval period, town growth had become associated with two very different activities in south-west England – the winning of metals and the production of cloth. In Cornwall the extraction of tin, copper and lead was undoubtedly more important than the manufacture of cloth although the distribution of fulling-mills or tucking-mills across the county in the twelfth, thirteenth and fourteenth centuries is a clear indication of the economic importance of cloth production. Unlike Devon, however, little of the Cornish output seems to have entered external trade; it must have been predominantly for domestic consumption.

Some of the markets associated with monastic houses subsequently grew, acquired charters, borough status, and permanent dwellings. But not all prospered like Bodmin, which was geographically well sited. Places such as St Germans collapsed completely with the dissolution of the monasteries in the sixteenth century, and Leland could only write of it as a 'poore fischer towne'. The magnificent Norman church still survives, but its priory has passed into private hands and what was once an active and prosperous town, sending two members to Parliament (until 1832), is now but a small village.

The Normans were responsible for introducing castles into the cultural landscape. These, too, attracted settlement and markets, which led on to borough status, but when the castle ceased to function as a strategic unit the associated town decayed if there was no other basis for its existence. Thus Trematon died and disappeared with the loss of the castle's strategic significance. Tintagel (Trevena) also declined towards the end of the medieval period, for it was ill equipped to take up fishing as an alternative occupation. Paradoxically, it now enjoys a temporary prosperity as a result of tourist interest in the castle, which was converted so romantically by Geoffrey of Monmouth into an ancient residence of King Arthur. On the other hand, Launceston survived the decay of

Dunheved Castle, as a result of acquiring other important administrative and commercial functions. Lostwithiel similarly survived the fall of Restormel (Plate 21) until a decline set in as a result of silting in the river.

A town could only survive and grow if it possessed natural advantages. The site value of Bodmin, for example, was of great importance, and there is little doubt that the town rapidly became the most populous place in the county in the Middle Ages and remained so until the sixteenth century. The earliest surviving charter, dating from the thirteenth century, reveals it as an important trading centre with many privileges and a strong religious life. Nowadays we can only guess at the ecclesiastical wealth of the town for nothing remains of the 'hospitals' of St George, St Anthony, and St Lawrence, and only a few fragments of the famous monastery of St Petrock can be seen in the priory grounds (Plate 17).

Launceston (Plate 25), too, was well sited. Not far away, the Tamar is joined by four rivers and there is a relatively extensive flood plain. A mile or two below this, the river disappears into hilly country in a series of deeply incised meanders. Some form of settlement near the entry of the old peninsula road into Cornwall, and with easy river-crossings, might almost be regarded as inevitable in the circumstances. The monastic establishment of St Stephen emerged in control of the area in pre-Norman times. With the Norman Conquest the district passed into the hands of the Count of Mortain who erected a castle on the hill of Dunheved, a mile south of the monastery and the river Kensey, sometime between 1066 and 1086. The market was removed from the monastery to the castle and the population migrated to Dunheved, bringing the name Launceston with them. A town was already growing around the foot of the castle mound by 1086. Eventually walls were built around the town and these were pierced by three gates, of which the South Gate still remains.

With the growth of the town in the later Middle Ages the houses spread downhill to the north. By 1250 we hear of the suburb of Newport ('new town') into which the Augustinian priory migrated from St Stephen's parish. Only scanty remains of the priory now exist by St Thomas's Church but many people pass through the priory's Norman doorway daily, for it now forms the entrance (not *in situ*) to the White Hart Hotel in the market-place. Launceston rivalled Bodmin in the medieval period, for its market and trade were a great source of wealth, whilst its position at the entrance to the peninsula made it a connecting link between Cornwall and the rest of England. There was no recognised county town of Cornwall, but Launceston played this part for many centuries, losing it officially to Bodmin only in 1835.

Truro (Plate 28) is another medieval foundation which has prospered because of a favourable site. In the vicinity of Truro several ridgeways converge upon the confluence of the rivers Calenick, Kenwyn, Allen and Tresillian. Below the confluence the river widens into a drowned valley which is tidal up to Truro. Despite these natural advantages, there is no evidence of the existence of any settlement before the late twelfth century. The town and parish then emerged as a result of the activities of Richard de Lucy, the feudal lord of Kenwyn. An older settlement existed nearby at Newham. This was of Saxon origin and later constituted a manor. At first, the two sites must have competed for trade, but eventually the superior position of Truro told, for in 1262 Newham lost its market and became subject to the reeve of Truro. The modern city of Truro has now completely absorbed Newham. The wealth of the town was based upon the coinage of tin, the weekly market, the annual fair and overseas trade. It steadily increased in size throughout the later Middle Ages and we find Richard Carew writing of it towards the end of Elizabeth I's reign: 'I hold it to have got the start of wealth of any other Cornish town and to come behind none in buildings, Launceston only excepted, where there is more use and profit of lodgings through the county assizes.'

Other Cornish towns which can trace their origin to the granting of medieval charters are Helston, Liskeard, Lostwithiel, Callington, Fowey and Penryn. The development of the rural manor of Henliston into a town dates from the early thirteenth century. King John made it a free borough, with extensive privileges, in 1201. Probably it was already a small town by this date. Occupying a strategic nodal position which controlled the entrance to the Lizard-Meneage peninsula, the town was also situated only two miles from the sea via the then tidal river Cober. The dependence of a town on geographical factors is dramatically illustrated by the temporary setback suffered by Helston when the growth of the Loe Bar in the thirteenth century cut it off from the sea. The Helston burgesses were forced to purchase rights in the port of Gweek, at the head of the Helford estuary, in an effort to offset this disadvantage.

Of almost similar age is Liskeard, another Domesday manor of some consequence, which obtained a charter, and a formal market and fair, in the mid-thirteenth century. Its position athwart the main road westwards from the Tamar, and away from the deeply-incised country to the south, has increased its importance as the chief market town of south-east Cornwall, and it has at various times derived added prosperity from the mineral and granitic resources of the adjacent Bodmin moors.

The picturesque town of Fowey began to germinate during the reign of Henry II. Henry's marriage with Eleanor of Aquitaine in 1152, which led to the acquisition by England of the rich provinces of south-western France, brought a new importance to the coastal harbours of south-western England. These now afforded the shortest crossing for military and commercial traffic. At least three towns in Devon and Cornwall owe their origin to this connection, all similarly sited on deep estuaries with commodious and sheltered anchorages – Fowey, Plymouth, and Dartmouth.

Fowey's first charter, setting it up as a borough, was granted by the prior of Tywardreath – 'the lord of the soil' – some time during the last quarter of the twelfth century. Both the site and origin of Fowey are almost identical with those of Dartmouth in Devon. Both towns lie about a mile inland from the mouth of their rivers (a clear defensive precaution), and in both the essential plan of the old town is a series of streets running parallel to the waterfront along the contours of a hill.

Lostwithiel, too, grew up during the twelfth century. When Robert de Cardinan gave it its first charter (or at least the earliest to survive) about the year 1194, he confirmed to the burgesses 'all the honours, dignities, liberties, and quittances . . . which my ancestors gave them of old on the day when they founded the town'. Penryn, on the other hand, was the creation of the bishops of Exeter, who were great borough-founders on their Devonshire manors also (as at Crediton and Ashburton). Today, and for a long time since, both Lostwithiel and Penryn have been supplanted by towns nearer the sea – by Fowey and by Falmouth.

Camelford first appears as a name about the year 1200, beginning as a river crossing in the rural manor of Lanteglos. It obtained a charter for a weekly market and an annual fair in 1260, and developed some faint urban characteristics, but it never came to much. Even today it has only a simple street-plan and is no more than a village set among fields that bear obvious signs of having evolved from open-field strips.

The comparatively late evolution of most Cornish towns out of older, rural manors is revealed by the fact that so many of them have no ancient parish church. Until the nineteenth century the parish church of Camelford was at Lanteglos (a clear indication of the mother-child relationship), that of Wadebridge was at St Breock, that of Launceston at St Stephen, and that of Bude at Stratton.

Many other Cornish boroughs were either still-born or died before they reached maturity. Grampound (Plate 26) is such a settlement which declined. Situated on the main medieval highway westwards, it was a crossing point of the river Fal. It is called Grauntpount in 1302, a name derived from the Norman-French *grand-pont* (great bridge). The bridge is first heard of in 1296. A street-village grew along the approaches to the bridge, and in 1332 received its first charter from the Earls of Cornwall, elevating it to the status of a borough. Grampound maintained its position until well into the fifteenth century, but thereafter declined, and Norden records that by Elizabethan times the inhabitants were 'few and poore'.

The modern tourist speeding along the A30 trunk-road through the single street of Mitchell (Fig.13, Plate 27) little realises its ancient history. A fair and market, together with the chapel of St Francis, were established at Meideshol as early as 1239 by Walter de Ralegh. It never came to much, but like several others of the failed boroughs was endowed with parliamentary representation under the Tudors and became one of the notorious rotten boroughs of the eighteenth cen-

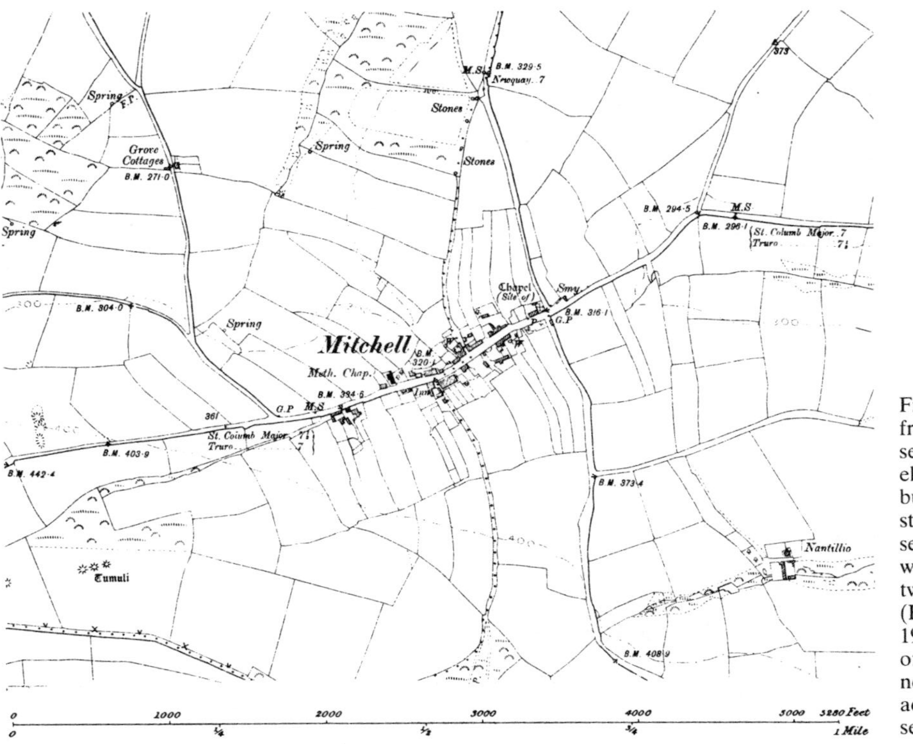

Fig. 13. Mitchell: a street-village dating from 1239 when a fair and market were set up on the medieval main road. The elongated strips appear to represent burgage plots rather than open-field strips. The late and artificial nature of the settlement is brought out by the way in which it overlies the boundary between two ancient parishes.
(Extract from OS Sheet 49 NW Revised 1906. A recent check revealed that some of the strip-fields have disappeared, two new farms and a sewage farm have been added to the west, but otherwise the settlement pattern remains the same.)

tury, though not so infamous as Grampound. Its two fairs had faded out by 1800, and by 1829 only seven inhabitants were entitled to vote. After 1832 Mitchell became, as it is now, a peaceful country hamlet.

The ports of Cornwall

Although land communications within the county were extremely difficult until the end of the eighteenth century, the penetration of the peninsula by numerous estuaries facilitated maritime movement as well as encouraging a partial dependence on the sea for food resources. The result was a proliferation of ports around the coast. Although some were engaged in a variety of activities, most fell into distinct categories related to fishing, mining or trading. Until the beginning of the Industrial Revolution in the mid-eighteenth century the volume of trade was relatively small, but thereafter a rapid expansion took place with the increased demand for Cornish minerals and the need to import coal and timber to service the mines and quarries. The increasing population also needed more food, and fishing prospered. The revolution in land transport of the nineteenth century and the eventual collapse of the mining and fishing industries inevitably led to the decline of many Cornish ports and a transference of most to the tourist industry. Few ports now function as they began; most are dominated by fleets of cabin cruisers and yachts which provide a colourful scene and alternative livelihood for many, but the character of the coastline has inevitably changed.

The fishing ports

Fishing around the Cornish coasts is of immemorial antiquity, but not until well into medieval times did it become a specialised occupation for whole villages. The fishing communities do not appear in the records until the fourteenth and fifteenth centuries. Polperro is noted as early as 1303, Port Isaac (Plate 29) in 1338, but Mevagissey (Fig.14, Plate 30) not until 1410. The explanation for their late appearance lies partly in the growth of a more organised industry, which enabled some

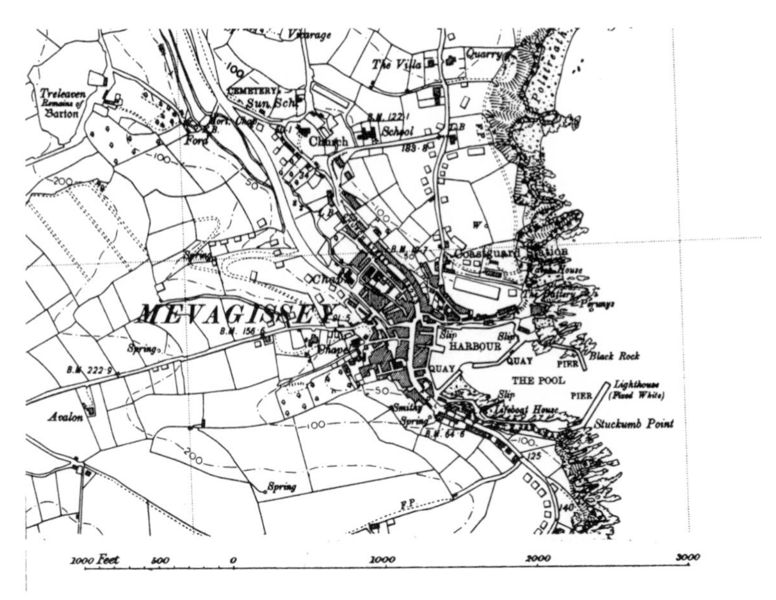

Fig. 14. Mevagissey: a fifteenth-century fishing port. The outer piers were constructed in the mid-nineteenth century.
(Extract from OS Sheets 59 SE and 60 SW Revised 1906 with additions 1938. The approach roads to Mevagissey now show a certain amount of infilling with the consequent loss of adjacent field boundaries.)

fishermen to employ others and dispose of the fish to the growing inland towns in Cornwall, and partly in the need for co-operative action to construct piers and protective works in the more exposed places. The engineering skill of the fifteenth century, which was creating bridges and churches inland, manifested itself on the coast in the form of piers and breakwaters. Mousehole, Newlyn, St Michael's Mount and Towan Blustry (Newquay, Plate 31), all had piers under construction in this century. Leland (about 1540) found Padstow 'a good quick (i.e. lively) fisher-town, but uncleanly kept'.

Bude seems to have developed somewhat later. It is first recorded as a name in 1400, when the Bishop of Exeter licensed a chapel there – probably for a small cluster of houses that lay too far from the parish church at Stratton – but it was a place of no consequence until Elizabethan days when (as at Clovelly in North Devon) a quay was built and a small harbour created on this wild and shelterless coast. Not until the nineteenth century, however, did it develop into a town expressly catering for holiday-makers.

Whilst the fifteenth century saw the first peak in pier and breakwater construction, a second phase was to follow in the nineteenth century with the expansion of the pilchard industry. New piers were constructed or outer breakwaters were added in many places, notably at Porthleven (1811–25), Polperro (1825–30), Mousehole (1850), Mevagissey (1860–5), St Ives (1864–7) and Newlyn (1866–8).

As well as the major fishing ports in the more sheltered localities, nearly every cove in Cornwall has at some time or other supported fishing activities. A mention of Kingsand, Cawsand, Polkerris, Gorran Haven, Portloe, Portscatho, St Mawes, Porthallow, Porthoustock, Coverack, Cadgwith, Mullion, Penberth, Sennen, Gurnard's Head, Portreath, Port Isaac, Port Gaverne, Port Quinn, sounds like a tourists' guide to Cornwall, but in all of these and many other coastal localities the discerning visitor will find traces of an earlier way of life now long since vanished.

Hake, ling, cod, pollock, mackerel and herring were all taken off the Cornish coasts, but the most important fish eventually proved to be pilchard. An organised industry permitted the seine-net method of fishing, and this system was fully developed by the time Carew wrote his *Survey of Cornwall*. From him we get a very detailed account of the method of fishing which lasted well into the present century. The industry in time built up a flourishing continental trade, especially to Italy, and throughout the latter half of the eighteenth and the first half of the nineteenth centuries several thousand fishermen were employed. The popular toast in Cornwall during this period ran:

> Here's health to the Pope, may he live to repent,
> And add just six months to the term of his Lent:
> And tell all his vassals, from Rome to the Poles,
> There's nothing like pilchards for saving their souls.

Today the entire fishing population of Cornwall numbers only a few hundred, but silent architectural witnesses of the former prosperity still remain. Most visitors to Cornwall will gain acquaintance with a huer's house (as at Newquay). This accommodated the huer or balker, who was posted on the cliff tops to locate the shoals of pilchards. The huer then directed the operations of the seine boats below by a series of signals. The fishing villages and ports are also characterised by the fish-cellar and the fish-palace, although hardly any now retain their original function. The fish-cellar was the ground-floor workroom of the individual fisherman, where he fumed, pressed, and pickled the pilchards. The bottom floors of these old fishing houses are now usually converted to other uses (shops, cafés and dwellings as at St Ives) but the discerning eye can detect their original form. The larger organisations had 'fish-palaces'. These began as rectangular courtyards with strongly-built walls on the inside of which were lean-to shelters or 'cellars'. In time dwelling accommodation was added above the cellars, and the courtyard houses so characteristic of parts of Newlyn and St Ives emerged. In the tourist areas many have become charming and picturesque residences, painted in pastel shades of blue and pink, and imparting a Mediterranean touch to the local scene.

A century and a half ago the atmosphere and aroma would have been very different indeed: Murray's *Handbook* says of St Ives in 1851 that it was 'most abominably tainted with the effluvia of the fish cellars'. Pounds suggests that several hundred of these cellars and palaces must have existed at one time in order to cope with the bulking and pressing of a season's catch of up to 50,000 hogsheads of pilchards. Mevagissey, Newlyn, Mousehole, St Ives and Newquay still have many interesting examples. Most of the cellars date from the century between 1750 and 1850: thereafter there was little new building as the industry began to decline.

The mining ports

The extraction of tin has been a feature of Cornish history for over 2,000 years. Initially the metal was obtained from alluvial deposits by streaming, a method which led eventually to the lodes from which the deposits had emanated. By the end of the medieval period, adit and shaft mining were supplementing the output from streaming, and silver and lead were also being extracted. Later copper was discovered. It was not, however, until the first phase of the Industrial Revolution between 1750 and 1850 that the rapid expansion of mining in Cornwall took place. Nearly all the metals obtained were intended for export to other parts of the country and until the advent of the railway link in 1859 movement was inevitably by sea.

The early tin trade was channelled through a small number of ports such as Truro, Lostwithiel and Fowey because of the system of coinage towns, but with the expansion of mining after the Industrial Revolution service ports were constructed in a large number of places adjacent to extraction points. Portreath on the west coast began in 1760 and went through several phases of expansion in 1800, 1824 and 1846. Hayle has its origins in the early eighteenth century but the port dates from Harveys' 'long wharf' of 1819. Devoran on the Fal estuary dates from 1826. These ports, along with Truro, built up a two-way trade with South Wales. Vast quantities of copper were exported to Swansea, the ships returning with Welsh coal for the mines and local copper smelting furnaces. In the east of the county mining activities similarly led to the construction of quays at Saltash, Forder, Millbrook, Halton Quay, St Germans and Cotehele. Little now remains of these 'ports', even the names of some will be unfamiliar to many.

Accompanying the nineteenth-century expansion of mining there was also a large increase in quarrying. Slate was leaving north Cornwall through Boscastle, Tintagel, Trebarwith, Port Isaac and Port Gaverne, whilst in south Cornwall granite from Carnmenellis was being exported via Penryn and from the Cheesewring via Looe. Most of this quarrying activity has died away during the twentieth century.

The one activity which has continued to grow is the extraction of china clay. Once again the associated port growth was initiated in the nineteenth century. There has been a succession of china-clay ports all closely located to St Austell Moor which is the main source of the clay. The construction of Charlestown by Charles Rashleigh and John Smeaton in 1800 marks the beginning of the organised export of china clay.

This port is perhaps now more famous for the mid-nineteenth century traveller's description of it:

> At first we could see nothing, but gradually our eyes accustomed themselves to the murk, and we made out that on one side of the harbour vessels were being loaded with china clay, and their crews were as white as millers. On the other side coal was being discharged, and the crews were as black as Erebus. The villagers were black or white according to which side of the port they resided on. While some were both black and white, like magpies.

The increasing export of the china clay eventually led to the construction in 1826 of Pentewan Harbour by Sir Christopher Hawkins and in 1828 of Par Harbour by the famous J. T. Treffry. In 1869, Fowey also emerged as an exporting point when its new Harbour Board constructed jetties in the estuary. Subsequent developments have been concentrated on Par and Fowey which now form the two main export points. Currently over a million tons of china clay per annum are being shipped from each of these ports. Fowey's capacity has been much increased by the construction of deep-water jetties and the replacement of the Par-Fowey rail freight line by a special road for china clay lorries only.

The trading ports

Most ports are engaged in multiple activities and trading would also have been characteristic, although on a minor scale, of the fishing and mining ports already mentioned. Other ports, however, have been predominantly engaged in general trade from their foundation. The difficult land terrain and the estuarine nature of the coast in Cornwall favoured sea communications rather than land connections until quite recently. It is not surprising, therefore, that in the past we find the growth of small trading ports at or near the head of estuaries where there were sometimes bridging points. Wadebridge, Tregony, Truro, Penryn, Helston and Lostwithiel are all medieval examples. The progressive silting of the estuaries, however, has resulted in the downstream migration of the ports: Wadebridge to Padstow; Tregony and Truro to Penryn and thence to Falmouth; Helston to Gweek; and Lostwithiel to Fowey. Some locations have virtually disappeared as ports, e.g. Tregony, others would seem to have little port life left as maritime trading activity becomes increasingly concentrated on the coastal sites of Fowey, Falmouth, Penzance and Padstow.

Fowey has had a long history of trading activity, emerging into prominence as a port in the early fourteenth century. It supplied some twenty-nine ships for naval operations against France in 1342. After 1400 when the Fowey river began to silt up rapidly, it took over Lostwithiel's tin trade. Although this was later lost to Truro, general trade continued until another boom period in the nineteenth century, when the construction of the railways led to large imports of timber, coal and general merchandise. A rail link to the Cornwall Railway and the emergence of a Harbour Board in 1869 resulted in the export of china clay, the construction of jetties and improved port facilities. As a deep-water port, Fowey can accommodate quite large vessels and its future seems assured.

Falmouth is situated on one of the best natural harbours in Britain, possibly in the world. Its sheltered deep-water roadstead can provide safe anchorage for an immense number of ships: it was of great value in the 1944 D-Day operation of the Second World War whilst it must have been a fascinating sight in the heyday of the nineteenth-century sailing ships. Originally Truro and Penryn functioned as the main Fal ports, but in 1661 a charter was obtained for the new town of Falmouth and in 1668 it became a Post Office packet station. It was the packet station combined with the decline of the upper Fal ports that promoted the growth of Falmouth. The situation at the mouth of the English Channel was ideal for packets to Portugal, Spain, the West Indies and to North and South America. Later, services were also introduced to the Mediterranean and to the East Indies.

With the advent of the railway and the steamship in the nineteenth century a new communications pattern emerged and by 1852 Falmouth had lost all its packet services – mainly to Southampton. But meanwhile the foundations for other services had been laid; depots for stores, ordnance wharves,

Plate 25 Launceston: the town at the foot of the Norman (Dunheved) castle mound, created shortly before 1086.

Plate 26 Grampound: the most notorious of the rotten boroughs of Cornwall. The rural nature of the medieval borough is well brought out in this view of the main street.

Plate 27 Mitchell: the single street (now part of the A30) of Mitchell, one of the failed Cornish boroughs.

Plate 28 Truro: an air view of the city looking north, showing the nineteenth-century cathedral dominating the centre.

Plate 29 Port Isaac: an example of a traditional Cornish fishing village now dependent on the tourist industry. The original settlement clusters in a valley at the head of a small bay. Protection for the fishing vessels was given by breakwaters. The more open settlement on the upper erosion surface is of recent origin.

Plate 30 Mevagissey: the inner harbour of the medieval fishing port, now largely given over to the tourist industry.

Plate 31 Newquay: the old settlement, known as Towan Blustry, clustered around the 'new quay' of the fifteenth century at the bottom of the picture. Across the bay is the Victorian seaside town.

Plate 32 St Austell: the twentieth-century central shopping precinct.

and a basin had already been built during the Napoleonic wars, and in 1860 the construction of Falmouth docks was started. This led to a ship repairing service and in the present century an oil tanker cleaning service. Falmouth has also witnessed periods of shipbuilding and fishing activity, and of naval activity during war emergencies (especially the Napoleonic and First and Second World Wars). Whilst its future is currently clouded by the decline in ship servicing it has much to offer in the way of ship facilities and should be able to respond quickly to any growth trends. The present-day forest of yacht masts in Falmouth Harbour and Carrick Roads is an indication of a current adaptation to the tourist trade.

Penzance has not the great advantages of Falmouth, but it does offer good protection from the northerly and westerly winds, so that it, too, was an early fishing and trading port, borough status being achieved in 1614. Later in the seventeenth century Penzance became a coinage town and this plus the export of tin and pilchards helped its prosperity until the decline of both industries in the second half of the nineteenth century. Meanwhile piers had been constructed in 1766 and 1785, a dry dock built in 1810, and further pier extension in 1811. In 1841 wharves followed and in 1845 the New or Northern pier was started. Further extensions took place in 1853 and 1870, and a floating dock became operational in 1884. These additions have provided Penzance with extensive harbour facilities for small coasting vessels. Penzance is a Trinity House depot for servicing lightships and lighthouses and the port is also the mainland terminal for services to the Scilly Isles. Its future, however, seems to be limited, with the growth in size of coastal vessels and the transference of its original fishing activity to the neighbouring port of Newlyn.

There are no major ports on Cornwall's northern coast. In the medieval period the Camel estuary provided facilities centred on Wadebridge which was also a bridging point. But this little port did not see its peak until the nineteenth century when small ships took away the granite from the De Lank Bodmin Moor quarries. The main difficulty has been the progressive silting of the Camel estuary, forming extensive sand banks of which one, the dreaded Doom Bar, became notorious. As a result Padstow emerged nearer the mouth of the estuary as a modern port, although it, too, is restricted by the available channel depths. Padstow's growth dates from the mid-nineteenth century although it has earlier origins. In 1843 a body of Harbour Commissioners was formed and an application was made for an Act to make Padstow a harbour of refuge. Shipbuilding was already a local activity and a regular steam-packet service was maintained to Hayle and Bristol, whilst emigrant ships also sailed from Padstow to North America. The coming of the North Cornwall Railway in 1899 delayed the decline of the port to some extent but the long-term trends combined with the navigational difficulties have now left Padstow with little more than a tourist trade.

The Tourist Towns

There are few towns in Cornwall that do not now qualify for inclusion in this category as the tourist trade is so widespread. This has not always been so, and a number of phases may be distinguished. Although, as elsewhere in England, it was the railway that provided the real basis for the organised tourist industry, traffic of this nature already existed in Cornwall from the early nineteenth century. The Napoleonic wars had cut off the continental resorts and many wealthy families began to visit the county, attracted by its remoteness, its mild climate and the fashionable summer bathing. The climate also brought many invalids for the winter, and Penzance became a renowned centre; W.G. Maton described it in 1794–6 'as the Montpelier of England'. At Bude Sir Roger Acland was building special houses for visitors in the early part of the nineteenth century and in 1814 the Lysons brothers recorded that cottages here 'furnish lodgings for such families as frequent the coast in the summer season for sea-air and bathing'.

The event which was to have such important consequences, however, was the opening of the Saltash Bridge in 1859. This joined the local railways, which had been developing in Cornwall since 1834, with the rest of England. The beauties of Cornwall, the fine bathing, and the mildness of the climate rapidly became known outside Cornwall and thereafter rail termini on or near the coast quickly grew as seaside resorts. In

Fig. 15. Newquay: the nineteenth-century seaside town built around the railway terminus. The fourteenth-century fishing 'port' of Towan Blustry lies to the north-west. (Extract from OS Sheet 39 Revised 1906 with additions to 1938. Since this date Trenance has been largely built over.)

the latter half of the nineteenth century hotels, boarding houses and other amenities were rapidly added to railheads such as Penzance, Falmouth, Looe, St Ives and Newquay (Fig.15, Plate 31). Bude and Padstow followed in the early part of the twentieth century. This rail-induced tourist traffic marks the second phase in the Cornish tourist industry.

The rise of the tourist centres at the railheads coincides with the decline of the fishing industry. It was accidental but fortunate that the shore conditions which favoured pilchard seine-net fishing, i.e. sheltered bays without strong currents and with sandy rock-free floors and beaches, were also ideal for bathing and for family holidays. This saved many purely fishing settlements, such as St Ives, from decay and ultimate disappearance. The transformation from a fishing port to a seaside holiday resort, and the growth of the rail termini as holiday centres, can be traced from the successive editions of Murray's *Handbook for Cornwall*. Newquay, for example, was in 1851 a village 'where the pilchard fishery is pursued on a considerable scale'. But by 1893 we read that 'the terminus of the Great Western Railway has made a small and inaccessible fishing village into a rising watering place'. In 1851 Padstow was an 'antiquated, unsavoury fishing town'. The beauties of the pilchard centre of St Ives when seen from a distance are described, but the traveller is warned that 'a descent into its streets, or rather lanes, will somewhat qualify his admiration'. By 1893, however, St Ives had acquired its artists' colony and an increasing number of visitors were arriving yearly. But the short-vacation summer tourist does not seem to figure so much in the early days. Falmouth is described as a 'winter health resort' until the end of the nineteenth century.

The third phase arises from the mid-twentieth century growth of road transport and the contraction of the rail network. The recent car explosion has not produced quite such dramatic results as the nineteenth-century advent of the railways, but the effect has been more widespread. The increased mobility afforded by the car and the coach has meant an increased ability to disperse over the face of the county so that now not only the remoter coastal sites but also the inland towns and villages have been drawn into the tourist net. New building to cater for the greatly increased volume of visitors is similarly well scattered, although nucleations are found in some of the more attractive coastal sites such as Polzeath, Mullion and Porthleven. It is estimated that a quarter of Britain's home holidays are now taken in the south-west which means that approaching ten million tourists now flood the region annually: the majority include Cornwall either as a base or for day visits and most arrive in the three summer months from June to August.

The twentieth-century expansion of the tourist industry has to some extent rescued the inland mining towns of the late eighteenth and early nineteenth centuries. It was during this period that the extraction of tin, copper, silver, lead, slate, granite and china clay all prospered. The boom also created a demand for small manufacturing and engineering establishments. Small hamlets and villages suddenly blossomed forth into towns, and centres such as St Just, Hayle, Redruth and Camborne (Fig.16) appeared. These towns bear witness to their nineteenth-century development. Monotonous rows of terrace houses, typical of the industrial town, are broken only by Italianate churches and public buildings. In the immediate vicinity are often found the ruins of the tin and copper mining industry. Somewhat similar in origin but a little later in development comes St Austell, but here the town still preserves its original function as a residential and administrative centre for the china-clay industry. Alone among the Cornish towns it also has a mid-twentieth century centre development with a pedestrian shopping precinct (Plate 32).

The prosperity of the mining and quarrying of this time was also reflected in the expansion and rebuilding of other established Cornish towns. As a result, the centres of many now have a typical Georgian appearance. Truro became a miniature Bath with theatre, Philharmonic Society and assembly rooms: here, too, the Lemons of Carclew built Boscawen Street and the street named after them. Lemon Street is one of the best-preserved Georgian streets in the country. Truro's famous granite cathedral is later in date. It was designed by J.L. Pearson in 1880, incorporating the south aisle of the old parish church of St Mary (1504–18) in the plan (Plate 28).

Another town of distinctly Georgian character is Liskeard,

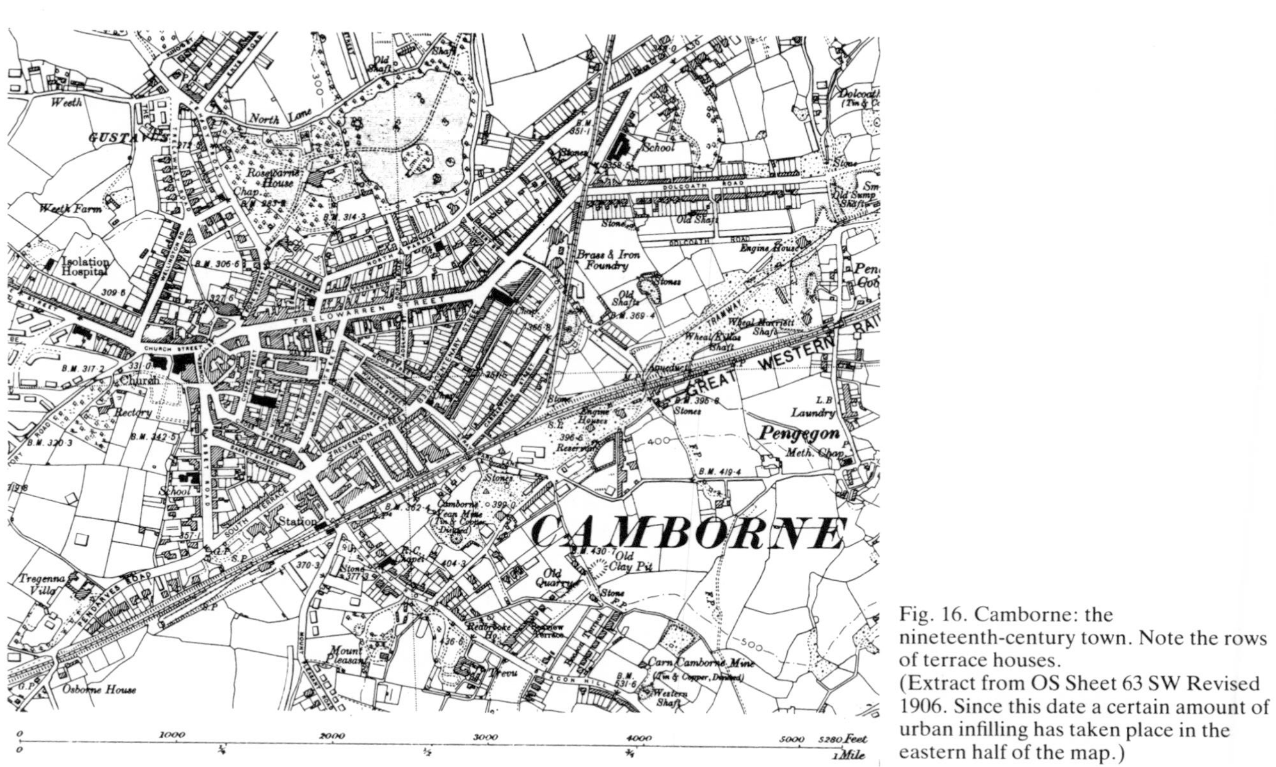

Fig. 16. Camborne: the nineteenth-century town. Note the rows of terrace houses.
(Extract from OS Sheet 63 SW Revised 1906. Since this date a certain amount of urban infilling has taken place in the eastern half of the map.)

where the town centre has moved away from the church to the Regency Parade. Here stuccoed, slate-hung, and stone-fronted houses alternate with more ambitious efforts such as the Market Hall (1821), Webb's Hotel (1833), and the Italianate town hall. Much of Falmouth is also of similar vintage; eighteenth-century terraces are common, and the early nineteenth century saw the addition of the Custom House, the Royal Cornwall Polytechnic, the Mathematical School, the Royal Hotel and numerous churches. Many domestic and public buildings in Bodmin and Penzance similarly date from this period.

Many of these inland and coastal towns now depend very largely on the year-round tourist and retirement industries for their livelihood. The urban ethos becomes a direct reflection of this dependence and each season exhibits a different character, the colourful crowds of summer contrasting with the quieter peace of winter.

Select Bibliography

Allen, J., *History of the Borough of Liskeard* (1856).

Gay, Susan E., *Old Falmouth* (1903).

Noall, Cyril, *The Story of St Ives* (1970). *Cornwall's Ports and Harbours* (1970).

Pearse, R., *The Ports and Harbours of Cornwall* (1965).

Peter, R. and O. B., *History of Launceston and Dunheved* (1885).

Pounds, N. J. G., 'Cornish Fish-Cellars', *Antiquity*, Vol. xviii (1944).

Roddis, R. J., *Cornish Harbours* (1951).

Toy, H. S., *History of Helston* (1936).

5. The industrial landscape

Tin and copper. China clay. Slate.
Igneous and other rocks.

THE EXPRESSION 'INDUSTRIAL landscape' normally conjures up a picture of belching chimneys, polluted air and untidy congested buildings. It speaks of a cramped and disharmonious encrustation upon the natural landscape. Cornwall has none of this. The coal measures are barren of the seams upon which industry might have been based, and manufacturing activity has played little part in the economic life of the county. Such industry as there is arises largely from servicing the mining, quarrying, maritime and agricultural activities.

Mining and quarrying have produced some well-known hydraulic and compressed-air engineering works in Camborne, Penryn and Camelford. Ship servicing has resulted in engineering works and peristaltic pump works in Falmouth, whilst boat and pleasure-craft construction may be found in a number of coastal locations, notably in Falmouth (Plate 33) and Fowey. Supporting electrical and marine-engineering activities are found in Penryn.

It is the tourist industry which, directly and indirectly, now employs a high proportion of the urban population. But this form of employment has its problems. It is seasonal with a peak that lasts at the best for little more than three months of the summer and it often produces a large surplus of female labour. In addition to the large number of hotels, garages, repair works, and transport depots catering directly for the tourist, there are also many small pottery, printing, leather, metal and fancy-goods activities. Few of these firms employ more than a handful of workers and they are scattered throughout the length and breadth of the county. Some of the larger units, however, include colour printing in St Ives, pottery and book binding in Redruth, the manufacture of fishing equipment in Falmouth and printing in Truro.

A new and interesting form of activity related to the tourist trade is the holiday attraction known locally as a 'grockle' or tourist trap. There are now well over a hundred of these scattered throughout Cornwall. Most of them consist of a fee-charging tourist attraction supported by car parking, restaurant and toilet facilities and the inevitable gift shop. The attractions range from the educational, such as the china-clay complex at Wheal Martyn, the tin plant at Tolgus, the slate quarry at Delabole and the craft museum at Camelford, to purely entertainment complexes, such as the miniature villages at St Agnes and Polperro, the Bird Paradise at Hayle, the Aero Park at Helston, the Poldark Mining at Wendron, the Age of Steam near Penzance and the miniature railways at Gwinear, Dobwalls and near Perranporth.

Additionally, many country houses and gardens have become tourist attractions, most having fallen into the hands of the National Trust in the post-war period. Few remain in private hands and even these are open to the public at certain times in the year. Among the more notable houses are those at Antony, Cotehele, Lanhydrock, Mount Edgcumbe, Trerice, Trewithen and St Michael's Mount. Among the gardens venues such as Glendurgan, Lanhydrock, Trewithen, Penjerrick and Trelissick are very popular.

These tourist attractions provide a valuable alternative to the beach for all ages throughout the season, but are especially useful in wet weather for those with families. They are now very much part of the Cornish scene, but from an employment point of view their contribution is rather limited.

Post-war efforts to resolve the employment problem have led to the introduction of no less than thirty-three 'mini-industrial estates' in the county, notably at Truro, Redruth, Liskeard, Penzance, Penryn, Falmouth, St Austell, Launceston, Saltash and Perranporth. Cornwall now has electronic engineering (Penzance), micro-processors (Falmouth), spiral stairways (Truro), reproduction furniture (Liskeard), laboratory apparatus (Falmouth), drafting films (Penryn), kitchen ware (Penryn) and PVC products (Launceston) diversifying the manufacturing scene.

Elsewhere small clothing factories have appeared in Camelford (pullovers), Portreath (ladies wear) and Launceston (baby wear). Fish-canning factories are found in Newlyn whilst the building industry has produced a number of associated activities such as aluminium fabrication, doors and windows in Camborne, blinds in St Austell, joinery in Truro, Camborne and Perranporth. Creameries at Camborne and near Penzance reflect one aspect of the agricultural base, whilst several of the ancient market centres now support agricultural engineering. Other miscellaneous manufactures include metal perforating (Hayle), plastic and bitumen roof coating (Bodmin), and tungsten carbide gauge blocks (Tor Point).

Although the statistics indicate that there are over two thousand 'manufacturing establishments' in Cornwall employing some 10,000 in all, the impact on the landscape is minimal, for the average establishment is quite small and rarely employs more than ten people. Much of the work is carried out in converted buildings tucked away in the back streets of the larger towns and there are only some 400 factory 'units' in the county. The casual visitor may be forgiven if he gains the impression that Cornwall has no manufacturing industry at all, but he is greatly surprised should he visit a Cornish Industries Fair. Yet if manufacturing industry is apt to be overlooked, it is difficult to move very far in the county without coming across extensive signs of past or present mining and quarrying.

Tin and copper

Although now of limited importance, pride of place in the industrial landscape of Cornwall must undoubtedly be accorded to tin. For many centuries it was Cornwall's chief export and its influence is manifest in many localities. It affected the landscape in two contradictory ways, accelerating on the one hand the enclosure of the waste land and its division into squarish fields by the miners, who for many periods were really miner-farmers; and on the other hand laying waste large areas of potential farmland. There is no record of the first extraction of tin, but it is generally thought to have become important in the late Bronze Age (after 1000 B.C.) when the trans-peninsular gold route developed across

Cornwall from Ireland to the European mainland. Tin as well as gold certainly moved along this route. The first written record may be that of Strabo, who tells of the Phoenician trade with the Cassiterides, but the precise location of these islands is open to discussion, and Camden's identification with the Scilly Isles is now suspect. Diodorus Siculus gives us a detailed account of the extraction, production and export of Cornish tin by Greek traders during the late Iron Age.

The mineral was obtained by a process known as 'streaming', a method which remained in use until late in the Middle Ages. A large number of valleys had become filled with detritus during glacial and post-glacial times and near the mineralised zones these deposits were highly charged with tin. The early 'streamers' dug over this material and washed out the tin, leaving behind a chaotic and hummocky landscape. Some of this land has been reclaimed, but in marginal areas, e.g. on Bodmin Moor and south of Lanivet, large tracts of derelict country still bear witness to the tin-streamers' activity. They were also responsible for accelerating the silting of the coastal submerged estuaries. The decline of medieval ports such as Tregony, Truro, Lostwithiel and Wadebridge was undoubtedly hastened by the large amounts of waste washed downstream from the 'tin-lands'.

We know little about the tin trade of Cornwall during the Roman occupation and the following Dark Ages. There is no reference to tin in any Anglo-Saxon document relating to Cornwall, nor is there in the Domesday Book. That tin-working had not entirely ceased is suggested by the levying of tolls on tin in certain Flanders towns in the late tenth century, for there was no other known source of tin but Cornwall. By the twelfth century there was a considerable revival and we hear of special courts or 'stannaries' for the tin areas at the end of the century.

There were four stannaries: Foweymoor (variously spelt) roughly corresponding to the present limits of Bodmin Moor; Blackmoor between the rivers Fowey and Fal and centred on St Austell; Tywarnhaile comprising the triangular area from St Agnes south to Truro and Redruth; and the united stannaries of Penwith and Kerrier respectively west and south of Kerrier. The documents relating to the stannaries provide an almost continuous data bank of information about tin extraction in Cornwall from 1156 right through medieval to recent time. They comprise not only the laws of the stannaries, but also the tinners' charters, the rolls of the mine courts, the Pipe rolls, the accounts of the receivers and auditors of the Duchy of Cornwall, and the figures for the annual production of tin. These records together with other Parliamentary and State papers were the means by which G. R. Lewis was able to produce his classic account of the stannaries in 1908.

Stannary parliaments were held at which laws were passed and a whole judiciary system grew up to cope with offenders, including the setting up of a prison at Lostwithiel. Tinners were exempt from military service and from market tolls. This situation reveals the remoteness of Cornwall from the rest of England during the medieval, and earlier, periods. The tinners were almost a law unto themselves as they had the right to divert streams for their purpose, to cut fuel, to search for and work freely for tin over areas of unenclosed common land, and they also enjoyed bounding rights described by Richard Carew in his classic 1602 *Survey of Cornwall* as follows: 'When a mine (or streamwork) is found in any such place the first discoverer aymeth how farre it is likely to extend, and then at the foure corners of his limited proportion, diggeth up three turves, and the like (if he list) on the sides, which they term Bounding, and within that compasses every other man is restrained from searching.' This was the miner's 'claim'.

In return for these privileges, the tinners were taxed on their product after smelting through a system of coinage. The actual process of coinage consisted of striking off a corner from each block of tin by hammer and chisel (the term 'coinage' being derived from the French *coin* – corner) and after assaying this sample, weighing the block to assess the dues. On payment of these the tin was then stamped with the Duchy seal. This process had to take place at designated centres and this is how the coinage towns emerged. These were originally Bodmin, Lostwithiel, Liskeard, Truro and Helston, but with the increasing development of tin westwards Bodmin and Lostwithiel eventually disappeared from the list and Penzance was added. As well as the duty payable to the Crown, the landowners also obtained a tin-toll normally amounting to about one-fifteenth of the quantity mined.

Theoretically there was a tight control on tin sales (which along with wool and lead formed the basis of England's commercial economy in medieval times) but there is little doubt that a considerable quantity never saw the light of any coinage hall. The remoteness of Cornwall from London and the scant regard of the population for excise duties, together with an open market in the Low Countries and ideal export smuggling conditions, produced a leak of now unknown proportion.

The records of the transactions in the coinage towns enable us to trace the gradual shift westwards of the focus of the industry in Cornwall, a process which was accelerated once true mining began to replace streaming. How the early prospectors traced the stream-tin back to the lodes and then began adit and shaft mining can be gleaned from accounts in Norden and Carew. Norden describes how the lodes were discovered 'by little stones which lye both in and nere the Brookes, and upon the mountaynes, wher the mettal lyeth'. Carew explains how 'they sink a shaft or pit seven or eight feet in depth, to prove whether they may so meet with the load'. When the mineral vein or lode was found it was followed but the depths reached were not great as drainage difficulties proved a limiting factor. Only adits and primitive pumping devices were available to clear the mines of water. Celia Fiennes confirms this picture in 1698 when describing St Austell, where 'there was at least 20 mines all in sight which employs a great many people at work, almost night and day, but constantly all and every day includeing the Lords day which they are forced to, to prevent their mines being overflowed with water'. Shaft mining seems to have begun in Devon in the late fifteenth century, and probably about the same time in Cornwall.

Yet another method of locating tin was to cut a trench at a steep angle across likely ground and then divert a stream into the trench. The stream would rapidly clear out material down to the bedrock and thus reveal any lodes. In so doing the hillside was gashed and a miniature delta would be formed at the foot of the hill. On other occasions larger streams were diverted so that the old bed could be worked over for the stream tin. All this activity played havoc with the natural surface and despite the regrowth of vegetation such areas often remain derelict. They form a distinctive pattern not only on the ground but also on the 1:25,000 Ordnance Survey Pathfinder maps.

During the early eighteenth century the character of the industry changed as deep mining became more general. This was possible partly because of the application of gunpowder to mining, the technique of blasting being employed in Cornwall after 1684, but mainly because of the technical advances in pumping engineering which enabled the pits to be kept dry. Morland had patented the plunger in 1675 but its development was slow and it was not adopted in any mine until 1796. In the meantime, Savery's unpractical steam engine of 1696 had been superseded in 1705 by Newcomen's steam engine which could keep a mine drained to a depth of 500 feet. So conservative, however, were the tinners we only find one such engine recorded in Cornwall in 1742. Thereafter there followed a rapid advance, partly because of the expansion of copper mining, and in the next thirty-six years more than sixty were erected.

Newcomen's engine in turn was displaced in the late eighteenth century by the improved Boulton and Watt pumping engine which increased the working depth to over 1,000 feet. The first Boulton and Watt engine in Cornwall was erected at Chacewater in 1777. In the following five years, twenty-one had been set up and only one of Newcomen's remained, which ceased in 1790. Further improvements by Trevithick, Hornblower and Woolf were to bring the Cornish mines into a relative high state of efficiency in the early nineteenth century. Other engines were also adapted for lifting the material out of the mines (a horse whim had previously been used), so that by the beginning of the nineteenth century each pit-head was acquiring a large and growing tip of waste material, an assemblage of buildings to hold the pumping and hauling engines, and the stamping mills and furnaces for the dressing and smelting of the ore. These erections were constructed of more durable slate-stone and granite and many have lasted, although no longer in use, to the present day. Previously, smelting had been carried on in thatched sheds, known as 'blowing-houses', by means of charcoal fires blown by bellows, and from time to time it became profitable to burn down the shed in order to recover tin particles which had become absorbed in the roof.

About the same time that deep tin mining became important, copper mining also developed. Copper ore was known to exist very early but had not previously been extracted in any quantity. It does not stand up to atmospheric weathering, being more often than not reduced to a mass of iron oxide and quartz: it was neither conspicuous nor easy to find, and there were no stream deposits. Extensive copper extraction, therefore, had to wait the development of deep-mining techniques, and was often initiated through accidental discoveries made when following the tin-lodes. The surface expression of the industry resembled that of tin-making, for the method of extraction and preparation of the ore followed that of tin in most respects. Tin and copper mines are inextricably mixed up and it is now difficult to distinguish them in a casual inspection of any derelict remains. However, the eventual development of the copper industry differed from tin in one important respect: large quantities of fuel were required for smelting and in the course of time it proved more economic to move the copper ore to plentiful fuel supplies in South Wales for the smelting process.

By comparison with tin extraction, which extends over 2,000 years, copper mining in Cornwall was short lived. Although mentioned by Carew in 1602, it was of limited significance before 1700 and was extinct by 1900. Yet in these 200 years copper far surpassed tin in value and tonnage and from 1750 to 1850 Cornwall's prosperity was largely based on copper. The demise of the industry in the 1860s was largely due to foreign competition from the New World and it led to a great exodus of Cornish miners. A pointer as to what was likely to happen to the industry had already been provided by the period between 1770 and 1800 which saw the rise and fall of the Anglesey opencast copper mining; this nearly caused the collapse of the deep-mined Cornish copper. Improved pumping efficiencies and the combination with the tin mining, however, kept the Cornish mines going until the exhaustion of the Anglesey deposits enabled a rapid expansion in the first half of the nineteenth century.

During the period 1750 to 1850 the Cornish connection with South Wales, and the Swansea area in particular, developed extensively as it was found less expensive to move the copper ore to the fuel (coal) for smelting than vice versa. Copper mining and copper smelting in Britain, however, were doomed with the rise of the great copper mines of Montana and Arizona in the mid-nineteenth century. Chile and Australia also entered the field and a steady decline of copper mining in Cornwall and copper smelting in Swansea took place between 1850 and 1900. During its productive period Cornwall had yielded nearly one million tons of copper from ten million tons of ore which had necessitated some forty million tons of veinstone being raised to ground level. Underground there were at least 1,500 miles of workings. Copper and copper alone had been responsible for the success of deep mining, for the introduction of widespread steam power for drainage, and for the creation of the Cornish mining ports and the associated mineral railways.

Whereas copper mining came and departed from Cornwall, tin extraction, either through streaming or mining, seems to have been almost continuous from prehistoric time to the present day although output has been very variable. The history of tin mining, particularly in the nineteenth century, is characterised by a series of booms followed by slumps and phases of mass emigration as a succession of overseas tin deposits were discovered and exploited. The Industrial Revolution from 1750 onwards naturally led to an increased demand for tin, but the improved machinery and methods of extraction of this period led initially to over-production which in turn depressed the market. A solution came, however, when the East India Company contracted to ship tin to China. Something like 2,000 tons of tin were then being consumed annually in China in the form of tin foil for religious ceremonies and for twenty-five years from 1789 Cornwall supplied approximately a third each year. This brought both stability and prosperity to the Cornish tin trade. But from 1820 onwards Malay alluvial tin began to enter the market and by the 1830s Cornwall had lost its world leadership and domina-

Plate 33 Falmouth: the dock area on the west side of the Fal estuary.

Plate 34 St Agnes: Grecian-like remains of the tin mining industry near Wheal Kitty.

Plate 35 Minions Mound: A derelict tin and copper mining area on the eastern edge of Bodmin Moor near Minions.

Plate 36 Wheal Jane Mine: modern tin mining at Wheal Jane three miles south-west of Truro.

Plate 37 Charlestown: the port constructed by Charles Rashleigh and John Smeaton in 1800 for the export of china clay.

Plate 38 Gunheath, St Austell: typical mid-twentieth century china-clay landscape on Hensbarrow Down.

Plate 39 Delabole: the great quarry at Delabole, the result of 400 years of excavation for slates.

Plate 40 Lamorna Cove: the remains of the granite quarries at Lamorna Cove.

tion in tin production, thereafter tin prices in Cornwall were gradually forced down to starvation levels.

The coinage dues (about 7 per cent of the price) then became an obvious economy target and after a great deal of agitation modifications were introduced in 1833 when additional coinage towns (Calstock, Hayle and St Austell) were added to the list and the frequency of the meetings was increased to once every six weeks. Whilst this improved the efficiency of the system the levy was still a burden on the industry and pressure for the abolition of coinage mounted steadily. The accession of Queen Victoria in 1837 provided the long-awaited opportunity and the whole coinage system was abolished in 1838.

The twenty years from 1830 to 1850 were marked by relative depression in the tin mining industry in Cornwall and although output was maintained, largely through the success of the Wheal Vor Company, the financial returns were low. There was large scale emigration to South Australia in 1835, followed by movements to Quebec and New York, and in 1847–9 further finds of copper in Australia and gold in California attracted still more Cornish miners. D.B. Barton writes:

> The rage for emigration from 1847–9 as a result of Australian copper and Californian gold was indeed phenomenal: in April 1847 it was reported that upwards of 700 persons have left Camborne parish within the last ten days for Australia and North America whilst two years later one Truro agent alone reported that he had received no less than 631 applications for emigration passages in the space of sixteen days . . . In three months of 1849 3690 persons left Plymouth for the Australian colonies and 1058 in one single week for Quebec.

By mid-century a more normal situation seems to have returned to the money and metal markets after the depression of the 1840s and another surge of production took place in both tin and copper in Cornwall for a few years. This was the period which saw the rise of Great Wheal Vor and Dolcoath (two legendary names in Cornish mining) and the development of deep-mined tin which appeared as the copper was exhausted.

Another depression was to come in the 1860s with the loss of the American market during the American Civil War but this was followed by the great tin boom of 1870–2 which was a direct consequence of an increased demand for tin from a rapidly-expanding canning industry combined with a slump in the Malayan output as a result of civil chaos in the area. The boom of 1870–2 was, in fact, the all-time high watermark of Cornish tin mining with the greatest number of active mines: some 230, employing 26,500. None had cause to suspect then that an almost unbroken fifty years of decline and depression lay ahead.

The immediate cause of trouble with the industry in Cornwall was the recovery of the Malayan area plus the discovery of extensive alluvial tin deposits in Queensland, Australia. These events combined with the opening of the Suez Canal in 1869 produced a collapse in tin prices and Cornish mines began to close rapidly. By 1877, only ninety-eight were operational and these survived only because of the introduction of dynamite and machine-boring tools. Another wave of emigration, this time to the diamond mines in South Africa, followed and the numbers employed in tin mining halved to 13,730 by 1878. For the next twenty years Cornwall struggled on with tin mining, but it was soon evident that the cheaper alluvial tin from the Malay Straits would, short of miraculous new finds, bring Cornwall to a halt. D. B. Barton records, 'The prophetic *obiter dictum* of Sir Stamford Raffles voiced to a junior member of the Bolitho family on the occasion of his visit to Wheal Vor in the 1820s that "you will live to see the day, my little boy, when the mines of Banca will eat up the mines of Cornwall" had, at length, come true' (Plate 34).

Worse was to follow because the soaring output of the Malay Straits was supplemented after 1895 by the development of tin mines in Bolivia, made possible by the completion of the Antofagasta and Bolivia Railway in 1892. By the turn of the century only about ten mines were still at work although these were all large and a considerable tonnage of ore was being milled. The First World War produced a contradictory state of affairs with the Cornish mines unable to meet the demand for tin because of lack of man-power. A post-war collapse of prices followed and this even brought the famous Dolcoath mine (which had worked since 1799) to an end in 1920. By March 1921 only one mine remained and all tin streaming had ceased. For a short while in the following year tin extraction in Cornwall stopped completely. Only the wind now whistled through the rusting head gear and broken window panes of the silent engine-houses. From being the world's only exploited source of tin Cornwall's output had dropped steadily to less than one per cent per annum (Plate 35).

By all the rules of economics this should have led to the end of tin mining in Cornwall but paradoxically the industry staggered on with various attempts to restart old mines right through the twenties and the depression years of the thirties. There were never more than a handful of mines operational at any one time and their output was insignificant by world standards. It says a great deal for the tradition and spirit of the Cornish venturers and miners that they refused to acknowledge defeat. The Second World War produced a minor transformation because of the importance of home supplies of tin (and wolfram) with the loss of Malaya in 1941, but the industry had fallen to such a low ebb that it proved difficult to boost output. The post-war period saw further minor slumps and booms largely related to price fluctuations. Post-war activity has been likened to the flutter of a new generation of moths into the old candle flame: the lure of instant riches with the fabulous strike is ever-present in the history of mining.

As this chapter is being written in the summer of 1982 there are still five mines actively working tin in Cornwall: these are South Crofty, Geevor, Wheal Jane (Plate 36), Pendarves and the resuscitated Wheal Concord, producing between them nearly 50 per cent of Britain's current consumption of 7,700 tonnes of primary tin a year. The last few years have also seen dredging for alluvial tin offshore near St Agnes and St Ives by Marine Mining (Cornwall) Ltd. There is undoubtedly a great deal of tin still left in Cornwall but its extraction ultimately depends on the world price of tin and the availability of overseas supplies.

Though mining was general in the mineralised zone certain

areas were more important than others, and the explanation is essentially geological. Tin was generally located in the granite areas, tin and copper came together in the aureole of altered rocks around the granite bosses; and the copper alone was found in the surrounding killas. The Penwith peninsula was one of the two most important districts, and nearly 300 mines, mainly for tin, have been worked in this small area: names such as Ding-Dong, Botallack and Levant are famous in Cornish history. At Botallack, about two miles north of Cape Cornwall, the tin lodes were pursued under the bed of the sea and the derelict buildings today make one of the most picturesque scenes on the Cornish coast. A further concentration occurs in the Camborne-Redruth area (Fig.16), but here copper eventually predominated and was largely responsible for the emergence of the late eighteenth-century town of Hayle, part of which still carries the name Copperhouse. Here coal was imported and some of the ore smelted, but the greater part ultimately found its way to South Wales for finishing, as the cost of transporting the coal proved to be greater than that of moving the ore. In this area names such as Wheal Virgin, East Pool, Dolcoath and Wheal Kitty were household words at the end of the last century. Here too, the characteristic landscape of the mining area is well exemplified with its heavy shapeless scars on the one hand and its pattern of small square fields on the other.

Another mining area lay around St Austell to the east of which copper was obtained, and to the west tin. Bodmin Moor and Hingston Down have also been a source of tin and copper, giving rise to mining villages such as Pensilva and Darite. Altogether some 550 mines have been active in Cornwall and these along with the medieval tin streaming have created considerable acreages of derelict land much of which remains unrestored to the present day.

Many other minerals have from time to time been extracted in association with the tin and copper: lead, zinc, silver, antimony, cobalt, tungsten, nickel, wolfram, arsenic and uranium have all been mined in varying quantities. But only lead, with a total production of around half a million tons, and possibly arsenic, can lay claim to any substantial output.

Cornish miners are now scattered over the face of the earth

from Arizona to Australia and Africa: it is said that wherever there is a hole in the ground there is a Cornishman at the bottom of it. Although the Cornish mining industry largely belongs to the past it has left an indelible mark on the present landscape in a variety of ways. In the Camborne-Redruth area the streets often run in the direction of a mineral vein – a relic of the time when the early miners followed the lodes. The abandoned workings and the simple rows of bleak grey granite houses of the miners are well known to travellers on the road from St Just to St Ives. Until quite recently derelict settlement sites were to be found but most of these have now been upgraded and reinhabited to meet the demands of the tourist industry. Elsewhere the old mining areas are characterised by acres of derelict land, or gorse and briar, with crumbling engine-houses and stamping mills: all now roofless, with vacant spaces for windows through which the wind blows mournfully throughout the winter months. Hard by each site stands a chimney stack, a gaunt sentinel often forming a conspicuous feature on the skyline. Sometimes the sheds and engine-houses have been quarried for building stone, and a solitary stack, a megalith of palaeotechnic man, alone remains as a silent witness of former prosperity. The lonely silhouette of a ruined engine-house and its stack beside it, seen on the skyline in the setting sun, is one of the abiding memories of the Cornish landscape (Plate 35).

China clay

In contrast to the grey sadness of the abandoned tin and copper areas we find the white sparkling landscape of the china-clay localities: a landscape unique in Britain although strangely owing its origin to events in China as long ago as A.D. 700. The manufacture of pottery or earthenware seems to have been a universal skill developed by *homo sapiens* in all parts of the world, a skill undoubtedly related to the widespread occurrence of many kinds of clay suitable for manipulation. Superior pottery or porcelain seems to have first appeared in China around A.D. 700 and it is likely that specimens reached Europe in the thirteenth century as a result of Marco Polo's travels. Its method of manufacture, however, remained a secret until the eighteenth century when the nature of the constituents was recognised by Bottger in Saxony: he realised the need to combine kaolin (a refined white china clay) and petuntse (a ground china stone) and further identified the association of both with altered granite. A porcelain works was then established in Meissen. The 'porcelain' works established in England in the eighteenth century could only produce a poor imitation as the secret was once again preserved – this time on the Continent. The two basic materials, kaolin and petuntse, had to be combined in the right proportions and fired at the right temperature to produce the hard white translucent and resonant porcelain.

It was a Quaker chemist and potter from Plymouth, by name of William Cookworthy (1705–80), who mastered the technique in England. Using accounts written by a Jesuit priest, Père d'Entrecolles, in China about 1712 and 1722 Cookworthy deduced the correct method and in 1745 acquired some kaolin and petuntse from an American potter, Andrew Duché, who had found the much sought-after ingredients in Virginia. Cookworthy then began a systematic search for the materials in Cornwall, discovering them first of all at Tregonning Hill west of Helston and subsequently in the parish of St Stephen's west of St Austell. It was not until 1768, however, that Cookworthy took out his patent for the manufacture of porcelain and the long interval of time after the discovery of the ingredients is doubtless a measure of the difficulty he had in mastering the technique of manufacture. The Plymouth china factory was moved to Bristol in 1770, partly because of fuel difficulties, and in 1774 Cookworthy retired, assigning his patent to Richard Champion who immediately applied for an extension.

These advances in porcelain manufacture naturally attracted the interest of the long-established Staffordshire potters among whom Josiah Wedgwood reigned supreme as a result of the construction of the famous Etruria factory in 1769. The Cookworthy patent effectively prevented imitation and also extraction of the ingredients: the attempt to extend it in 1775 by Champion was vigorously contested by the Staffordshire potters, with partial success for Wedgwood and his partner Turner, in that it subsequently became possible for the Staffordshire potters to obtain the materials from Cornwall although it was to be some time before they could make the 'hard' porcelain. Wedgwood came to an agreement with a Mr Carthew of St Austell in 1779 for the supply of the materials. It was not long before Champion, having lost his monopoly of the supply of the raw materials, was forced to close the Bristol factory and the Staffordshire potters then took over the process with the Wedgwoods again dominating the manufacture.

The cost of the china clay and china stone to the Staffordshire manufacturers was mainly in the transport of the material, facilities for this being poor at the time. Almost inevitably the possibility of establishing the industry in Cornwall was considered, with the idea of using coal from Swansea as the nearest source of fuel. Subsequent improvements in transport such as the Trent-Mersey canal, the construction of Charlestown harbour in the 1790s, and the introduction of special cargo ships, contrived, however, to reduce transport costs of the clay below that of coal and the proposals for a Cornish pottery works faded away.

After 1800 bone china became fashionable and demand for the clay and stone continued to rise despite the Napoleonic Wars. A report in 1807 records seven china clay works active in the St Stephen's area west of St Austell, to each of which was annexed a china stone quarry. The pits were shallow, averaging only nine to eighteen feet in depth, and the maximum production in any one pit was only 300 tons a year. The china clay was extracted by methods very similar to those used in tin streaming.

The end of the American War of 1812 and the Napoleonic Wars in 1815 reopened the American and European markets for the Staffordshire potters and a large expansion of production took place. Local Cornish 'clay venturers' began to replace the Staffordshire potters in a 'clay rush' on to Hensbarrow Down and the foundations were laid for a number of nineteenth-century Cornish fortunes.

The period from 1820 to 1858 was marked by an almost continuous increased demand for china clay, partly because of the surge for pottery products with increasing population, but also because of the new uses for china clay in the textile and paper industries. As it proved expensive to deepen existing pits, expansion took place laterally by opening up numerous small additional works. Thus the 1820 total of twelve established works had grown to eighty by 1845, so that by the mid-nineteenth century Hensbarrow Down was being heavily assaulted by the clay diggers. In 1852 there were some 7,200 men, women and children working the clay and stone quarries in this area, producing between them 65,000 tons of china clay and 22,000 tons of china stone each year.

Other areas were also being explored for the clay and stone. In 1827 there was a revival of interest in Tregonning Hill, in 1830 pits were opened near Towednack, three miles south-west of St Ives, and in 1839 at Treganhoe near Sancreed, three miles west of Penzance. During this period the pits began to deepen and the pumping devices for dewatering became necessary. The technological knowledge to solve this problem was available in the adjacent tin and copper mines. There was a close relationship between tin and clay as working for the one resource often led to the discovery of the other, and on occasions both commodities were being extracted from the same pit.

As each clay pit deepened and its output increased, it became more difficult to remove the waste sand from the pit by the traditional 'hand shamelling'. Some eight tons of sand might result from every ton of washed clay. Horse-whim wagons on inclined rails overcame this problem, tipping the waste into 'burrows', and in so doing initiating much of the china-clay landscape of today. During this period, various experiments were also made in exporting the clay and stone by different methods, routes and ports. Among the ports Charlestown (Plate 37), Pentewan, Fowey, Par and Newquay were all tried but none realised at the time that Fowey and Par were destined to become the major export points for china clay.

The second half of the nineteenth and the first part of the twentieth centuries saw the third phase of the development of the china clay industry. From 1858 to 1914 there was a continuous increase in the number of works although some were short lived. Whereas in 1858 there were eighty-nine active china clay pits of which two topped 2,500 tons per annum, by 1878 there were 120 pits working of which a large number topped 6,000 tons per annum. By 1914 a further increase to 159 pits had taken place and several topped 9,000 tons per annum. Some had by then reached depths of 300 feet and more. In the same period prospecting took place on Bodmin Moor and in the 1870s several well-developed 'slads' or hollows with kaolinised floors were discovered and the present Bowaters and Stannon pits were initiated. Development was at first hampered by transport difficulties, these pits all being remote from road, rail and port facilities. This period also saw the beginning of amalgamations between some of the major producers, and the emergence of some of the legendary names such as Lovering, Stocker, Martin and Pochin, which were to dominate the china-clay trade for many decades to come.

The late nineteenth-century technique of extraction involved the washing down of clay into the base of the pit where the coarser silica waste settled out immediately. The clay stream was then pumped to the surface where the mica and remaining quartz were separated out in mica drags. The residue was then introduced into settling tanks and later to drying sheds and storage sheds (linhays).

Some of these constructions now form distinctive 'archaeological' remains in the landscape. Close by were vast tips of waste and straggling lines of clay workers' cottages, often distributed haphazardly and forming no clear settlement plan. By the turn of the century problems of waste disposal began to trouble the industry. Lateral disposal killed future potential workings and the landlords would not permit infilling of old pits as this prevented speedy re-opening; this only left vertical disposal and in the first half of the twentieth century the burrows were gradually replaced by vast cones of white quartz sand producing, along with the pits, a unique 'lunar' landscape (Fig.17, Plate 38). This landscape is itself now in process of change into a 'mesa' form as new tipping regulations (following from the Aberfan disaster) produce flat-topped tips.

By the beginning of the twentieth century, a wide range of additional uses had been found for china clay. Porcelain had

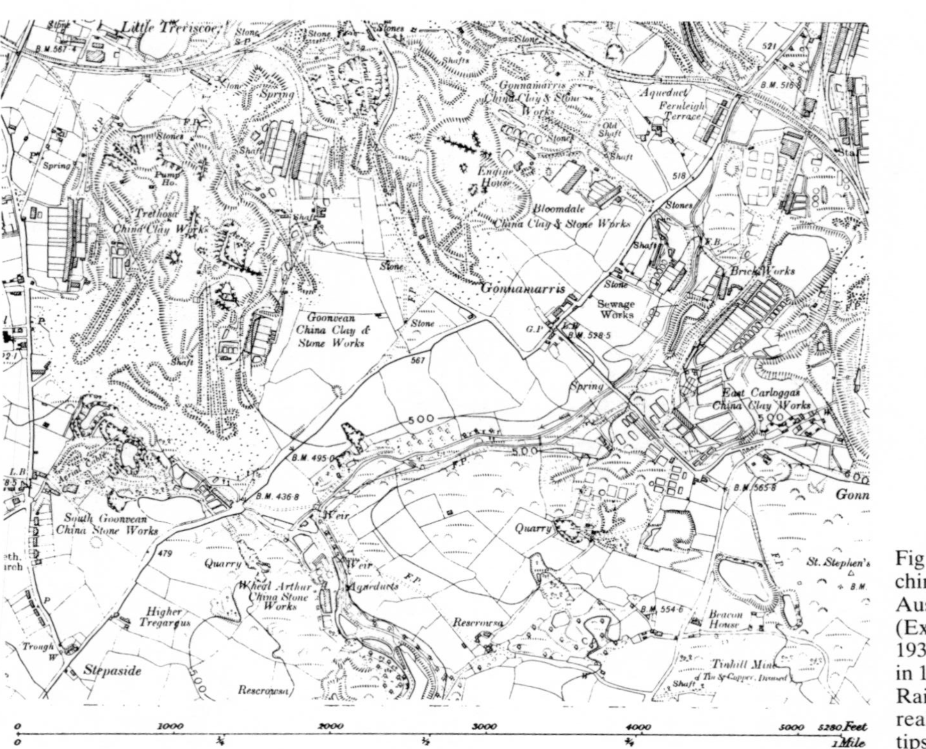

Fig. 17. Gonnamarris: a transient china-clay landscape north-west of St Austell.
(Extract from OS Sheet 50 NW Revised 1932. This area is almost unrecognisable in 1982 as a result of new workings. Railway lines have disappeared, roads realigned, new pits have appeared and tips extended.)

already been overtaken by its use in paper making and textiles, and soon paints, distemper, plaster, linoleum, household and toilet requisites, pharmaceuticals and artists' materials were added to the list, whilst even the waste products were being used for tiles and bricks. Increasing amounts were being exported overseas and shortly before the First World War over 800,000 tons of clay a year were being produced, of which 75 per cent went overseas where English china clays held a virtual monopoly.

This success story was badly hit by the 1914–18 war, partly because so many overseas markets were in enemy hands and partly because of the success of the submarine war. The difficulties led to the formation of a limited liability company for marketing which was called Associated China Clays Ltd. This had sixty-six founder members representing 90 per cent of the industry. The integration of the major producing companies was a natural follow-on to this development and in 1919 English China Clays emerged controlling half of the industry's capacity.

The expected post-war revival was slow to come, partly because of the development of alternative clay sources overseas and partly because of the run-down during the war. By 1921 output was still only half the pre-war boom level. However, a gradual return to more normal trading conditions came towards the middle and end of the decade combined with a new technology. Electric centrifugal pumps for dewatering, electric hydraulic monitors for washing down the clay, filter presses to accelerate the drying process, electronic separation of the clay and mica instead of mica drags, motor lorries for transport, packing by bags instead of casks, all combined to increase productivity, reduce costs and undercut foreign competition.

The world slump of 1931 damaged this recovery because of the temporary loss of much of the American market. Half the pits closed and the recession led to the amalgamation of the three main producers into English China Clays Lovering Pochin and Co. Ltd. which covered 75 per cent of the industry with a potential output of over a million tons per annum. One big advantage of the amalgamation was the introduction of an advanced research department to improve the quality of the clay products, to seek new uses, and investigate new outlets for the product.

The Second World War again depressed the industry because of the heavy dependence on overseas markets. Production dropped to a third of the pre-war output and the labour force was cut by 60 per cent. A concentration scheme was introduced and for a while production went right back to the level of 1876.

Post-war conditions, however, brought another boom situation and for a while the industry had difficulty in meeting the demand owing to a shortage of labour and coal (for fuel). The need to export to improve the balance of payments and clear the American debt brought government assistance and, combined with plans prepared during the war then being operated by English China Clays Lovering and Pochin, the industry climbed back to its pre-war output, so that by 1966 E.C.L.P. alone was producing two million tons of clay a year representing 85 per cent of the total British output.

Acting as a focus for the Hensbarrow Down china-clay area and very much dependent on the industry is the town of St Austell. It had become 'a considerable town' of nearly 4,000 inhabitants by 1801 and it is now a leading urban centre of Cornwall very different from the time when Leland described it as 'a poor village'. It is the only Cornish town to boast a post-war central redevelopment scheme with pedestrian precincts.

Another technological revolution also took place in the post-war period: the clay was now being extracted in great quantities on a large scale from a much smaller number of large pits (twenty-four all told), productivity being improved by bulldozers, dumpers, trenchers, excavators, mobile cranes, automatic monitors, conveyor belts, mobile continuous separators, and rotary driers. The scale of the industry is now completely different from that of the nineteenth century and much of the landscape then created is disappearing rapidly and a new vista is taking its place. The numerous small excavations have given place to huge open conical pits several hundred feet deep and up to half a mile in diameter. More than a hundred smaller pits have been abandoned or absorbed into larger excavations. Abandoned engine-houses, drys, linhays and labourers' cottages, which had gradually become overgrown with ivy and brambles, have been bulldozed away for the newer and larger pits or have been engulfed by the ever increasing white quartz tips. There was a time when eight months passed before the clay was dry enough for sale but today it is only a matter of eight hours between being washed out by the monitor and being ready for loading at the quayside. Both Fowey and Par now have the capacity to export over a million tons of china clay each year. In 1977, 573 vessels docked at Fowey for clay and over 1,000 at Par.

With an annual production rate of china clay now around two to three million tons, the question inevitably arises as to how long the industry can continue at this high level. Estimates have ranged from between 100 to 500 years. Whatever the answer it is clear that, like tin and copper, china clay extraction must eventually pass into history, but before it does so it will have created a sequence of unique landscapes: the original small-scale excavations of the eighteenth century developing in the first half of the twentieth century into a lunar-like landscape of burrows, tips and ghostly volcanic-shaped cones interspersed with turquoise white-cliffed lakes (Plate 38). This landscape itself is now being gradually changed into a flat-topped mesa-like scene with modern tipping methods. Like the Cheesewring the end result will doubtless long outlive human occupation of the area.

Slate

Yet another extractive industry in Cornwall which has left its mark on the landscape is slate quarrying. This is of very ancient origin but no authentic records of its beginning have so far come to light. As early as the fourteenth century, Cornish slate was being used in large quantities at Restormel Castle, and sent by sea for buildings elsewhere. Norden described the Menheniot slate in 1584 as the best in Cornwall. The industry may have arisen spontaneously some time in the thirteenth century as a result of the demand for building and hedging stone, when it was probably discovered that the slate could be split into thin and light forms suitable for roofing. As a result, we now find throughout the geological formation known as the Devonian, which makes up the greater part of Cornwall outside the granite areas, widespread excavations of varying size and age. Time has now softened the smaller and earlier quarries which once gashed the hillsides and moorlands, but in some localities slates of exceptional quality were discovered and an export trade developed.

As early as 1602 Carew indicated that the export trade was well established, for he says of Cornish slate: 'in substance thin, in colour fair, in weight light, in lasting strong: and generally carrieth so good regard, as (beyond the supply for home provision) great store is yearly conveyed by shipping both to other parts of the realm and also beyond the seas into Brittany and the Netherlands.' Quarries gradually grew larger, notably in and around Liskeard, Helston and St Teath, with the greatest concentration occurring between Delabole and Tintagel. The latter group of quarries is entirely due to the distribution of altered Devonian mudstones, which have been changed by the granitic intrusion of Bodmin Moor into hard compacted slates, of which the most famous is the Delabole blue.

Slate has been continuously extracted from this area now for over 400 years. There are records of sales in the fifteenth century, whilst slate tombstones in the nearby St Teath churchyard go back to 1580. The Old Delabole Slate Company archives contain documents dating from the seventeenth to twentieth centuries. Many quarries were opened up during this period, mainly worked by small bodies of men with little capital. Fluctuations in demand and the working out of good beds often caused abandonment of the smaller workings. In the nineteenth century, the use of dynamite and steam power and the introduction of engines favoured the larger concerns with more capital and gradually amalgamations took place until eventually the greater part of the industry came under the control of the Old Delabole Slate Company. This was originally formed as a joint stock company in 1841 and consisted in the first instance of several adjacent pits. These are vividly described in Murray's 1859 *Handbook for Devon and Cornwall* as follows:

> The quarries present one of the most astonishing and animated scenes imaginable. The traveller suddenly beholds three enormous pits, which, excavated by the uninterrupted labour of centuries, are encompassed by the dark blue hills of rubbish, continually on the increase, and slowly encroaching upon the domain of the farmer. The scene is enlivened by a throng of men busily engaged in various noisy employments, while wagons and horses are everywhere in rapid motion, and steam engines are lifting with a harsh sound their ponderous arms, and raising loaded trucks from the depths of the pit, or masses of slate of several tons weight, which are seen slowly ascending guide-chains to stages which overhang the quarries . . . About 1000 men are employed in these works, who raise on an average 120 tons of slate per day, which, manufactured on the spot into roofing slates, cisterns, and other articles are exported to various parts of the United Kingdom and to France, Belgium, the West Indies and America.

The continual working of the several quarries owned by the company at Delabole eventually led to their coalescence in one vast pit. This enormous quarry, several hundred feet deep and with an average diameter of over a quarter of a mile, is the largest single open excavation in England (Plate 39). Around the quarry are the rubble banks and spoil heaps of rejected waste, covering well over a hundred acres of land. Today the noise and bustle so vividly described by Murray no longer exists, but the quarry, along with its working museum, has become a tourist attraction in north Cornwall.

Other large quarries have existed in the Trebarwith valley and near Tintagel, and even the sea cliffs have been quarried along this coast; the hand of the slate quarryman has indeed made its impress upon the landscape in this locality. The effect might well have been greater if Cornish slate could have overcome transport charges and competed more strongly with Welsh slate in the Midlands and Belgian slate in south-east England during the nineteenth century, and with both home and imported manufactured tiles in the twentieth century. There was a minor boom in the Second World War when overseas supplies were cut off and much slate was needed for the repair of buildings damaged in air raids; Cornwall's output of slate then rose from a pre-war average of about 17,000 tons per annum to nearly 90,000 tons in 1943. The post-war period has seen a gradual decline in demand for roofing slate as it has proved difficult to compete in price with manufactured roofing tiles.

Slate has had other uses in Cornwall as well as supplying roofing materials. Examples of its wide range of use can be seen in the unique village near the Delabole quarry. Here not only the walls and roofs of the older houses are made of slate, but also the floors, lintels, window-sills and chimney pieces; not to mention a variety of domestic articles ranging from rolling pins to ash trays. Slate is widely used too for headstones in the churchyards, the inscribed slate headstones and tombstones of Cornwall form a distinct local art, and their lettering and design merit a closer study than has yet been accorded to them.

Igneous and Other Rocks

Cornwall has always occupied a high place in the output of igneous and other rocks among the English counties. In recent years production figures well in excess of a million tons per annum have been recorded. In the Culm Measures country numerous small quarries have yielded stone for local use in buildings, and the same is true of the slate of the Devonian Measures. Some rocks, e.g. the dove-grey hornblende picrite of Polyphant near Bodmin, and the hypabyssal basic igneous 'Catacleuse' stone from near Padstow, have been worked for ornamental and monumental purposes.

Small quarries, mainly for roadstone, are especially found scattered over the areas where igneous rocks have been intruded. Basalts, elvans, gabbros, dolerites and rocks of the metamorphosed aureoles which resist erosion and attrition, are all worked. Some quarries, strategically placed for transport, have developed long-distance markets, as for example near Penzance, and have grown to a considerable size. Roadstones will not stand the cost of transport very far, but building stones with special qualities can travel further, and in the past much of the igneous production has been made up of granite which has been exported to specialised markets.

Cornish coarse-grained granite is very resistant to wear and pressure, and also occurs in larger and more regular masses than the finer grained granite found elsewhere in the British Isles. This fact was a discovery of the nineteenth century. Initially the demand for granite was met by the 'moormen' who used the natural boulders and blocks which lay strewn upon the granite uplands. Records show that Smeaton's famous Eddystone lighthouse of 1759 was built of 'moorstone' whilst Dartmoor was a source of granite for much of London up to the early part of the nineteenth century. The eventual exhaustion of the surface stone led to systematic quarrying. In Cornwall William and John Freeman, Stone merchants of Westminster, London, opened up the Penryn district for granite from 1840 onwards. Quarrying brought to light the 'sounder' rock from beneath the surface and the full value of granite for docks, bridges, lighthouses and other civil engineering works was soon realised. Naval and commercial dockyards in particular generated a demand in the latter part of the nineteenth century and Cornish granite will be found in Bombay, Swansea, Belfast, Keyham, Gibraltar, Cardiff, Famagusta, Dover, and Buenos Aires. Other architectural works include lighthouses (Tyne, Fastnet, Folkestone), bridges (Vauxhall, Kew), and buildings (New Scotland Yard, the Old Bailey and many public buildings in London). Most of the quarry scars and the great screes of granite waste in Cornwall date from this period, and will long continue to bear witness to it, for many centuries must pass before any vegetation can obliterate this activity.

Since granite is bulky and heavy, nearness to railways or tide-water determined the siting of most of the larger quarries. Fortunately, none of the granite masses is far from the coast. Extensive quarrying operations have taken place at Gunnislake, Kit Hill, the Cheesewring, and De Lank in the Bodmin Moor area; at Colkerrow and Tregarden near Par on the flanks of St Austell Moor; in the Lamorna district of the Penwith peninsula (Plate 40); and in the greatest concentration on Carnmenellis Moor centring on the port of Penryn. Within a short space of time following the opening up of this area by Freeman's there were over ninety pits being operated by organised moormen. Tresahor, Polkanuggo, Rosemanowas, Maen Rock, Mabe and Carnsew contain literally scores of quarries and this area was the chief source of Cornish granite, with Penryn fully equipped with dressing sheds, storage accommodation and loading quays. It is mainly from Penryn that Cornish granite has been exported all over the world.

In Cornwall much of the historic record is embedded in this rock. Prehistoric menhirs and stone circles, medieval churches and crosses, bridges and docks, and Truro Cathedral, have all been built with this enduring native stone. Cornish houses, too, have been built of it, from the circular huts of Bronze Age man, high up on the moors, to the nineteenth-century 'villas' of successful tradesmen and mine-captains in the seaside towns, over a space of nearly 4,000 years.

Perhaps one of the most dramatic illustrations of the close inter-relationship of the physical and man-made landscapes can be seen on the south-eastern flanks of Bodmin Moor. Here Nature has produced the granite tor of the Cheesewring, with its fantastic weathered slopes and block-strewn moorland landscape. Close by, prehistoric man has erected the standing megalithic stones at Trethevy, the stone circles of The Hurlers, and a granite fort on Stowe's Hill; medieval crosses dot the moorland road, and granite churches and holy wells are to be found in the surrounding villages. And nineteenth-century man has, in a way, erected an even larger memorial to his activities in the enormous excavation for granite on the Cheesewring, the waste heaps of which will testify to his quarrying powers for thousands of years to come.

Like all the other extractive industries of Cornwall, granite has had its booms and slumps. Norwegian and Swedish granites have at times been strong competitors and the introduction of reinforced concrete has provided an alternative building material, but the main problem has been the volatile nature of the demand for public works. Current output does not match the high figures of the last century but there would be no difficulty in expanding the industry should the need arise.

One of the legacies of the extractive industries of Cornwall which does not figure in the guide books is the very large amount of derelict and waste-land in the county. At least 7,800 acres of derelict land remain from metalliferous mining. Subsidence is common and the land is very uneven with spoil heaps up to fifteen feet in height, all of which have deterred reclamation for either agricultural or urban use, quite apart from the fact that the soil in many areas has a poisonous arsenical residue. The main areas of dereliction are in the neighbourhood of Redruth and Camborne, north of Liskeard, east of Callington and at St Just-in-Penwith. All these areas are clearly seen both on the ground and on the Ordnance Survey maps.

Another 3,000 acres are given over to pits, tips and other forms of china-clay dereliction. The bulk of this area is in the St Austell Moor region where some thirty square miles of land is dominated by the industry and is now fit for little else but china-clay extraction. A smaller area is also found on Bodmin Moor. Slate and granite and roadstone quarrying collectively add several thousand more acres of dereliction so that it is not surprising to find that Cornwall appears very near the top of the county list for derelict land in England.

Select Bibliography

Barton, D. B., *A History of Copper Mining in Cornwall* (1961). *The Mines and Mineral Railways of East Cornwall and West Devon* (1964). *A Guide to the Mines of West Cornwall* (1965). *A History of Tin Mining and Smelting in Cornwall* (1967).

Barton, R. M., *A History of the Cornish China Clay Industry* (1966).

Collins, J. H., 'Seven centuries of tin production', *Trans. Mining Assoc. and Inst. of Cornwall*, Vol.iii. 'Four centuries of copper production', *Trans. Mining Assoc. and Inst. of Cornwall*, Vol.iv.

H.M.S.O. *Working Party Report on China Clay* (1948).

Jenkin, A. K. Hamilton, *The Cornish Miner* (1927).

Lewis, G. R., *The Stannaries: A Study of the English Tin Miner* (1924).

Ordish, H. G., *Cornish Engine Houses* (1967 and 1968).

Pounds, N. J. G., 'China Clay Industry of South-West England', *Economic Geography* (1952).

Rowe, John, *Cornwall in the Age of the Industrial Revolution* (1953).
Towse, R. J., 'Port Development and the China-Clay Trade of Mid Cornwall', *Geography* Vol. 63 (1978).

6. The pattern of communication

Roads. Ferries. Canals. Railways. Airfields. Telecommunications.

ONE OF THE most striking features of the large scale maps of Cornwall is the complicated pattern made by the roads. From one end of the county to the other they form a fine lacework, linking together the thousands of tiny dots that represent the farmsteads and hamlets, and themselves brought together at intervals, by the thicker red lines of the main roads. Though the great mass of the traffic now flows along the main roads, the basic pattern – the one that really interests the historian of the landscape – is that of the lanes, narrow, deep-set, and twisting, that take little or no account of what happens in the next parish but pursue their sequestered way independently from Tre- to Pol- and on to Pen-, from one grey farmstead to another between granite faced hedgebanks, under the shade of rustling trees and bushes. Altogether these lanes form thousands of miles of quiet trackways for human beings and their cattle, and they have been in continuous use for anything from 600 to 3,000 years. Beside them, the main roads – with some exceptions – are things of yesterday.

Next to the lanes in antiquity are probably the ferries, for one cannot go far in Cornwall without coming to a deep estuary or a fast-flowing river; and then, a little later in date, came the earliest stone bridges, from the thirteenth century onwards. Later still, there were the coach roads and the turnpike roads, in the seventeenth and eighteenth centuries. Almost simultaneous with the turnpike roads were the first canals, though Cornwall had few of these, by reason of its topography. Within forty years of the first canal, the first railway was constructed (a 'tram road' built between 1809 and 1818); and, with the spread of the railways in the 1830s and 1840s the canals and the turnpike roads declined, though they did not disappear from the landscape. Finally, in the twentieth century, came the main trunk motor roads, the 'by-passes', and the airfields, all of them making their own individual contribution to the landscape.

Roads

The prehistoric trackways are not easy to locate but can be detected from various finds of artefacts and from traces of settlement. These reveal two dominant lines of movement, the more important of which was across the county, linking the English Channel with St George's Channel. This was the Bronze Age and Iron Age trade-route between Ireland and Brittany, and must have arisen to avoid the dangerous sea passage around Land's End. Various trackways crossed the peninsula but, because of the absence of good harbours on the north coast, only the Hayle and Camel estuaries were important on that side. From Hayle the Land's End isthmus was crossed to Mount's Bay, while from the Camel several routes were used to reach the south coast. The Camel valley was followed to somewhere near the site of Bodmin and thence into the Fowey valley, a second and more southerly course lay via the Fal estuary, whilst, as Crawford has shown, a third ancient route passed over the St Breock Downs, Goss Moor and Hensbarrow Down to the sea near Pentewan.

Cutting across these north-south routes was a trackway running up the length of the peninsula. Beginning in Mount's Bay it crossed the Carnmenellis area and Hensbarrow Down, and then proceeded either over or to the north-west of Bodmin Moor, making a connection with the rest of England near Kilkhampton. The direction of this route was undoubtedly determined by the wide barrier of the Tamar to the south-east.

On the strength of milestones discovered at St Hilary, Breage and Tintagel, antiquaries have argued that Cornwall was traversed by a Roman road, supposed to follow in part the prehistoric peninsular trackway. No indisputable evidence has come to light to support this view, and Cornwall was probably without any real Roman roads, although short tracks from selected ports to the tin areas may well have existed. Such short connections would easily account for all the known Roman milestones and other Roman traces.

The early ridgeways – most of which probably date from Iron Age times, from the century preceding the coming of the Romans to the rest of England – form the basis of a good deal of the secondary road system of modern Cornwall. The exact course they follow bears a close relationship to the topography, which is nearly always difficult for roads in Cornwall: the deep, narrow and wooded valleys were avoided in favour of the easier gradients of the open land of the interfluves. The roads converging on Truro illustrate this well.

The network of lanes extended and grew slowly all through Celtic times, linking the *trevs* one to another. As the surface of the ground was cleared of moorstone, the boulders and blocks were carried to one side and built up to form the boundaries of the little fields that were being reclaimed from the 'waste', and yet others were used to line the narrow lanes. The granite facing of the Cornish hedgebanks, where they line the lanes, was probably devised to keep the soil of the fields from being washed down, or otherwise slipping, into the lanes, so making them impassable. These lane-walls, when built high enough, were consolidated with a layer of earth and turf on top, and on this bushes and even trees have succeeded in rooting themselves.

Often a boulder or a block of moorstone was too massive or too deeply embedded to be moved, and was incorporated into a hedgebank or a lane-wall, which might make an abrupt change of direction to do so. Hence arose many of the apparently inexplicable irregularities in the early field-boundaries and in the course of the ancient lanes. Fields and lanes were constructed piecemeal, on a small scale, over a long period of time, made by hand, or with primitive hand-guided tools, over many centuries. Therein lies much of the unending charm of the countryside.

The founding of villages following the Saxon Conquest, and the building of churches, each led to the extension of the lane pattern. In a land of dispersed settlement, for the most part, the church was most times built in a central position, and to it a number of church-paths were trodden out from all over the parish. But we must not forget that often, too, the site of the new parish church – in the centuries just before and just after the Norman Conquest – must have been determined, in the absence of any village, by the existence of cross-roads that had already come into being for another reason.

The great period of colonisation that followed the Norman Conquest completed the intricate network. Hundreds of new farms came into existence and lanes were made to join them together, not all at once but as human wont and usage dictated. With the rise of the market-towns and boroughs from the twelfth century onwards, these tiny local lanes acquired a wider significance, linking farmsteads and hamlets not only with each other but also with their nearest market a few miles away.

The rise of the market-towns and the growth of the tin trade, the cloth trade and the fishing industry further enlarged the horizons of the Cornish country people. This promoted the emergence of the main roads, linking one market-town to another over a dozen miles of country, or connecting an inland town to its local port a few miles down-river. By about 1300 it is likely that something recognisable as 'main roads' had come into being, built up for the major part by incorporating short sections of earlier lanes and tracks that happened to fit into the general direction. Even so, the main roads were hardly more than glorified lanes: they might have stone bridges where they crossed streams instead of fords or shaky timber structures; they might be a little wider in places where no ancient walls shut them in; they might have some of the worst bends evened out of them, and take a short cut now and then up a precipitous hill. Still, they are the beginning of the main roads as we know them, and that is how their course was first determined, in the twelfth and thirteenth centuries for the greater part, and by the needs of medieval trade.

A great road, known as the Royal Cornish Way, ran down the backbone of Cornwall, just as the A30 does today, but not taking exactly the same route. The oldest ridgeway had entered the county in the extreme north-east, near Kilkhampton, so avoiding any crossing of the Tamar. As early as the eleventh century, a bridge had been built over this river – at Bridgerule, which is called *Brige* in the Domesday Book of 1086 – but this lay far upstream and did not save many miles. The building of Launceston Castle between 1066 and 1086, however, brought about a more important diversion, for this was almost certainly followed by the construction of Polston Bridge over the Tamar, about two miles to the east. This then became the main road into Cornwall from London and Exeter, so that in the late fifteenth century we find one of the earliest travellers to go round England – William of Worcester – referring to Launceston as the 'beginning of Cornwall'.

The present A30 road boldly surmounts the wastes of Bodmin Moor after leaving Launceston, but the medieval main road ran along its northern flank, through Downhead and Davidstow, and thence turned south-westwards through Camelford, probably along the present A39 to the ford over the Camel at Wadebridge. That this was the line of the thirteenth-century road we deduce (for there are no maps to tell us) from the setting-up of a borough at Camelford in 1259, and the setting-up of a weekly market and two annual fairs at *Wade* in 1312. *Wade* is probably derived from the Old English word *waed*, 'a ford', and here the main road crossed the head of the Camel estuary. *Wadebridge* appears in the fifteenth century and clearly relates to the construction of the bridge in 1468. Beyond Wadebridge, the road proceeded by St Columb Major to Mitchell, where a 'borough' had been set up with a weekly market and an annual fair in 1239, and so by the old ridgeway through Trispen down into Truro.

An alternative crossing of the Camel estuary was used at an early date involving a ferry between Rock and Padstow. This is recorded as early as 1337 (Henderson), and is the route shown in Ogilby's *Britannia*, published in 1675. This ferry was approached from Camelford by way of the marked ridgeway that runs through Delabole and St Endellion.

Ogilby shows two other recognised roads into Cornwall in the seventeenth century. According to his map, the main road from Exeter to Truro ran via Dunsford to Chagford, thence across the heart of Dartmoor to Postbridge and Merrivale to Tavistock, and thence entered Cornwall over New Bridge and proceeded via Liskeard, Lostwithiel and Grampound to Truro. New Bridge, over the Tamar, was not built until the second quarter of the sixteenth century.

The only other medieval road into Cornwall from outside was that which crossed the Tamar mouth at Plymouth by the

Cremyll passage to Mount Edgcumbe, and thence went by Millbrook and Crafthole to Looe. Here a fine medieval bridge, nearly 400 feet long was built between 1411 and 1436. Before that date, travellers must have used the round-about inland road through Liskeard and Lostwithiel, or else crossed the Looe estuary by ferry. Probably the road was in use at least from the fourteenth century, for the next ferry it makes use of – at Bodinnick across to Fowey – dates from that time. Beyond Fowey the medieval road ran via Grampound into Truro, or via Tregony and Philleigh to Marazion, Penzance and Sennen.

There were a number of other locally important 'main' roads in medieval Cornwall. We can deduce their approximate course from the whereabouts of the numerous medieval stone bridges which still survive, most of which were erected with the aid of indulgences during the fifteenth century. No fewer than three of these handsome bridges remain over the middle reaches of the Tamar. Of these Horse Bridge is the oldest (1437), though the beautiful Greystone Bridge came very shortly afterwards (1439, Plate 43), and is probably the work of the same builder. New Bridge, a few miles downstream from Horse Bridge, was built about 1530–40.

Other medieval bridges are to be seen at Wadebridge, built about 1468 and called by Carew 'the longest, strongest, and fairest that the Shire can muster'; at Lostwithiel, dating from 1437; and at Yeolm Bridge, over the Ottery, 'the oldest and most perfectly finished bridge in Cornwall', and certainly fourteenth century in date. Those who wish to seek out the other ancient bridges of the county, of which there are rather more than a score, will find an excellent guide in Henderson and Coates's *Old Cornish Bridges and Streams*. The fine medieval bridges at Polston and Looe were, it should be noted, entirely rebuilt in the nineteenth century.

The Reformation marked the end of the great period of bridge-building in Cornwall, and the responsibility passed to the justices of the Quarter Sessions. But the justices soon found it difficult to maintain the existing bridges let alone construct new ones. Perhaps this reflects the advantage of the indulgence method of raising money compared with the rating system! After the Reformation no new county bridges were built in Cornwall until the turnpike era of the late eighteenth century.

The system of indulgences had also been employed to maintain the roads, and these suffered in like manner after the Reformation. Travellers' descriptions in the seventeenth and eighteenth centuries contained numerous complaints about the poor condition of the roads, although the routes in Cornwall rarely became completely impassable as they frequently did in the clay-vales of south-east England and the Midlands. Celia Fiennes, travelling through the county in 1698, 'passed over many very steep stoney hills' and 'steep precipices great, rocky hills' and also noted that 'there are many holes and sloughs where ever there is clay ground'. A little later Tonkin wrote that the roads were badly kept and overgrown by hedges, and suggested that they should be much better maintained because suitable materials were always to hand. The same point was also made by Borlase in the middle of the eighteenth century, more particularly with reference to south-west Cornwall.

The presence of carriages and coaches might perhaps have accelerated improvements. As it was, pack-horses, mules and ponies formed the chief means of transporting goods and passengers in Cornwall until well on into the eighteenth century. The arrival of Charles I by coach in Lostwithiel probably marked the appearance of one of the very first four-wheeled vehicles to be seen in the county, but as Henderson shrewdly remarks 'we must remember that he had several thousand men to get him out of the mud and it was the month of August'. Another century was to elapse before the regular appearance of a coach upon the Cornish scene, and this, the famous Hawkin's coach, is still preserved in the Truro museum.

In the construction of the turnpiked roads, parts of existing routes were joined by entirely new sections and the roads were all carefully graded to take wheeled traffic. Whereas in the past roads had followed the ridges between the valleys and then plunged down into the valleys, so that relatively level sections alternated with precipitous descents and ascents, the new turnpikes were cut along wooded river valleys and maintained gentle gradients as far as possible. Although often an expensive undertaking, the work was well done and the turnpike phase was responsible for the construction of some picturesque routes which delight the modern motorist.

Cornwall was in the forefront of turnpike-road construction. Nationally the great era of highway building was from 1760 to 1792 during which time over 750 Turnpike Acts were passed by Parliament. Prior to this, however, a start had been made on the Falmouth Road, a route established in connection with the Post Office packet service from Falmouth. A short turnpike had been constructed as early as 1754 from Falmouth to Grampound via Truro, but the first major advance came in 1759 when a start was made on turnpiking the old road from Launceston to Truro by way of Camelford, Wadebridge and St Columb. In 1760, a turnpike was established from West Taphouse to Liskeard and Cremyll, and schemes were afoot to build a new road across Bodmin Moor. But another nine years were to pass before this road was authorised (1769). It ran from a point three miles south of Launceston to an inn called the Indian Queen, ten miles beyond Bodmin, and gave a direct route over the top of the moors. It soon took the bulk of the mail and passenger traffic to Falmouth and west Cornwall, and still retains its pre-eminence as the modern A30. Other turnpikes were established between the more important towns, and in time Wadebridge was connected with Padstow and Bodmin, Truro with Redruth, Redruth with Falmouth, Helston with Redruth, Truro with St Agnes, and Bodmin with Lostwithiel.

Thus the new roads came gradually one by one, and the valleys of the Glynn, Ladock, Lanivet, Lamellan, Pencalenick and Perran-ar-Worthal, once deserted, were opened up with smoothly graded roads which threaded their way through miles of beautiful woods. Precipitous lanes which once led into places such as St Austell, Ponsanooth, Truro, Helston and Grampound were now replaced by finely graded descents. However, the full effectiveness of the new roads did not emerge until the improved surfacing techniques of the nineteenth century had been introduced by Thomas Telford (d.1834) and John McAdam (d.1836). The latter came to Cornwall in 1798 as a navy victualling officer at Falmouth. It was here that he experimented with roadmaking using the local Cornish greenstone as a base. He became general surveyor of all roads in 1827 whilst his grandson William was surveyor to the Truro Turnpike Trust for the period 1825–36. It was along these improved roads that the great mail and passenger coaches thundered, ablaze with their brightly uniformed guards, during much of the nineteenth century (Plate 41).

With the turnpike roads came other additions to the landscape. Tolls were collected by keepers posted at intervals along the roads. The keepers lived in toll-houses set close to the roadside, and constructed so that traffic approaching from either direction could be seen from within. The posts were often located in lonely places, as for example near Lockengate, south of Lanivet. The architectural features of these houses are very distinctive and many still exist, now functioning as normal dwelling-houses or farm labourers' cottages. Another important addition resulted from the need for servicing the passengers and horses on these routes. This brought forth a series of coaching inns or changing houses, such as the Norway Inn at Perran Wharf (Plate 42), the Royal Hotel at Truro, the Falmouth Arms at Ladock, Indian Queen on Goss Moor, the Royal Hotel in Bodmin and the famous Jamaica Inn at Bolventor. The Royal Hotels in Truro and Bodmin, alas, no longer exist, having recently given place to stores and offices.

Another visible link with the turnpike trust era is the numerous milestones which the trusts commissioned. Most are of stone but some are cast in iron (chiefly in south-east Cornwall). Some stones are very plain showing only an initial letter and a figure, e.g. those in the Glynn valley between Bodmin and Liskeard, or between Bodmin and Camelford. Between Truro and Indian Queen, however, there are triangular stones with cast-iron plates showing distances to Falmouth and London – a relic of the packet run to Falmouth. There are older milestones on the Royal Cornish Way in the vicinity of Mitchell, square in plan with a pyramid at the top. Additionally, there are to be found all over Cornwall curious milestones of local origin. This is a fascinating topic which has yet to receive detailed study.

Despite the improvements to the communication network

the density of traffic must, by modern standards, have been light. The *West Briton* of 2nd October, 1857 carries a letter from an aggrieved traveller commenting that, 'At all times of the day and night are to be found pigs and donkeys straying on these roads, and at night time I understand that it is no uncommon occurrence to find one of the latter animals asleep in the middle of the road'. Similarly, the St Austell Petty Sessions of February 1861 records a fine of ten shillings on John Kent for allowing his wagon 'to pass through the town of St Austell, without anyone in charge of the same, he being more than three-quarters of a mile behind, at Mount Charles in that parish'.

A road problem of quite different dimensions now faces Cornwall in the last quarter of the twentieth century. It is estimated that a quarter of Britain's home holidays are taken in the south-west, which means that approaching ten million holiday-makers now visit the region annually: the great majority include Cornwall either as a base or for day trips. As a result of the Beeching rail cuts of the 1960s, over 90 per cent of the visitors now arrive by road (85 per cent by car and 5 per cent by coach). As the holiday season is concentrated into the three summer months of June, July and August, the congestion on the roads at peak periods (usually the Saturday change-over day) has to be experienced to be believed. A major problem facing planners and local authorities in Cornwall is how to increase mobility and accessibility without disturbing the character of the region.

The situation has, of course, been aggravated by the construction of the M4 and M5 motorways which have brought the greater part of south-east England, the Midlands and South Wales within easy reach of Cornwall. The improved A38 road from Exeter to Plymouth is also of motorway standard and is linked to Cornwall by the new Saltash suspension bridge (Plate 44): but the motorist is rapidly made aware of different conditions as soon as he enters Cornwall. As a result the radical improvement of the main routes, the construction of a spine road, and the provision of relief roads and by-passes have been under continuous debate since the beginning of the car explosion in the mid-fifties. Some 'improvements' have been made but these are often alien to the

Cornish landscape and have an adverse effect. The remoteness of Bodmin Moor, for example, has been destroyed by a highway (substantially four-lane) which now updates the A30. Something of the earlier character can still be sampled, however, if the traveller follows the old track through Temple. On the other hand the peace of some towns has been preserved by the construction of by-passes, e.g. around Liskeard, Bodmin, Launceston, Redruth, Camborne and St Columb Major. The recent Redruth by-pass is of interest in that it by-passes an earlier by-pass of the nineteen thirties which had become absorbed in the built-up area. Modern motorway concepts should, however, preserve recent routeways for traffic alone.

Concomitant with the road traffic problem there has been a parking problem in or near the towns and tourist centres. In the height of the season acres of metal shimmering in the sun confront the visitor to any popular location. The capacity of many a site is indeed often limited by car-parking facilities as most car owners are reluctant to walk far from their cars. This preserves the character of some historic sites and beaches although at the expense of locations with less restricted facilities. Other ideas which have been adopted to meet the challenge of the car include the construction of car parks on the outskirts of centres such as Padstow, St Ives and Newquay in order to reduce internal congestion: and the establishment of pedestrian precincts in tourist-dominated centres such as Polperro and Looe.

Within Cornwall the bulk of the present trunk-road system consists of single two-lane carriageways supported by a dense network of mainly one-lane tracks, all of which are of substandard width and often poorly aligned according to modern motoring ideas. These produce the charm and character of the county for nine months of the year, but frequent chaos results in the summer months. The problem for the future is undoubtedly the resolution of the conflict between the preservation/conservation lobby and the improvement lobby, in order to achieve the greatest benefit for the majority without fundamentally disturbing the essential character of the countryside.

Ferries

Closely connected with certain of the routes are the ferries. Cornwall possesses a larger number of these than any other English county and many are of great antiquity. Three ferries, Torpoint, The King Harry, and Bodinnick, are nowadays capable of handling motor vehicles, while passenger ferries still operate at Flushing, St Mawes, Padstow, Polruan, Cremyll, Helford, Greenbank (Falmouth), Restronguet, Malpas, Portcuel, Antony and occasionally elsewhere.

The oldest and most important of the ferries were those crossing the Tamar at Saltash and Cremyll. These, and other now abandoned ferries at Halton and Calstock, were attached to their respective manors, and records of their use go back to the thirteenth century. Torpoint is, in comparison, a mere youngster, as it was created in 1791 by an Act of Parliament. Now, however, with the demise of Saltash ferry as a result of the new suspension bridge, it has become important along with Cremyll in linking Torpoint and Millbrook with Plymouth.

The Bodinnick ferry over the Fowey goes back to the fourteenth century. The earliest reference to it so far discovered is dated 1344. The well-known King Harry Passage across the Fal is probably of the same age. The origin of this name has long excited speculation, but Charles Henderson was probably right in associating it with Henry VI, to whom a small chapel, which stood on the eastern side of the passage, had been dedicated. Most of the ferries had adjacent passage-houses, some of which are of considerable antiquity.

Canals

Coastwise shipping was limited in its ability to penetrate the complete length of some of the estuaries, and this problem was doubly aggravated by the growing size of ships and the steady shrinkage of many channels through silting. By the seventeenth century it had become necessary to transfer goods to barges in order to ascend the rivers, and in this way Lostwithiel could be reached on the Fowey, Morwellham on the Tamar, Tideford on the Tiddy, Landrake on the Lynher,

Plate 41 Boscastle: road travel in 1913, a four-horse coach leaving the Wellington Hotel.

Plate 42 Perran Wharf: road travel in 1982, the old coaching inns take on a new lease of life. Cars parked outside the Norway Inn on the Truro-Falmouth turnpike road.

Plate 43 Greystone Bridge: from the Cornish side looking into Devon, built in 1439 over the Tamar, one of the finest fifteenth-century bridges still in daily use.

Plate 44 Saltash: Brunel's railway bridge of 1859 and the modern road suspension bridge of 1961.

Plate 45 Bude: the lock entrance from the sea to the Bude Canal constructed in the 1820s.

Plate 46 Bodmin: one of Brunel's nineteenth-century railway viaducts near Bodmin.

Plate 47 Godrevy lighthouse: constructed in 1859 on Godrevy Island, this lighthouse controls a wide stretch of the west Cornish coast.

Plate 48 Morwenstow: the Composite Signals Organisation satellite station.

and Sandplace on the Looe. Efforts were naturally made to lengthen the stretches of the rivers already used, and as early as the reign of Charles I a rather ambitious scheme was passed through the House of Commons to make all the rivers of Cornwall completely navigable. But the country was soon embroiled in the Civil War and nothing came of the project. A little later, in 1667, Trevanion attempted to improve the Fal up to Grampound, but the work proved too costly for completion.

The first real canal in Cornwall dates from 1773 with the attempt to link Mawgan Porth, St Columb and Porth (near Newquay) for the inland carriage of sand, manure and coal, and for the export of stone. This canal was the brainchild of John Edyvean and it introduced the principle of the inclined plane, which was later to prove so successful elsewhere in Cornwall, in place of locks. The barges were all fitted with wheels in order to negotiate the inclined planes but water was still the main motive power for the lift. Two portions of this canal were built. One from Trenance Point above Mawgan Porth for about five miles past Porth Farm, Moreland, Lower Lanherne, New Farm, Trevedras and Bolingey to Whitewater. There was an inclined plane at Trenance up which the boats were hauled. The second, shorter section ran from Lusty Glaze south of St Columb Porth past St Columb Minor to Rialton with another inclined plane at Lusty Glaze. The canals were opened between 1777 and 1779 but operated only until 1781: they have long since faded into the countryside but their routes can be traced with the aid of large scale plans.

This time was the heyday of canals in England so that it is not surprising to find a number of schemes being proposed for Cornwall despite the terrain. Most foundered long before any turf was cut. The Padstow-Lostwithiel and Polbrook Canal scheme of 1793–6, the Helston Canal project of 1796, the Hayle-Camborne Canal proposal of 1801, and the Retyn and East Wheal Rose scheme of 1821 are examples of projects which literally never got on to the ground.

In the 1820s, however, one of Cornwall's most successful canal ventures, the Bude Canal (Plate 45) began to take shape after several abortive efforts. John Edyvean was again the initiator as early as 1774: John Smeaton (1778), Edmund

Leach (1785), Lord Stanhope (1793), Robert Fulton (1794) were amongst those who kept the project in being, but it was not until an Act of 1819 that work actually started and in 1823 the first section of the canal was opened. Eventually the canal was to extend to North Tamerton, Bridgetown and Druxton with feeds to the Alfardisworthy reservoir and Holsworthy – a total distance of over thirty-five miles. The canal was a remarkable piece of engineering, the longest tub-boat canal then in existence, with six inclined planes in place of locks. The goods carried were chiefly sea-sand, lime, manure, coal, culm, timber, salt and grain. The canal continued in operation for over seventy years: its demise was largely related to the coming of the railway to Holsworthy and Bude in the 1890s. It then became part of a water supply scheme for a while. The old reservoir, now known as Tamar Lake, was transferred to the Devon Water Board in 1967. From Burmsdown to Hele Bridge much of the canal has been sold. Below Hele to Bude sections are in local authority ownership and in Bude itself the old broad waterway is used for recreational purposes. The Marham Church to North Tamerton and Bridgetown sections are now completely abandoned but, with the inclined planes, there are parts which remain very much in evidence in the present-day landscape, and the canal route can be traced across country without difficulty.

Another successful canal connected Liskeard to Looe. This opened in 1828, again after several abortive attempts dating from Edmund Leach's 1777 proposal. Sand, lime and coal were the basis of its initial success but in 1837 the Caradon copper mines were opened up and soon the canal was carrying copper ore outwards, to be followed by granite from the Cheesewring quarries, so that from 1846 onwards it became for a time very profitable. By 1860, however, a railway line paralleling the canal had been constructed and the canal traffic declined thereafter, ceasing altogether by the beginning of the present century.

The last canal to be built in Cornwall was actually constructed in connection with a railway scheme. This was J. T. Treffry's Par Canal of 1847. The canal ran from the sea harbour at Par to Pontsmill where it connected with the Treffry tramway. It was barely two miles long and was used for tin and lead ores as well as china clay; it functioned until 1873.

Railways

Cornwall's contribution to the history of railway development is more significant than is commonly realised. A plaque on a building in Cross Street, Redruth, records that 'here lived William Murdock (1754–1839) who made the first locomotive here and tested it in 1784'. It is true that this was only a model but Murdock was soon followed by Richard Trevithick, born at Carn Brea in 1771, who seems to have been the first to run a trial locomotive on rails in 1802. Some authorities have placed this event in Cornwall but more recent research suggests the Darby foundry at Coalbrookdale in Shropshire with which Trevithick was associated at the time.

It was the development of the mineral tram roads associated with tin and copper mining that put Cornwall ahead of many other counties in the railway era. Based at first on gravity combined with horse traction most of the individual mineral lines eventually became connected and employed steam traction. The first of the horse-drawn gravity tramways was the Poldice to Portreath line which served the copper mines around Scorrier and St Day. This was built between 1809 and 1818 and continued in use until about 1865. It was followed by the important Redruth and Chasewater Railway constructed between 1824 and 1826 which, with its extension to Devoran on the Fal, served the rich copper area of Gwennap. In the 1830s traffic on this line was in excess of 60,000 tons annually. A combination of gravity and horse traction was used until 1854 when two steam tank locomotives were introduced. This line actually lasted until 1915 although a receiver had been appointed in 1879 following upon the closure of the copper mines.

A third mineral line was the Pentewan Railway constructed in 1829 to facilitate the transport of china clay from the St Austell area to the harbour at Pentewan; locomotives were introduced on this line in 1874. Although not officially allowed, passengers were in fact conveyed on this line for 3d.

a time, presumably in the clay wagons as the only saloon carriage available was that built for the Hawkins family in 1875. The line lasted until 1918.

The Bodmin and Wadebridge Railway which followed the three preceding mineral lines marked an important step forward in catering for passengers and employing steam traction from the outset. Conceived and promoted by Sir William Molesworth in 1831 it received assent in 1832 and opened in 1834. The primary purpose of the railway was to convey sea-sand from Wadebridge to the farmlands of the Camel valley but passenger coaches were also employed and cheap day excursion tickets were soon introduced. A special excursion in 1840 even conveyed passengers to Bodmin to witness the public execution of the Lightfoot brothers; the *West Briton* newspaper recorded the presence of a crowd of between 20,000 and 25,000 at this event. In 1846 the Bodmin and Wadebridge was bought by the London and South Western Railway but it was not until 1895 that a connection to the parent company's line was made, after the connection to the Great Western system at Bodmin Road in 1887. The Wenford Bridge branch of the old Bodmin and Wadebridge still conveys considerable quantities of china clay from Stannon on the edge of Bodmin Moor to the main line at Bodmin Road,

The Hayle Railway, constructed between 1834 and 1837, covered an area from Redruth and Portreath westwards to Hayle; with its various branches a network of some seventeen miles appeared before the end of 1838. Both horses and steam locomotives were employed, the locomotives being locally built in the Copperhouse Foundry. A passenger service was introduced in 1843 and a contemporary report noted, 'we are glad to learn that although the train went three times over the lines during the day, no accident of any consequence occurred'. This line initially included rope-worked inclines and small sections of it are still in use today.

The West Cornwall Railway was formed in 1846 to reconstruct the Hayle Railway and extend it to Truro and Penzance but it was not until 1855 that the extensions were completed. That it got off to a good start can be gathered from the following report in the *West Briton* newspaper for 3rd August, 1855.

> The weather was fine, and the West Cornwall Railway having advertised cheap excursion trains for that day, an immense number of people took the opportunity afforded them of enjoying a day's pleasure. Shortly after eight o'clock in the morning, a train of forty-five carriages, propelled by three engines, was despatched from Truro station, the number in the train at starting being 1,016. At the stations between Truro and Camborne large additions of teetotallers and others were made to the train, which on its arrival at Penzance consisted of eighty-four carriages. The engines were sent back for the people left behind at the Hayle and St Ives stations, who were brought down in a train of twenty-six carriages; and besides these, the ordinary train from Truro, took on ten extra carriages from Camborne, full of people who could not be accommodated in the first train that passed from Truro earlier in the morning. Altogether, with the attraction of the teetotal celebration, and the opportunity of a cheap excursion, the number conveyed to Penzance on the line this day was 5,612 and the receipts of the Company amounted to £285. 19s. 5d.

Excursions were not only local affairs: on 22nd June, 1860 the *West Briton* records a 'cheap excursion train from Scotland to the Land's End, arrived at Truro on Tuesday evening, at 7.15. The train consisted of eight carriages, containing 400 excursionists, of whom 300 went on to Penzance the same evening. The excursion was organised by Mr Cook, of Leicester.' This was one of Thomas Cook's early ventures.

Brunel was involved in the construction of the West Cornwall Railway and the battle of the gauges was by then in full swing, Cornwall by this time having acquired a mixture. In 1866, the West Cornwall was taken over by the Great Western and the broad gauge was laid throughout so that both broad- and narrow-gauge trains could be catered for. The St Ives branch was opened in 1877 as part of the West Cornwall line and it had the distinction of being the last section of railway constructed for Brunel's broad gauge.

The Cornwall Railway emerged in 1846 with plans to link Plymouth, Truro and Falmouth, together with several branches, but work progressed slowly as the project was really dependent on the link with the Great Western over the Tamar at Saltash. Brunel's masterpiece (Plate 44) was opened on 4th May, 1859 and subsequent events were to make this a historic date in the evolution of the Cornish landscape as thereafter the county lost its isolation and became wide open to English influences.

The Royal Albert Bridge over the Tamar was a mid-Victorian wonder – over 700 yards long and containing 4,000 tons of iron, it rose 100 feet above the river. A further feature of the Cornwall Railway beyond the bridge was the large number of viaducts, no less than thirty-one being necessary between Saltash and Truro. These again are mainly attributable to Brunel. Originally built of timber on masonry piers they spanned the deep valleys in a majestic fashion, producing some breath-taking views from the carriage windows. The timber spans were replaced after 1871 by masonry structures or iron truss girders and these are the viaducts we see today, often with the old masonry piers alongside (Plate 46). The problem of the terrain also forced the engineers to locate stations at some distance from the then centres of Liskeard, Bodmin, St Austell and Truro, although subsequent expansion of the two latter towns has brought the stations into the present urban areas. The single line from Truro to Falmouth was opened in 1863 and this involved eight further viaducts.

The Liskeard and Caradon Railway was another mineral line incorporated in 1843 and opened in 1844 with further branches in 1846. This was constructed to extract the copper of the Caradon mines and the granite of the Cheesewring area. The railway took the materials to the Liskeard and Looe Canal at Moorswater and thence by barge to Looe for export. Eventually the canal was filled in and the Liskeard to Looe Railway replaced it. The Liskeard and Caradon Railway initially was another gravity and horse-traction combination and passengers were conveyed in wagons only unofficially as accompanied luggage! In the course of its life many shorter feeder lines were built in the area and an extension across Bodmin Moor to Launceston nearly came to fruition. Various halts, stations, bridges, long since abandoned, can be traced from this period. The Great Western Railway worked both the Liskeard and Looe, and the Liskeard and Caradon, lines from 1909. The Caradon section was closed in 1916 and the Looe section was absorbed by the Great Western Railway in 1923.

In central Cornwall an enterprising landowner from Fowey by name of J. T. Treffry began in the 1840s a series of tram roads to serve the china clay and granite quarries of the St Austell area. He also had visions of linking the north and south coasts of Cornwall and an important step was taken in this direction with the Newquay Railway of 1849. Treffry's various railways eventually grouped together, along with the Tamar, Kit Hill and Callington lines to form the Cornwall Minerals Railway. Various further developments took place in the 1870s with branches being constructed to Fowey, Carbis and Perranporth. The Cornwall Minerals Railway lost its identity in 1896 on absorption by the Great Western Railway.

The London and South Western Railway had acquired the Bodmin and Wadebridge Railway in 1846 but it was to be many years before a connection to the parent body was made. Acting through the Launceston and South Devon Railway, the London and South Western was pushing its tracks into the remoter parts of Devon, reaching Halwill in 1879. This stimulated entrepreneurs in north Cornwall to form the North Cornwall Railway to serve an area devoid of rail tracks. It was not until 1899, however, that the line from Padstow through Wadebridge and Delabole to Launceston was complete. Wadebridge and the connection with the Bodmin and Wadebridge had been reached in 1895, and a further line had been thrown out to Bude from Halwill in 1898. Eventually taken over by the Southern Railway, this northern route acquired, in 1927, the famous Atlantic Coast Express which acted as a foil to the Great Western's Cornish Riviera Express.

The Great Western Railway completes railway construction in Cornwall. This railway was really an amalgamation of existing lines so far as Cornwall was concerned, although it had stimulated the construction of the southern route. Step by step the Great Western acquired the West Cornwall Railway, the Cornwall Railway, the Cornwall Minerals Railway, the

Liskeard and Caradon, and the Liskeard and Looe lines so that by the turn of the century it dominated the southern services. The broad gauge came to an end in 1892 when the mammoth task of converting the line to standard gauge between Exeter and Truro was completed in two days with the aid of 5,000 men distributed along the track. The next thirty years saw bridges strengthened or rebuilt and the line gradually doubled so that eventually the only remaining single track was that over the Royal Albert Bridge. Another short addition took place between 1903 and 1905 with the construction of the Chacewater, Perranporth and Newquay line: the first Cornish Riviera Express ran on 1st July, 1904 whilst the early part of the century also saw a number of mineral sections both closed and extended as adjustments were made to the changing economic situation.

The direct contribution of the railways to the landscape of Cornwall will be obvious to the discerning traveller: the deeply-incised topography necessitated long sweeping curves, high embankments and deep cuttings which alternate with short tunnels, lofty viaducts and dramatic bridges. Few English counties can produce such spectacular stretches of railway track as are found in Cornwall. Undoubtedly the most dramatic is the succession of lofty viaducts along the old Great Western line through south Cornwall (Plate 46).

Today, however, there is another aspect of the direct contribution to the landscape which, alas, is now only too familiar throughout Cornwall. This is the pattern of abandoned lines closed in part by the collapse of tin and copper mining and granite quarrying, but mainly by the Beeching cuts of the 1960s. Most of the Ordnance Survey's maps of Cornwall now have numerous 'track of old railway' symbols on them and the railway enthusiast or historian has more than ample scope for tracing abandoned lines in the landscape. Generally speaking, the closures have taken place in the reverse order to that in which the lines originally appeared and today only the main line from Plymouth to Penzance with the branches to Newquay, Falmouth and St Ives remains of a complex network built up in the nineteenth century. There was even debate in the 1970s and early 1980s (the Serpell Report) as to whether this section of the Western Region should be kept, but with the energy crisis of the 1980s there are some who see a possible resuscitation of railway transport.

Perhaps the indirect effect of the railways upon the landscape has been even more significant. The opening of the Saltash Bridge heralded the beginning of what might well be called 'the second English invasion' of Cornwall. The county at last lost its isolation from the rest of England and the infiltration of cultural influences from across the Tamar was much quickened. The basis of the economic life of Cornwall began to change as the mining and fishing industries decayed and were replaced by the tourist and holiday industry. Old towns and villages altered their character and new ones grew at rail-heads on the coast. Agriculture began to change from a subsistence type of farming to more specialised dairy farming, and the growth of early vegetables and flowers for export from the county. Building materials increased in variety, and architectural styles were for long in a state of flux as new ideas entered the Duchy.

The arrival of the internal combustion engine in the twentieth century has, of course, spread many of these influences into parts of the county which had not been touched by the railways. But the car has not produced such violent changes as the railway wrought, for there has been merely a switch from rail to road traffic, and many ancillary tourist services for which the railway was originally responsible are now common to both. Furthermore, the modern motorist inherited a road-pattern which was already largely completed by the mid-nineteenth century. Apart from renewing an old prosperity along these lines of communication, the present century has not seen any real major change in the road pattern other than the construction of the by-passes to towns such as Liskeard, Bodmin, Launceston, Redruth and Camborne, and the widening and straightening of some of the worst sections. As we have seen, the road network handed down from the Middle Ages and the turnpike era is in the main ill-adapted to the flood of traffic which pours into the county every summer. What the twenty-first century, with diminishing supplies of petrol, will bring remains to be seen.

Airfields

Cornwall has few airfields for the need is rarely great and the terrain rarely favourable. However, the county occupies a strategic position in relation to the western approaches to the British Isles, and a number of military and naval airfields were constructed during the Second World War of which some still remain. Their siting was essentially geographical, in nearly all cases the flat Pliocene erosion surfaces were chosen. Within the airfields most of the earlier landscape pattern has been swept away. Some, e.g. at St Eval, Mullion, Perranporth and Davidstow, have since been abandoned and the land has reverted to agricultural use, but two important airfields remain at Culdrose near Helston, and St Mawgan near Newquay. Their wide, open, hedgeless and treeless areas, with great concrete runways, hangars and huts, seem strangely foreign to Cornwall, although serving such an important function.

Telecommunications

No description of the impact of communications upon the landscape of Cornwall would be complete without a reference to lighthouses and radio. It is perhaps not surprising that Cornwall's strategic position with reference to the western approaches and its lengthy coastline of 268 miles (the longest of any county in England) has produced a number of historic lighthouses. The original Lizard light dates back to between 1619 and 1630. Another very early light was installed at St Agnes in the Scillies in 1680 and this operated for 231 years until 1911 when it was replaced by Peninnis Head on St Mary's. The famous Eddystone Reef lighthouse was first completed as early as 1698 but the present tower, built of De Lank granite, is the fifth to be constructed on this spot. The Longships Reef light was first displayed in 1795: Bishop Rock, Godrevy (Plate 47) and Wolf Rock followed in 1847, 1859 and 1870 respectively. Elsewhere on the mainland are a succession of lighthouses such as St Anthony, Penzance, Newlyn, Tater-Du, St Ives, Pendeen and Trevose, which provide assistance for shipping on one of Britain's most dangerous coasts.

Cornwall has also figured prominently in the story of radio for it was at Poldhu near Mullion that Marconi succeeded in 1901 in transmitting the first wireless signal across the Atlantic. Poldhu Radio Station subsequently became an important research centre but it was closed in 1934 and the site cleared in 1937. A granite memorial has been erected on the cliff edge and a search in the adjacent fields will reveal traces of the transmitters of those early days. It was as a direct result of the Marconi experiments that the Canadian and South African beam transmitters were built near Lanivet (Bodmin) in 1926 and 1927. Finally in 1962 the Post Office established at Goonhilly Down, only two and a half miles from Poldhu, the first satellite communication ground station in Britain. Cornwall had thus contributed to and witnessed all forms of communication from the Falmouth mail packet service of 1688 to the Telstar satellite almost three centuries later. A further satellite station has now been established by the Composite Signals Organisation at Morwenstow (Plate 48).

Select Bibliography

British Road Federation, *Roads and the West Country*.

Fairclough, A., *Cornwall's Railways* (1970).

Grundy, G. B., 'Ancient Highways of Devon and Cornwall', *Archaeological Journal*, Vol. xcviii (1941).

Hadfield, Charles, *The Canals of South West England* (1967).

Henderson, C. and Coates, H., *Old Cornish Bridges and Streams* (1928).

Noall, Cyril, *Cornish Mail and Stage Coaches* (1964).

7. Land-use patterns and the landscape

Townscape. Farmscape. Wildscape. Rurban fringe. Marginal fringe.

We have so far been largely concerned with an analysis of the minutiae of the landscape, probing the origins of prehistoric sites, of hedges and boundaries, communication lines, settlement sites, hamlets and towns, and the impact of agricultural and industrial activities. It is, however, an amalgam of all these aspects that presents itself to the visitor and the resident – an amalgam that changes not only with time but also with space – an amalgam that could be confusing, difficult to comprehend and describe, unless some attempt at a geographical synthesis is made.

The simplest synthesis is the urban/rural approach, but this is of little assistance in understanding the problems of the landscape. A more realistic approach is through the patterns of 'scapes and fringes' proposed by the Second Land Utilisation Survey of Britain. Five very broad and inclusive patterns or territories have been recognised, each of which can if necessary be sub-divided to produce more complex refinements. The five patterns of landscape which are readily detectable both on the ground and on the map consist of three 'scapes' – townscape, farmscape and wildscape, and two 'fringes' – the rural/urban (rurban) fringe lying between townscape and farmscape and the marginal fringe found between the farmscape and wildscape.

Townscape

Townscape, with which we are most familiar, is the fully urbanised area consisting of a mixed pattern of houses, shops, factories, parks, roads and railways. Its key feature is the

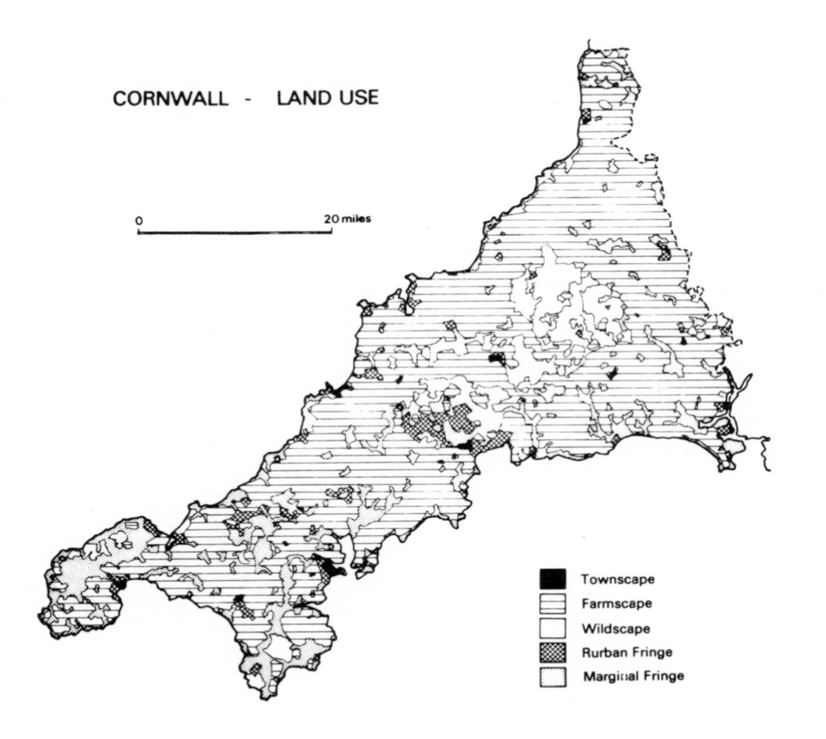

Fig. 18. The land-use patterns of Cornwall according to the Second Land Utilisation Survey of Britain undertaken in the 1960s.

dominance of settlement. Farmland and vegetation are either absent or sufficiently sparse and subordinate to be absorbed without damaging the essential urban aspect. So far as Cornwall is concerned the origin, development and character of the urban area forming the townscape have been dealt with in chapter 4 (Plates 28, 51, 53, 54). Whilst an important element in the landscape, true townscape only occupies 0.5 per cent of the land surface in Cornwall as by far the greater part of the settlement is scattered in the rural/urban (rurban) fringe territory.

Farmscape

Farmscape is characterised by agricultural use – either pastoral or arable in the widest sense and including small patches of woodland and small settlements. A good deal of variety exists within this major territory and change over a short time-span is often noticeable as farmers respond to economic fluctuations. As 68.8 per cent of the land surface of Cornwall occurs in this territory it tends to dominate the landscape and we shall return below to consider its changing face (Plates 50, 55).

Wildscape

Wildscape is dominated by natural vegetation, as in mountains and moorlands, heaths and marshes, and woodlands. Some wildscape provides a nearly natural wildlife habitat; other areas have been impoverished by clearance of their natural woodland cover but have adapted as semi-natural habitats. Still others have been reforested, or are used as unimproved grazings. Some are occupied by lakes. All are much more sparsely inhabited than farmscape (Plate 49). Surprisingly, the percentage of land in Cornwall to which this description applies only amounts to 4.9 per cent, much less than the percentage for England and Wales as a whole. This reflects the fact that, apart from Bodmin Moor, Cornwall lacks really extensive tracts of wilderness such as are found in parts of northern England and central Wales. Much of the Cornish wildscape has disappeared as a result of agricultural inroads and it is the marginal fringe territory which is in greater evidence (see below). The essential areas and character of the Cornish wildscape have been touched upon in chapter 1.

Rurban fringe

Between the scapes we find the fringes. These, in the geographer's eye, are zones of conflict where the respective scapes are battling for dominance: dominance often related to changing economic circumstances. Between townscape and farmscape we may find either a narrow or wide rural/urban band or rurban fringe where the town has begun to make inroads upon the countryside in a patchy pattern of development. As settlement invades the farmland, it casts an urban shadow of trespass and damage and may make the surrounding land uneconomic to farm. The wastefulness and injustice of urban sprawl was recognised in the 1930s and one of the chief aims of the Planning Act of 1947 was to replace sprawling development by compact urbanisation. The modern objective is infilling in the rurban fringe to upgrade it into townscape, and avoidance of sprawl in virgin farmscape to prevent it being downgraded into rurban fringe.

Cornwall, like all other English counties, has its rurban fringe and some 4 per cent of the land surface falls into this territory. The problems in Cornwall are related in part to the modern holiday cottage and retirement bungalow, many acres of which are to be found in areas such as Polzeath and Rock on the north bank of the Camel. Larger rurban areas have also been created by past and present mining and quarrying. The china-clay area of Hensbarrow Down is a typical rurban mix of quarries, tips, cottages, derelict areas, small holdings and patches of rough vegetation. The old metal-mining area near Camborne and Redruth also features as rurban fringe, with its derelict sites, many of which are now overgrown with colonising vegetation. An increasing awareness of the need for landscape conservation is, however, gradually eradicating the worst of the eyesores and bringing some order to what would otherwise be a somewhat chaotic situation.

Marginal fringe

The last of the five land-use patterns lies between farmscape and wildscape. This is the marginal fringe which is another zone of conflict. It is typified in Cornwall by the landscape of parts of the Penwith peninsula and the borders of Bodmin Moor. Improved and unimproved land are interlocked in a patchy pattern, where the better land is reclaimed or the worse land reverts to nature in response to economic booms or slumps in food prices. In some areas long-term patches of unimproved land may be colonised by woodland, or planted, and so give rise to a more stable and attractive marginal subtype. Cornwall has, *in toto*, some 21.8 per cent of the land surface falling within the marginal-fringe territory, an amount well above the national percentage.

With some 68.8 per cent of the land surface of Cornwall in the farmscape territory, it is not surprising that the first impression acquired by the visitor is of a rural-agricultural landscape. This impression is reinforced by the fact that over half of the marginal-fringe land is farmland also. This means that by far the greater part of the landscape is farmland which by now might be thought to have reached some degree of both maturity and stability. A steady state or static condition is, however, illusory and there is a slow continuous process of change going on depending upon the changing methods and technology of farming. The appearance of the landscape alters accordingly.

In the eighteenth century, considerable quantities of grain were grown in south-east Cornwall as well as in the middle and western parts in response to the demand from the metalliferous mining districts. The best soils carried wheat and the poorer soils rye, oats and barley. Barley in particular occupied large areas in the north of the county between Newquay and Port Isaac – an area then known as the granary of Cornwall. Much of the farming was essentially of a subsistence character, with small family farms providing a generally low productivity. The unenclosed moorlands were extensively used as grazings for cattle and sheep, the dispersed locations of the granite masses giving many farms a mixture of land holdings.

Plate 49 Wildscape: Bodmin Moor with Brown Willy, the highest point (1,375 feet) in Cornwall. The massive earthen bank in the foreground marks the limit of medieval cultivation.

Plate 50 Farmscape: an air view of the country near St Neot looking south. Note the wooded valleys and the farms of the erosion surfaces.

Plate 51 Townscape: an air view of Camborne, an early nineteenth-century industrial town which grew out of a medieval hamlet. See also Plate 28.

Plate 52 Mousehole: part of the west coast of Mount's Bay showing the pattern of small fields with high protective hedges on the sheltered eastern facing slopes used for horticulture.

Plate 53 Fowey: Customs House Hill.

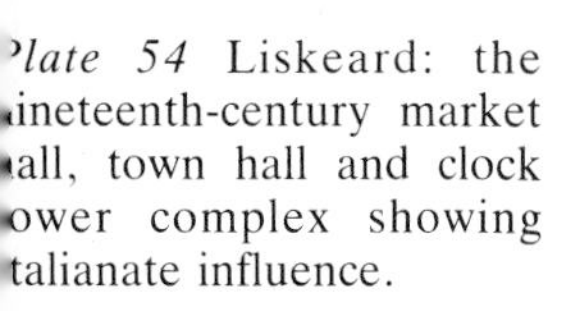

'late 54 Liskeard: the ineteenth-century market all, town hall and clock ower complex showing talianate influence.

Plate 55 Godolphin Cross: a medieval lane with a twentieth-century dairy herd typifying the Cornish farmscape. Note the granite-faced hedgebank.

The second half of the nineteenth century saw a significant change as a result of the Corn Laws of the 1840s, the decline of the mining and fishing industries, and the agricultural depression of the 1870s. There was a steady switch from corn growing to mixed farming and pasture. Apart from the plough-up campaigns of the two world wars, this has been the pattern of agriculture in Cornwall in the twentieth century.

Dairy activities have been aided by the development of good rail and road communications and the establishment of a number of milk factories, and as a result pig-keeping has also become important. The railway links further stimulated the production of special early crops and horticulture has flourished.

The outstanding landscape effect of these slowly evolving trends has been to produce a dominance of grass fields. Improved grass now occupies 55.45 per cent of the land surface and pasture is the basis of much of the farming in the region as well as the key to much of its prosperity. The Cornish farmer practises a system of long leys of from four to eight years so that it is difficult to make a distinction between permanent and temporary grass: often fields are ploughed only when they begin to show signs of infestation or a need for reseeding. In many areas permanent grassland may be restricted to river flood-plains or steep hillsides: in Cornwall the river meadow is rare but the steep hillside which is too difficult to plough is very common; these inevitably carry permanent grass.

The grass supports dairy cattle, beef cattle and also sheep. Dairy cattle in particular increased after the Second World War in response to improved transport facilities in east Cornwall and improved processing facilities at milk factories in west Cornwall. Markets for east Cornwall are now readily accessible in the Midlands and the London area, whilst the creameries at St Erth, Lostwithiel and Camborne cater for west Cornwall. As a by-product of the increase in dairy cattle there has been a little realised upsurge in pig keeping which has been fostered by the small size of the agricultural holdings and the availability of local skim milk and of swill from the urban areas. As a result, pig keeping is now common in the Lizard and Penwith peninsulas, in mid-Cornwall and south-east Cornwall. The region now supplies large numbers of store pigs to other areas for fattening.

Beef cattle and sheep will also be found on some lowland farms, but this activity is more characteristic of the upland areas where farming impinges upon the wildscape and marginal fringe appears – fields going in and out of use according to market conditions and government grants and subsidies for the keeping of stock. Throughout the region a considerable part of the sheep and cattle production is destined for fattening in other areas of lowland England. Currently some 800,000 head of cattle and sheep will be found in Cornwall during the main grazing season.

Arable land, as might be expected, is much less in evidence in Cornwall than in the rest of England. Only 12.84 per cent of the land area is given over to cereal production as compared to a national percentage of 18.57. The post-war years have indeed seen a continued decline in wheat, oats and mixed corn (dredge) in Cornwall, but these grains have been largely replaced by barley and the total arable acreage tends to remain the same. Wheat has never been suited to the damp climate of south-west England and for many years dredge corn, a mixture of oats and barley, was more typical of the Cornish scene. One grain supports the other against wind and rain, they draw nutrients from different soil levels and it is unusual for them both to fail at the same time. New strains of barley, especially the Proctor, and government subsidies have, however, more recently favoured barley production. It must also be borne in mind that the crop is important not only for feeding to animals but also for the supply of straw. The balance between barley and dredge is likely to alter in the future as new strains of oats appear and agricultural policies at the government level are modified.

The third major land use giving character to the landscape which will strike the discerning visitor is the complex of activities grouped together under the general term horticulture. The total area devoted to horticulture in Cornwall is not large – some 2.22 per cent which is less than the national figure of 3.76 per cent of the land area – but much is concentrated on the south coast of the county and hence more noticeable. Turnips, swedes, mangolds, potatoes and kale may be found generally throughout Cornwall, supporting the life of both man and beast on the farms, but the special climatic conditions of the southern coastal zone permit the growth of early high-value crops that will overcome the cost of transport to more distant markets. The risk element for these enterprises is high as frost and cold winds or disease may decimate crops whilst competition from elsewhere may reduce sales. Bulb and flower producers now have to contend with forcing techniques in glasshouse cultivation, early potato growers have to meet competition from Pembroke, the Channel Islands and some continental countries. Broccoli growers face imports from France and Italy and in the overlap season from Kent and Lincolnshire. It is the out-of-season crops that probably compete more effectively than the early crops: broccoli, anemones and violets during the winter season are hence safer than the early narcissi, daffodils, potatoes, spring cabbages and strawberries. In adjacent Devon, glasshouse cultivation and a specialisation in tomato production has appeared, but this has yet to extend to Cornwall.

Horticulture is concentrated in four main areas: the Scilly Isles, the Penzance-Mount's Bay area, the west bank of the Fal, and the west bank of the lower Tamar. In some parts, notably the Scilly Isles, the growth of shelter hedges of tamarisk, veronica and escalonia to protect the plants against the wind produces a unique kind of landscape. Wind also plays a dominant role in concentrating horticultural locations on the west banks of the Fal and Tamar, and it encourages the continuance of well-sheltered tiny fields in the Penwith peninsula, notably near Mousehole (Plate 52).

True wildscape in Cornwall accounts for only 4.9 per cent of the land surface and is made up of heathland, moorland, rough pasture, woodland and coastal dune areas. There are now few large continuous areas and even Bodmin Moor has lost much of its original isolated character. Agricultural incursions at the edges of the traditional granite moorlands have converted much of the wildscape into marginal-fringe land: most of the Penwith peninsula and the whole of Carnmenellis have been so transformed, whilst china-clay extraction and tin mining on Hensbarrow Down have also effectively removed most traces of the ancient wildscape.

Smaller separate wildscape areas also occur on the serpentine rock of the Lizard peninsula (Goonhilly Downs) and there are some notable coastal dune complexes at Gwithian and Penhale Sands. The ancient wildscape of St Breock Downs on the sandstone between Newquay and Wadebridge has now, however, passed into the marginal-fringe category.

All the moorlands now provide considerable pasture areas for beef cattle and sheep and also ponies. All the areas have been nibbled away at the edges by adjoining farms as efforts have been made to take in fields and improve the pastures: there are even a few small farms in the centre of Bodmin Moor itself. In some areas, poor drainage gives rise to the development of rushes which grade into reedy moors and open cotton-grass moors which are difficult to utilise. This is a feature of the northern part of Cornwall and more especially the Carboniferous Culm measures. Steep valley slopes are also often covered in bracken or other rough vegetation as near Port Gaverne and Tintagel.

The Cornish cliffs also carry a narrow fringe of heathland made up of gorse, heather and bracken which may become quite wide in places. As already noted, areas of blown sand are extensive at Hayle, Gwithian, Perranporth and in the Scilly Isles. These often exhibit the sequence of developing vegetation and some parts have been improved for permanent pasture. Rough marsh pasture is further found in the valley floors of the Lynher, Camel and Allen valleys.

There are no important forest lands in Cornwall but 5.76 per cent of the land surface now carries woodland. This is an increase over the pre-war figure of 3.5 per cent and reflects efforts to expand the acreage of trees. Most of the woodland is in central Cornwall on the steep slopes of river valleys such as the Camel, Allen, Fowey, West Looe and the Fal. Some efforts have been made to reclaim the moorland by planting, for example at Wilsey Down between Launceston and Camelford. However, the Forestry Commission has had to recognise that Cornwall is not one of the country's potentially important forest areas, as moorland and heathland, which would elsewhere be ideal for planting, are here too exposed to the fierce Atlantic gales. Afforestation could only be achieved by the slow and gradual building up of shelter belts.

The final 'land-use' of significance in the landscape is the derelict and disused land. This can occur in any of the five territories noted. As we have seen, Cornwall has nearly twice the national percentage of derelict land and in some areas it is a major element in the landscape. Paradoxically, however, derelict land in Cornwall is less offensive than elsewhere in Britain and in some cases may even be said to be a tourist attraction, adding its own peculiar charm to the scene! From a distance at least, there is something unique, one might almost say a mystique, about the sparkling white china-clay tips and pits of Hensbarrow Down north of St Austell: something awesome about the enormous excavations in the Carboniferous slate region between Delabole and Tintagel, and in the granite quarrying on Bodmin Moor near the Cheesewring. Time and vegetation have also softened the effects of medieval tin-streaming and nineteenth-century tin and copper mining in the Redruth-Camborne area. The solid but gaunt chimney stacks of the abandoned engine-houses have become industrial monuments to this phase of Cornish history. Surrounded by bracken and gorse-covered mine spoil they have a charm of their own and produce an ethos which is essentially Cornish. Human activity has indeed here added variety to the landscape and produced tourist attractions which contrast with the picture of dismal derelict land in other parts of Britain.

Though Cornwall has been well served by its early cartographers, their maps of the county give little indication of the details of land-use. Thus the maps of Saxton (1576), Gascoyne (1690), Norden (1584–1625), Overton (1712), Kitchen (1750) and Borlase (1758) give little or no idea of the extent of the cultivation of Cornwall or of the wasteland. The first accurate indication of the moorland area does not come until the Ordnance Survey's one-inch map of 1813 followed by Greenwood's map of 1827. We have to wait until the geographically-sponsored First Land Utilisation Survey of Dudley Stamp in the 1930s and the Second Land Utilisation Survey of Alice Coleman in the 1960s before any detailed land-use knowledge becomes available in map form.

Select Bibliography

Coleman, Alice, 'Land-Use Planning, the Second Land Utilisation Survey', *The Architects' Journal*, Vol.19 (Jan 1977).

Roberson, B. S. and Stamp, L. Dudley, *The Land of Britain Part 91 Cornwall*, First Land Utilisation Survey (1941).

8. Conservation in Cornwall

The National Trust. The Countryside Commission. The Nature Conservancy Council. The Cornwall Naturalists' Trust. Other bodies.

THE IMPORTANCE OF conserving the landscape has been increasingly realised in Great Britain since the end of the Second World War. Those familiar with the general measures which have been taken as a result of various Acts of Parliament together with voluntary action, will not be surprised to learn that much of Cornwall is now subject to planning restrictions, conservation and preservation orders. Eight major authorities now own, administer or are responsible for the conserved areas: four of these, the Countryside Commission, the Nature Conservancy Council, the Forestry Commission and South West Water are official government bodies; the remaining four, the National Trust, the Cornwall Naturalists' Trust, the Royal Society for the Protection of Birds and the Woodland Trust, are private organisations (Fig. 19).

The National Trust

The first steps towards conservation were taken at the end of the nineteenth century when some enlightened individuals began to realise the heavy price that was being paid for industrialisation; cities strangling the countryside, opencast mining, quarrying and slag heaps despoiling the landscape, air pollution destroying the vegetation. These and other aspects of decay in the landscape led to the foundation of the National Trust in 1895 by Miss Octavia Hill, Sir Robert Hunter and Canon Rawnsley. Their plan was to set up a Trust for the Nation that would acquire land and houses worthy of permanent preservation.

One of the Trust's first acquisitions was in Cornwall at

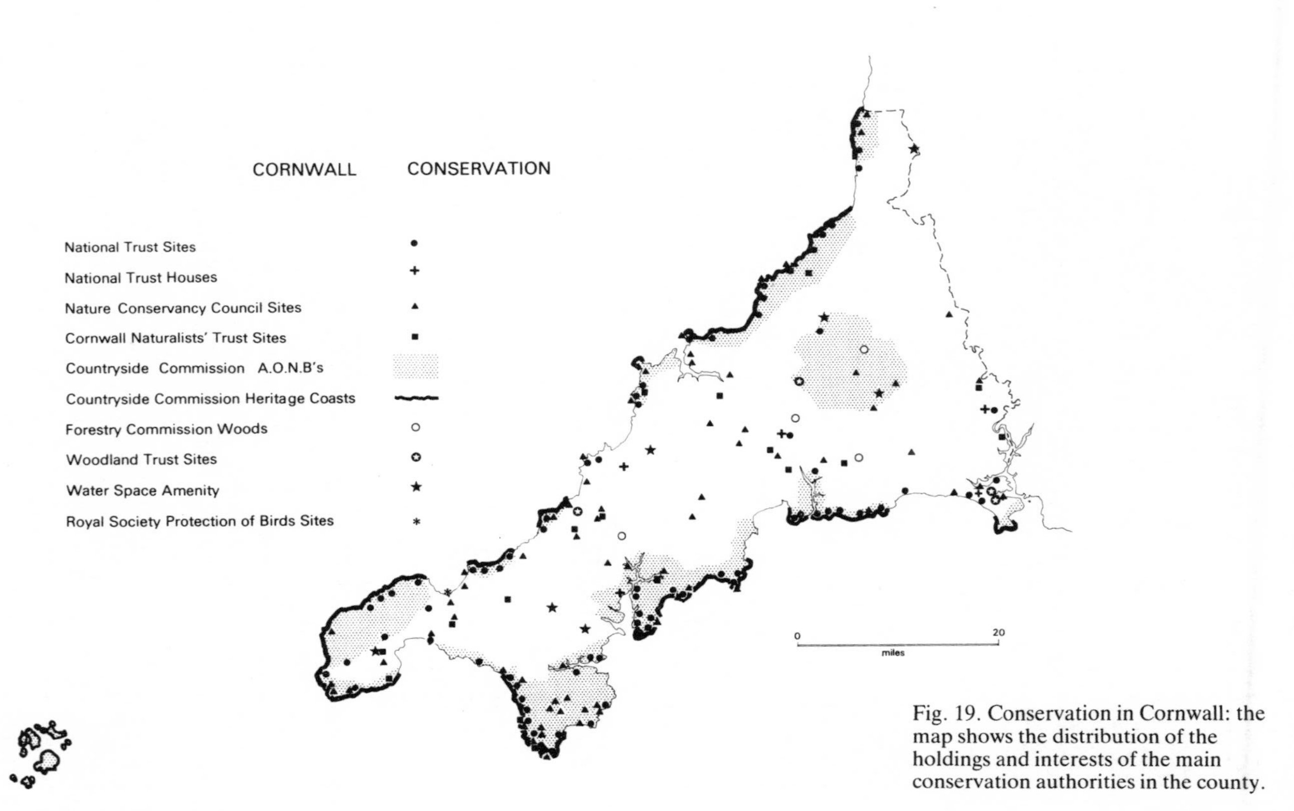

Fig. 19. Conservation in Cornwall: the map shows the distribution of the holdings and interests of the main conservation authorities in the county.

Barras Nose to the north of Tintagel. The explosion in tourist accommodation and the building of the Great Western Railway's King Arthur Castle Hotel at Tintagel which followed the arrival of the railway in North Cornwall in the 1890s, led to an intense local reaction and an appeal for funds to save the coastal cliffs and Barras Nose in particular. Barras Nose was acquired in 1897 and subsequently the cliffs and coast between Tintagel and Trebarwith became Trust property (Plate 57).

Today well over 10,000 acres of land in Cornwall are owned by the National Trust and more than 2,500 acres are protected by covenants. As might be expected, the Trust's holdings are concentrated along the coast: in fact a substantial proportion of the coastal strip has either been donated to the Trust or is in some form of protective covenant. Additionally, since the end of the Second World War, many of the large inland country houses in Cornwall together with their grounds have passed to the National Trust either as a result of, or to avoid, death duties on estates.

Along the coast, notable Trust holdings include Morwenstow where some sixty acres form a memorial to the eccentric parson-poet, the Reverend Stephen Hawker (1835–74). Southward and west of Kilkhampton is Coombe Valley which contains the site of Old Stowe House whence Sir Richard Grenville set out in the *Revenge* in 1591 to win everlasting fame 'at Flores in the Azores'. North and south of Crackington Haven several miles of coastal cliffs were given to the Trust as a tribute to aircrews killed in the Battle of Britain in 1940. South of Cambeak is the fearsome Strangles and the famous High Cliff which is featured in Thomas Hardy's novel, *A Pair of Blue Eyes*; at 731 feet this is the highest cliff in Cornwall.

Continuing south, Boscastle Harbour, the Palace Stables and some 300 acres of the Valency valley are now in the care of the Trust (Plate 56). The jetty at Boscastle was rebuilt by Sir Richard Grenville in 1584 and is almost as good today as it was 400 years ago. We have already noted the coast from Barras Nose at Tintagel to Trebarwith Strand and there is a further section at Tregardock now in the hands of the Trust; these precipitous cliffs are of slate and have not only been quarried but the 'strands' have been used for the export of slate from the cliffs and from neighbouring Delabole.

Another substantial section of the coast from Portquin to Polzeath is now largely owned by the Trust; Portquin epitomises the guide-book picture of a Cornish fishing village, whilst Pentireglaze at Polzeath is the scene of Baring Gould's nineteenth-century thriller, *In the Roar of the Sea*. The acquisition of Pentire Point and Rumps Point has saved the Iron Age cliff castle and a notable geologic and physiographic part of the coastline from bungalow development. Much of the coast between Padstow and Newquay is still in private hands but the famous Bedruthan Steps – the rocky islets south of Park Head – are now Trust property and attract many summer visitors (Plate 58). Conditions in winter can be quite different, for this is another notorious stretch of Cornish coast feared by the captains of nineteenth-century sailing ships. The importance of shipwrecks in the local economy at this time is well seen in the commemorative rhyme which followed an incident in 1850 when the *Good Samaritan* sailing out of Liverpool went aground at Bedruthan:

> The *Good Samaritan* came ashore
> To feed the hungry and clothe the poor,
> Barrels of beef and bales of linen,
> No poor man shall want a shillin.

Much of Crantock Beach and Kelsey Head south of Newquay is also Trust land but it has been left to the Ministry of Defence to 'conserve' Penhale Sands where a military establishment was set up after Dunkirk in 1940 on some 3,000 acres.

At St Agnes Beacon over 400 acres are now cared for by the Trust, preserving a unique piece of tin-mining landscape from the last century (Plate 34); many roofless engine-houses and circular stacks form a silent memorial to a way of life which lasted into the 1920s. From the old coal and timber importing harbour of Portreath to Godrevy Point there are five miles of magnificent cliffs all now owned by the Trust. This stretch includes the famous Reskajeage Downs and Hell's Mouth sections and is noted for its splendid displays of sea pinks, violets, thyme, stone crop, bladder campion, kidney vetch, valerian, samphire and ferns. Seals breed in the caverns at Navax Point and can often be seen in the adjacent Fishing Cove.

In the Penwith peninsula the Trust's coastal holdings are somewhat patchy but notable additions include Hor Point near St Ives, Zennor Head, Rosemergy Cliff, Mayon Cliff near Sennen, Pedn-mem-an-mere Cliff at St Levan, Treen Cliff and Penberth Cove. The next major Trust acquisition is St Michael's Mount which annually attracts one of the highest visitor counts in the country: this is followed by a clutch of properties at Gunwalloe Church Cove, Mullion Cove and Predannack Head. It was from this locality in 1901 that the first transatlantic wireless signal was sent by Marconi to Newfoundland: the masts, cables and shed have long since vanished from the site but a stone memorial recalls the historic event. At Predannack there is a great tract of true Lizard scenery, a wilderness related to the serpentine rock and exposure to the Atlantic gales, which carries a unique flora and many rare plants in the heath and bog. A similar Trust property of eighty acres lies above and to the east of Kynance Cove which is another visitors' 'honeypot' in the Lizard.

East of the Lizard the Trust again has a scatter of coastal sites: Bass Point south of Landewednack, the spectacular blow-hole of the Devil's Frying Pan at Cadgwith, Black Head south of Coverack, and Carne on Gillan Creek bring us to the Helford river. On the north side of this picturesque inlet is Mawnan Shear and Rosemullion Head which are also in the Trust's safe keeping.

East of Falmouth lies the beautiful peninsula of St Anthony in Roseland where the Trust owns the whole of the headland opposite to St Mawes, stretching back to Froe Creek. Northwards at the head of Gerrans Bay lies Carne, probably the country's largest round barrow (Plate 12), fortunately now in the care of the Trust, and nearby is the fine scenery of Nare Head, Rosen Cliff, Kiberick Cove and the coast south of Portloe, most of which is Trust property. Another substantial Trust holding occurs east and west of Dodman Point, which has an unenviable reputation in sailing circles for the large number of wrecks which have occurred here as a result of the offshore currents.

Apart from three acres at Bodrugan's Leap north of Gorran Haven the Trust owns nothing in Mevagissey Bay and St Austell Bay until the great Headland of The Gribbin is reached, but thereafter for nearly ten miles the coastal strip is almost wholly Trust property. This is another stretch noted for its unique botanical cover: ilex, beech, rhododendron, sea buckthorn can all be seen, whilst near Gribbin Head is Menabilly Barton, made famous as Manderley in Daphne du Maurier's *Rebecca* (1938). This was the home of the Rashleigh family whose influence permeates Fowey.

Much of Bodinnick on the east side of the Fal estuary is held by the Trust which now cares for the Hall Walk as a Second World War memorial: adjacent to the walk is the great monolith of granite commemorating Sir Arthur Quiller-Couch's association with Fowey. From Polruan to Polperro there are eight miles of Trust property consisting largely of undisturbed cliff not easy of access: this is another section of coast noted for its botanic diversity, sea holly, sea kale, sea bindweed, centaury, thyme, mallow, orchids (notably Lady's Tresses) are all present. To the east is the great sweep of Whitsand Bay culminating in Rame Head; little of this stretch, however, is Trust land apart from Higher Tregantle Cliff and Sharrow Point.

Inland the Trust's holdings are nearly all associated with the large country houses and gardens which have passed to the Trust since the end of the Second World War. The undoubted jewel of these acquisitions is Cotehele House and its grounds of some 1,200 acres which include two miles of the Cornish bank of the river Tamar below Calstock together with the Morden valley and the famous hanging woods (Plate 23). Cotehele is unique in being the most authentic untouched surviving example of a fortified manor rebuilt in the late medieval tradition. Originally the home of the Cotehele family it passed to the Edgcumbes in 1353 as a result of marriage, but it was Sir Richard and his son Sir Piers Edgcumbe who remodelled the old fortified manor in the late fifteenth and early sixteenth centuries. Cotehele was largely abandoned by the end of the seventeenth century when the

Edgcumbes moved to a larger mansion near Plymouth. This move was providential in that the Tudor building and its contents at Cotehele remained untouched: the house contains a fine collection of Jacobean and Stuart furniture as well as seventeenth-century tapestries. The gardens at Cotehele have been restored to their former beauty and they now rank high in botanic appeal with a unique collection of magnolias, fuchsia, rhododendrons, azaleas, hydrangeas, eucryphias, hoherias, ferns and gunneras set amongst stone terraces, pools and granite walls against a background of ash, sycamore, maple and tulip trees.

The second largest Trust house in Cornwall is Lanhydrock House (Plate 59) near Bodmin set in a 1,000-acre site which includes another fine garden and park, and much of the wooded valley of the river Fowey between Glynn and Restormel. This was the home of the Robartes family until Viscount Clifden gave the property to the Trust in 1953. The house dates from 1620, was largely rebuilt in 1780, suffered a disastrous fire in 1881, after which it was rebuilt to the original plan. The late Lord Clifden was responsible for many of the trees which now grace the estate – magnolias, flowering ash, copper beeches, swamp cypress and tulip trees in particular are interspersed with azaleas and rhododendrons; the famous avenue of beeches and sycamores goes back to 1648.

Of greater historic interest perhaps is Antony House near Torpoint: this is probably more vividly associated with Cornish history than any other extant building. The estate came into the possession of the Carew family in the late fifteenth century and it was here that Richard Carew wrote the famous *Survey of Cornwall* in 1602. The family suffered grievously during the Civil War but eventually recovered and the house was rebuilt between 1701 and 1721. In the course of time the estate passed to the Pole family and, in the nineteenth century, Antony entered its golden age. The Carew-Pole family still contribute to the social and political life in Cornwall but the house and grounds became Trust property in 1961.

On a similar scale and probably better known because of its garden is Trelissick near Feock (Plate 60). Although founded on a building of about 1750 the present house mainly dates from the mid-nineteenth century. The gardens are largely the work of the Copelands from 1937 onwards: many hydrangeas, azaleas, magnolias, rhododendrons, maples, nothofagus, eucalyptus, tree ferns, cedars, cypresses and geans were planted together with a great variety of bushes and shrubs, producing an all-the-year round interest in the garden.

By way of contrast, the interest at the fourteen-acre Trerice estate south-east of Newquay is concentrated on the house which, like Cotehele, has undergone little alteration since its construction by Sir John Arundell in 1572–3 (Plate 61). It is built in the familiar medieval plan with a screens passage entered from the porch with the great hall beyond. The latter is lit by a vast window of twenty-four lights whilst the solar is equally well illuminated by a great semi-circular bay window.

Finally two gardens complete the Trust's holdings in Cornwall. Over forty acres at Glendurgan near Mawnan Smith constitute a notable valley garden which drops down to the Helford river. This is the home of the Fox family and contains the famous laurel maze planted in 1833, as well as a great profusion of exotic plants. Secondly, at Trengwainton in Madron, near Penzance, there is a sheltered valley garden of over 100 acres containing many sub-tropical species, including a large number from south-east Asia collected by Kingdon Ward. The house and grounds were once part of the Arundell estates in Cornwall, but passed to the Bolitho (tin mining) family in the nineteenth century.

The Countryside Commission

A second major conservation force appeared in 1949 with the passing of the National Parks and Access to the Countryside Act. This Act came after a long series of reports dealing with land use and conservation, the most notable of these being the Scott Report (1942), the Dower Report (1945) and the Report of the National Parks Committee (1947). The increasing pressure of population upon diminishing land resources in Great Britain has inevitably produced attempts at comprehensive town and country planning, where efforts have been made to balance the needs of industry, housing, transport, agriculture, forestry, military use and recreation. Partly out of the need for recreation and partly because of the need for conservation, there emerged the National Parks Commission. This Commission demarcated a number of national parks and also designated certain localities as 'Areas of Outstanding Natural Beauty' (AONBs, Fig.19). The Commission was also interested in long-distance footpaths.

Cornwall was an obvious area of attention and the Commission very early recommended that much of the county should be declared a National Park. However, in spite of the general welcome given to the proposal, local doubts and reservations subsequently arose and in June 1953 the Cornwall County Council requested that the project be deferred *sine die*. The Commission replied that it could not acquiesce and asked for a reconsideration, but the Council declined. The net outcome of further negotiation was not a national park but the designation by 1954 of the Cornwall Coastal Path extending for 268 miles round the entire coast, and the designation by 1959 of some 360 square miles of the county as 'Areas of Outstanding Natural Beauty'.

The National Parks Commission has now been replaced by the Countryside Commission. The latter has retained the national park, AONB, and long-distance path concepts, but has additionally developed the country park idea along with picnic sites on a smaller scale. In Cornwall the long-distance coastal path remains the core of the Commission's interest, passing through an almost continuous belt designated as AONB land and with sections highlighted as Heritage Coasts. Inland, Bodmin Moor has been designated an AONB whilst so far one country park has been named at Mount Edgcumbe, west of Plymouth, and two picnic sites established at Respryn Bridge, near Lostwithiel, and at Wacker Quay, south of St Germans.

The Nature Conservancy Council

In addition to the need for national parks for recreational purposes, the post-war approach to land-use planning also revealed the need for conservation of areas where our native flora and fauna can continue to exist and be scientifically studied. The Nature Conservancy (now the Nature Conservancy Council) was established for this purpose at the same time as the National Parks Commission. The Conservancy has the power to acquire land for nature conservation and can also enter into management agreements with landowners in order to conserve designated sites of special scientific interest. It gives advice on nature conservation to government and all those whose activities affect our wildlife and wildscape. In contrast to some other conservation bodies, it sometimes finds it necessary to limit public access to certain 'Sites of Special Scientific Interest' (SSSIs).

It is the duty of the Nature Conservancy Council to inform local planning authorities of the existence of SSSIs in their area. In return, the local planning authorities are required to consult the Nature Conservancy Council on any planning applications they receive for sites incorporating SSSIs to enable the Council to advise them of the effects any proposed development will have on the scientific interests. The local planning authority then takes the advice into account when adjudicating on the application.

In Cornwall the Nature Conservancy Council has designated more than sixty sites of Scientific Importance mainly for their geological, geomorphological, botanical or ecological interest: the sites are scattered throughout the peninsula although there is a tendency to find them in the coastal zone, located in AONBs and on National Trust land. This coincidence is welcome as it should ensure their preservation. Additionally, there is one National Nature Reserve in the Lizard where the Conservancy has been purchasing land in order to ensure the survival of the unique Lizard heathland and coastal habitat: nearly 1,000 acres of the peninsula and the cliffs at Mullion and Predannack have now been acquired. Not only is the serpentine base unique in this area, but at least fifteen species of rare British plants occur, notably the hairy greenweed (*Genista pilosa*), western clover (*Trifolium occidentale*) and the land quillwort (*Isoetes histrix*). Inland there is a mixed maritime heath characterised by the western gorse (*Ulex gallii*), purple moor grass (*Molinia caerulea*) and Cornish heath. Numerous *Allium* growths have developed in the shallow soils overlying the serpentine and here there occur wild chives (*Allium schoenoprasum*), the green-winged

Plate 56 Boscastle: the sixteenth-century harbour. The inner jetty was rebuilt by Sir Richard Grenville in 1584. The outer jetty was damaged by a mine during the Second World War but has been repaired.

Plate 57 Tintagel: part of the castle walls and foundations of interior buildings on 'The Island'. Barras Nose in the background.

Plate 58 Bedruthan Steps: stacks and islets produced by marine erosion. Now in the keeping of the National Trust.

Plate 59 Lanhydrock House: a seventeenth-century house and home of the Robartes family until acquired by the National Trust in 1953.

Plate 60 Trelissick Gardens with the river Fal in the middle distance. Now National Trust property.

Plate 61 Trerice: the sixteenth-century Elizabethan home of the Arundells built in 1572-3. Now National Trust property.

Plate 62 Drift Reservoir near Penzance. Cornwall has seven surface reservoirs all of which contribute to conservation as well as to water supply.

Plate 63 Pencarrow House near Bodmin. A seven-bay, three-storeyed mid-Georgian house but with seventeenth-century work behind and inside.

orchid (*Orchis morio*) and the dwarf rush (*Juncus capiatus*). The cliffs support important colonies of sea birds such as guillemots, kittiwakes, razorbills, herring gulls and shags and, as will be clear from the smaller-scale maps, the Lizard is an important landfall for migrant birds.

SSSIs in Cornwall range from Bodmin Moor, Phillack and Upton Towans Amble Marshes, Loe Pool and Boconnoc Woods to Coverack Cliffs, Kynance Cove, Cligga Head, Bedruthan Steps and the Cheesewring Quarry, covering a great variety of geological and botanical interests.

The Cornwall Naturalists' Trust

Accompanying these official conservation moves in the post-war period, there has also been a welcome surge of public interest which, in the 1960s, led to the foundation of naturalist trusts throughout the country on a county basis. Cornwall, in common with all other English and Welsh counties, now has its Naturalist Trust founded to own, lease and manage properties. The Trust now holds the freehold of five properties at Hawke's Wood near Wadebridge, the Hayman Reserve near St Agnes, Kemyl Crease at Lamorna, Red Moor at Lanlivery and Ventongimps Moor near Perranporth. It has leasehold arrangements on six other sites, notably Kynance Cliffs, Lower Predannack Cliffs and Mullion Island, the Luckett Reserve and Peter's Wood at Boscastle: whilst land agreements have been signed for another six sites, more especially Pelyn Woods near Lanlivery, Pendarves Wood at Camborne and Porthcothan valley near St Eval.

Other bodies

More recently two other official national bodies have become actively engaged in conservation matters and both have interests, although limited, in Cornwall. The Forestry Commission, dating from 1919, was founded with the major objective of growing timber to meet possible war-time emergencies. It has been realised since the end of the Second World War, however, that most of the forests created offer considerable opportunities for recreation and that many of the acquired forests have a considerable conservation potential. Forest walks, nature trails, picnic points, camping, wildlife watching, fishing and trekking are some of the activities now possible in many forest parks, whilst other specialist stands of timber merit conservation and restrictions on access. As we have seen, Forestry Commission holdings in Cornwall are limited but there are a number of 'open' woods, notably Cardinham Woods near Bodmin where there are walks and nature trails (Riverside Walk, Panorama Trail, Bluebell Walk and Silvermine Trail); Deerpark Wood in a tributary valley of the west Looe river with picnic sites and forest trails; Halvana Wood on Bodmin Moor with picnic site and forest trail (Plate 8); and St Clement Wood north of Truro with forest trails. Some of the Forestry Commission land is leasehold and the woods may not be open to the public: the most common constraint is that the landlord has reserved the sporting rights and wishes wildlife to be undisturbed. Local signs usually indicate the extent to which Forestry Commission land is open to the public.

A more recent conservation authority is the water supply industry. Although the multiple use of water reservoirs is the main objective and recreation again dominates, the water supply industry finds itself acting as a conservation agency because of its effect on wildlife. In Cornwall, South-West Water is the responsible authority and there are some seven reservoirs, several having picnic sites and nature trails, whilst some have boating and sailing facilities. All have bird watching but with restrictions (permits needed) because the reservoirs are almost the only large expanses of fresh water in the region and are therefore important areas for wintering wildfowl and waders on migration. The reservoir are:

Argal and College	(Bird watching, fishing trails)
Porth	(Bird watching, fishing)
Crowdy	(Bird watching, fishing)
Siblyback	(Bird watching, fishing, sailing, trails, water skiing)
Tamar Lakes	(Bird watching, fishing, sailing, trails).

Stithians	(Bird watching, fishing, sailing, water skiing)
Drift (Plate 62)	(Bird watching, fishing)

Finally, there are two national organisations in the private sector that are beginning to make an impact on conservation in Cornwall. The Royal Society for the Protection of Birds has done valuable work in promoting an interest in bird conservation throughout the country and it now has its own hide and information centre in Cornwall in the Hayle estuary. Founded in 1889, the RSPB is Europe's largest voluntary wildlife conservation body with a membership of over 330,000. It is assisted in its work in Cornwall by the Cornwall Bird Watching and Preservation Society which dates from 1931 and now has a membership of over a thousand.

A more recent private organisation is the Woodland Trust, formed in 1972 to conserve specialist woodland. It is now the largest non-commercial woodland estate holder in Britain and it has acquired three properties and leases one other in Cornwall: Shute Wood Trevellas near St Agnes, Benskin's Wood, St John near Torpoint, and Lavethan Wood Blisland near Bodmin have all been bought or donated, whilst Antony Wood near Antony has been leased to the Trust by Sir John Carew-Pole.

It will be clear that a widespread public conscience about conservation in Cornwall exists. This extends to local authorities and to private residents responsible for the care of ancient monuments, houses and gardens. Arwenack House in Falmouth, Boconnoc House near Lostwithiel, Caerhays Castle near Mevagissey, Mount Edgcumbe adjacent to Plymouth, Place House near Padstow, Pencarrow near Wadebridge (Plate 63), Port Eliot in St Germans, Tregothnan near Truro and Trewithen near Probus are all well-known houses and gardens achieving a high level of maintenance. Cornwall's historic castles at Launceston, Restormel, Tintagel, Pendennis and St Mawes are all in the care of the Department of the Environment: only Trematon is still privately owned and occupied by the Duchy of Cornwall.

The general distribution of the various conservation interests in Cornwall is depicted in Fig.19. The high density of the conservation interests is immediately apparent as is also the concentration in the coastal zone. This reflects the fact that the outstanding natural endowment of Cornwall is its magnificent cliffed coastline which adds up to some 200 miles of the total 268 miles of coast. These cliffs account for one-third of the English cliffed coast. There seems little doubt that in future almost the whole of the Cornish coast will be preserved for posterity.

Select Bibliography

Bere, Rennie, *The Nature of Cornwall* (1982).

Countryside Commission, *The Coastal Heritage* (1970). *The Planning of the Coastline* (1970).

Fedden, Robin and Joekes, Rosemary, eds., *The National Trust Guide* (1973).

Laws, Peter, *Guide to the National Trust in Devon and Cornwall* (1978).

National Parks Commission, *The Coasts of South-West England* (1967).

9. Epilogue

THE CORNWALL OF the twentieth century is a synthesis of the labours of more than a hundred generations of men working ant-like through the ages upon the natural landscape. Our exploration of this man-made landscape has been both historical and geographical, but we have not been concerned with the rebuilding of past geographies, nor with a strictly historical analysis of individual elements in the changing scene. Instead we have tried to interpret the present landscape, drawing attention to the activities of earlier generations of which traces still remain. And how rich Cornwall is in these remains! As long ago as 1883 the historian J. R. Green in his classic, *The Making of England*, pointed out that, 'the ground itself, where we can read the information it affords is, whether in the account of the Conquest or in that of the Settlement of Britain, the fullest and most certain of documents'.

But no landscape is static and even as we study what it has become it is in process of becoming something different. We are the spectators of a transient scene. The process is never ending whether man is there or not, but the presence of man will often accelerate the rate of change; although at times he appears to achieve a balance which may persist for several generations, ultimately some new factor favours alteration and once again a new transformation takes place.

Cornwall is much more than piskies at Polperro, the bathing at Bude, or the surf riding at Sennen. It is a county with a landscape which for its interest, continuity, and fascination is unique in England. Looking back, the intelligent traveller will remember not only the delights of swimming in quiet little bays and the pleasures of Cornish cream teas eaten in the open air. He will also call to mind, and dwell upon, the various landscape patterns: the bleak moors of the granite bosses and the sun-drenched rocky coves of an indented coastline; the small, irregular fields of Celtic origin, and the rectangular fields of more recent creation; the dispersed settlement dating from prehistoric time, and the nucleated groups of historic time; the intricate pattern of deep, narrow lanes handed down from medieval days and the grandeur of the vistas from what is left of nineteenth-century railway construction; the grey sadness of the abandoned tin-mining areas and the sparkling activity of the china clay districts. Prehistoric monuments, remote and majestic Norman castles, beautiful Elizabethan manor houses and sturdy medieval churches, fascinating fishing ports with their silver-washed, low-pitched roofs, old granite farmsteads on the moorland edge – all these and much more contribute to the picture and excite one to explore further. And if the traveller is anything like the writer, the pursuit of this delightful and inexhaustible task will take him again and again into the field in search of the secret history of Cornwall.

SELECT BIBLIOGRAPHY

Berry, C., *Cornwall*, The County Books (1949).
Betjeman, J., *Cornwall*, A Shell Guide (1964).
Camden, W., *Britannia* (1637).
Carew, R., *A Survey of Cornwall* (1602).
Chope, R. Pearse, *Early Tours in Devon and Cornwall* (1918).
Davidson, Robin, *Cornwall* (1978).
Defoe, D., *A Tour through England and Wales* (Everyman edition).
Fox, C., *Personality of Britain* (1947).
Halliday, F. E., *A History of Cornwall* (1959).
Henderson, C., *Essays in Cornish History* (1935).
Jenkin, A. K. Hamilton, *Cornwall and its People* (1946).
Jenkin, A. K. Hamilton, *The Story of Cornwall* (1950).
Lysons, D. & S., *Magna Britannia* Vol iii *Cornwall* (1814).
Malim, J. W., *Bodmin Moors* (1936).
Maurier, Daphne du, *Vanishing Cornwall* (1967).
Maxwell, I. S., *Historical Atlas of West Penwith* (1976).
Mee, Arthur, *Cornwall: The King's England Series* (1960).
Millward, Roy and Robinson, Adrian, *The South West Peninsula* (1971).
Moll, H., *A New Description of England and Wales* (1724).
Morris, C., ed., *The Journeys of Celia Fiennes* (1947).
Munn, Pat., *Bodmin Moor* (1972).
Murray, J., *Handbook for Travellers in Cornwall* (11 editions 1851–93).
Norden, J., *Topographical Description of Cornwall, 1584* (1728 edition).
Page, W., *Victoria County History of Cornwall* (1906).
Pevsner, N., *The Buildings of Cornwall* (1951).
Rowse, A. L., ed., *The West in English History* (1949).
Rowse, A. L., *Tudor Cornwall* (1969).
Shorter, A. H., Ravenhill, W. L. D. and Gregory, K. J., *South West England* (1969).
Smith, L. T., ed., *The Itinerary of John Leland 1535–43* (1906–10).
Stokes, A. G. Folliott, *Cornish Coast and Moors* (1928).
Todd, A. C. and Laws, Peter, *Industrial Archaeology of Cornwall* (1972).

Index

Most places mentioned in the text and listed in the index are shown on the Ordnance Survey's 1:50,000 Landranger maps and can be located quickly by means of the National Grid Reference which follows each entry. It should be noted that some place names have alternative spellings and others occur more than once: in the latter case it is customary to add the parish or district name e.g. St Just-in-Roseland, St Just-in-Penwith.